This book is due on the last date stamped below.
Failure to return books on the date due may result
in assessment of overdue fees.

FINES	.50 per day	

U.S. HOMELAND SECURITY

A Reference Handbook

Other Titles in ABC-CLIO's
**CONTEMPORARY
WORLD ISSUES**
Series

Books in the Contemporary World Issues series address vital issues in today's society such as genetic engineering, pollution, and biodiversity. Written by professional writers, scholars, and nonacademic experts, these books are authoritative, clearly written, up-to-date, and objective. They provide a good starting point for research by high school and college students, scholars, and general readers as well as by legislators, businesspeople, activists, and others.

Each book, carefully organized and easy to use, contains an overview of the subject, a detailed chronology, biographical sketches, facts and data and/or documents and other primary-source material, a directory of organizations and agencies, annotated lists of print and nonprint resources, and an index.

Readers of books in the Contemporary World Issues series will find the information they need in order to have a better understanding of the social, political, environmental, and economic issues facing the world today.

U.S. HOMELAND SECURITY

A Reference Handbook

Howard Ball

CONTEMPORARY WORLD ISSUES

A B C CLIO

Santa Barbara, California
Denver, Colorado
Oxford, England

Library of Congress Cataloging-in-Publication Data
Ball, Howard, 1937-
    U.S. homeland security : a reference handbook / Howard Ball.
        p.   cm. — (Contemporary world issues)
    Includes bibliographical references and index.
    ISBN 1-85109-803-8 (hardcover : alk. paper) — ISBN 1-85109-804-6
(ebook)   1. United States. Dept. of Homeland Security—History.
2. Terrorism—United States—Prevention—History.   3. National
security—Law and legislation—United States—History.   I. Title: US
homeland security.   II. Title.   III. Series.
    HV6432.4.B35 2005
    353.3′0973—dc22

                                                        2005021789

08 07 06 05   10 9 8 7 6 5 4 3 2 1

This book is also available on the World Wide Web as an eBook. Visit abc-clio.com for details.

ABC-CLIO, Inc.
130 Cremona Drive, P.O. Box 1911
Santa Barbara, California 93116-1911

This book is printed on acid-free paper   .
Manufactured in the United States of America

For Sophie

Contents

Preface

This book is an examination of the factors and events that led to the creation of a new leviathan, the Department of Homeland Security (DHS), in 2002. As with so many new creations in government, its genesis lay in the ruins of the tragic September 11, 2001, terrorist attacks on the symbols of America's military and financial might, the Pentagon and the World Trade Center skyscrapers.

One month after 9/11, President George W. Bush issued an executive order creating the Office of Homeland Security. Eight months later, President Bush called for the creation of a cabinet-level Department of Homeland Security. On November 25, 2002, he signed the Department of Homeland Security Act of 2002. In little more than fourteen months, one of the largest governmental reorganizations in U.S. history was begun. It is still going on and will continue to do so for many years—perhaps decades, if the experts are correct (see chapter 3).

In 1947, during the administration of President Harry S. Truman, there took place a major reorganization of the executive branch. The U.S. Department of Defense was created, made up of the old War Department, the Navy Department, and the Department of the Army. The Central Intelligence Agency, the nation's foremost foreign intelligence-gathering agency, was established (just in time for the beginning of the half-century "Cold War" against the Soviet Union—the "evil enemy," as President Ronald Reagan called it—and its surrogates around the globe). In addition, the National Security Council was created to provide the president and his national security advisors with advice and counsel regarding the strength and intentions of our new enemies.

This defense establishment, combining military and intelligence-gathering and analysis, has provided all presidents since

Truman with foreign and military policy analysis and advice—as well as providing the implements of war whenever the decision was reached in the White House that war was the necessary option for the United States to use in its confrontations with the enemy.

From the late 1950s until 2002, America's national security policy was premised on the principle of mutually assured destruction. Both the United States and its surrogates and the Soviet Union and its surrogates had hordes of atomic weapons and the capacity to deliver them to the enemy by intercontinental ballistic missiles, submarines, or bombers. U.S. policy included the notion of "no first strike" but instant retaliation with its nuclear arsenal if attacked by the Soviet Union. It was, simply, a reactive national security strategy.

The 9/11 attacks led, in a single year, to three major legislative and presidential actions: (1) passage of the USA Patriot Act of 2001, (2) passage of the Department of Homeland Security Act of 2002, and (3) creation of a radical change in U.S. national security policy strategy. In September 2002, President Bush announced the new policy in a government publication entitled *The National Security Strategy of the United States of America* (see Korb 2003). The essence of the radical change was contained in Part V of the new policy document. Entitled "Prevent Our Enemies from Threatening Us, Our Allies, and Our Friends with Weapons of Mass Destruction," it clearly stated the national security policy change: "We must deter and defend against the threat *before* it is unleashed. . . . Given the goals of rogue states and terrorists, the United States can no longer solely rely on a reactive posture as we have in the past. . . . We cannot let our enemies strike first. . . . To forestall or prevent such hostile acts by our adversaries, the United States will, if necessary, act *preemptively*."

This radical change went against the foreign policies of preceding presidents back to the beginning of the Cold War; starting with Democratic president Harry S. Truman (1945–1953) and Republican president Dwight D. Eisenhower (1953–1961). In 1953, the newly elected President Eisenhower said about the Cold War against the Soviet Union: "All of us have heard this term 'preventive war' since the earliest days of Hitler. I don't believe there is such a thing; and frankly, I wouldn't even listen to anyone seriously that came in and talked about such a thing" (Maharidge 2004, 191).

Because of the events of September 11, 2001, the national government just one month later created an act that gave law enforcement personnel enormous criminal procedure powers to identify probable terrorists and their supporters in the United States and abroad. Passage of the DHS Act was the effort to consolidate the almost two dozen disparate federal agencies working to protect domestic security into one behemoth bureaucracy. And finally there was the radical change in national security policy that preceded by six months the first preemptive war in U.S. military history: the Iraq invasion of March 2003. After 9/11, the Department of Defense functionally reverted to its pre-1947 title: it again became the Department of War—in both Afghanistan and Iraq. And, less than one month after 9/11, the Office of Homeland Security (OHS) was created; its first director, Tom Ridge, reported directly to President Bush on the necessary steps to take to provide homeland security from future terrorist attacks on American soil. The homeland had to be prepared for this possibility. By November 2002, the OHS was transformed into the newest executive department: the Department of Homeland Security, with Tom Ridge its first secretary.

A brief comment about the naming of the new federal executive department is appropriate here. Many persons in the United States are extremely uncomfortable with the name given to the DHS. The phrase "homeland security" was first used in a Department of Defense Report in 1997 (Becker 2002, A10). For many, the name conjures images of totalitarian Nazi Germany. In Germany, the term *heimat*, homeland, "came to have an unfortunate association with Nazism" (Freeman 2003, 1).

The phrase was quickly adopted, however, by the Bush White House following the 9/11 attacks by the Al Qaeda terrorists. After 9/11, the front in the war against terror was not a foreign battlefield, it was the "*home* front." And the Bush administration "settled on 'Homeland Security' [because] it was intended to recall home and hearth, and to assure Americans" that the Bush White House was doing all it could to insure "homeland" tranquility (Becker 2002, A10; Maharidge 2004, 157).

Peggy Noonan, a highly respected conservative columnist for the *Wall Street Journal*, has given voice to those who object to the use of the phrase: "The name Homeland Security grates on a lot of people, understandably. *Homeland* isn't really an American word, it's not something we used to say or say now. It has a vaguely Teutonic ring—*Ve must help ze Fuehrer protect ze Home-land!*—and Republicans must always be on guard against sounding Teutonic. Who could argue? Not me." (Noonan 2002, 17)

I agree with the criticism voiced by Noonan and others (Kaus 2002, 1). If I had the power, I would change the title of this new federal department to Department of Domestic Security. However, until the designated political actors take such action, if they ever do, the new federal agency created in November 2002 is the Department of Homeland Security. That name, however uncomfortable this author and many others are with it, is the one used in this book about providing domestic security to all persons residing in the United States.

Howard Ball
Richmond, Vermont
July 2005

References

Becker, Elizabeth. 2002. "'Prickly Roots' of Homeland Security." *New York Times*, August 31, 1A.

Freeman, Franklin. 2003. "The Homeland Security Department and the Northern Command." http://geocities.com.

Kaus, Mickey. 2002. "The Trouble with 'Homeland.'" *Slate*, June 14. http://slate.msn.com.

Korb, Lawrence J. 2003. *A New National Security Strategy in an Age of Terrorists, Tyrannies, and Weapons of Mass Destruction*. New York: Council on Foreign Relations.

Maharidge, Dale. 2004. *Homeland*. New York: Seven Stories.

Noonan, Peggy. 2002. "Homeland Ain't No American Word." *Wall Street Journal*, June 14, 17.

Introduction

You can't just willy-nilly destroy everything just because you have a message.

> —*U.S. Senator Charles E. Schumer (D-NY),
> August 4, 2004, after the U.S. Coast Guard, acting on an
> anonymous tip that a container ship carried a
> deadly cargo of hazardous material in a shipment
> of over one million lemons, boarded and seized the
> cargo. Upon testing, the lemons found to be harmless
> but were destroyed nonetheless (Ramirez 2004, A11).*

Of course we need to screen airline passengers, but I
think there is a better way. . . . People must be treated
with respect.

> —*Diane Dimond, August 30, 2004, after seeing her
> 78-year-old father, who was diagnosed with an inoperable
> lymphoma, humiliated by a "burly screener forcing my
> frail father to stand at attention—arms spread—for a wand
> search . . . and then take off his shoes (Dimond 2004, 12).*

"We don't want to let you in, we don't think you
should come in," [British novelist Ian] McEwan recalls
being told by an immigration official. . . . He says: "I'm
not immune to the argument that you need Homeland
Security to help counter terrorists; America has a lot of
enemies, more now than ever. But this sort of thing increases its isolation."

> —*Elena Lappin,* New York Times, *July 4, 2004*

"I tried to get on a plane back to Washington," [U.S.
Senator Edward] Kennedy [said]. "You can't get on the
plane" [he was told]. "I went up to the desk and said,

'I've been getting on this plane, you know, for 42 years. Why can't I get on the plane?'" [The ticket agent] said, "We can't tell you."
—*Rachel L. Swarns,* New York Times, *August 20, 2004*

The ease with which foreign travelers and immigrants have entered the United States in past decades created a dangerous situation for the nation. Until recently, members of Al Qaeda and other terrorist organizations found it immensely easy to legally enter the United States. Once inside the country, their targets are "literally limitless. That is the drawback of living in the world's most open society, America's Achilles' heel" (Brzezinski 2004, 8).

This was definitely the case before the attacks of September 11, 2001. Because of general disinterest in tracking the movements of terrorists from overseas into the country, and secure with the comfort of the nuclear shield created in the decades-long Cold War against the Soviet Union, U.S. defense forces did not—and still do not—have an accurate count of the number of terrorists in America—persons ostensibly planning for some kind of terrorist action inside the country.

Protecting the homeland against any and all [such domestic] assaults was an entirely new area for the U.S. government in 2002. . . . This [terrorist] enemy keeps too low a profile. Hiding among us, they might live next door, or sit next to us in business class. This enemy uses freedom as a cover, turning the American way of life into its most potent weapon. (Brzezinski 2004, 10)

There is no hard and fast knowledge of the number of Al Qaeda cells in the United States in 2005, nor is there any knowledge of the number of members in these cells, their relationship to other Al Qaeda cells, and their relationship to other non–Al Qaeda cells in the United States. It has only been since 9/11 that federal and state law enforcement and information-gathering agencies have begun to develop sophisticated screening protocols for use by customs and law enforcement personnel at the nation's hundreds of entry point sites.

Because of the casualness in the screening of incoming visitors, as well as the lack of appropriate funding for domestic security needs, national security actions taken by the U.S. government after alleged terrorist cells have been discovered have not been very successful. The terrible consequences of such porous entry points into the United States have led to the creation of very real doomsday scenarios by many observers. "If a ten-ton nuclear weapon . . . exploded in Times Square," wrote Nicholas D. Kristov in 2004, "a fireball would reach tens of millions of degrees Fahrenheit." He continued, "It would vaporize or destroy the theatre district, Madison Square Garden, the Empire State Building, Grand Central Terminal, and Carnegie Hall. The blast would partly destroy a much larger area, including the United Nations. On a weekday, some 500,000 people would be killed. Could this happen? Unfortunately, it could—and many experts believe that such an attack, somewhere, is likely." (Kristov 2004, A26)

The example Kristov presented was not a totally hypothetical situation. On October 11, 2001, just one month after the 9/11 Al Qaeda attacks, "aides told President Bush that a CIA source code-named Dragonfire had reported that Al Qaeda had obtained a 10-kiloton nuclear weapon and smuggled it into New York."

The CIA found the report plausible. The weapon had supposedly been stolen from Russia. Russia is reported to have lost some of its nuclear materials, and Al Qaeda has mounted a determined effort to get or make such a weapon. And the CIA had picked up Al Qaeda chatter about an "American Hiroshima." President Bush dispatched nuclear experts to New York to search for the weapon and sent Dick Cheney and other officials out of town to ensure the continuity of government in case a weapon exploded in Washington instead. But to avoid panic, the White House told no one in New York City, not even Mayor Rudolph Giuliani. (Kristov 2004, A26)

"We're racing toward unprecedented catastrophe," warned former Secretary of Defense William Perry (1993–1997) about the possibility of such a nuclear weapon being smuggled into the United States by terrorists and detonated in Manhattan (Kristov 2004, A26). At the heart of Perry's and others' concerns is the reality that the borders, ports, and rivers of the United States are so porous that such a scenario is scarily possible.

It is not only the possibility of the detonation of a nuclear bomb that keeps homeland security personnel awake at night. More than three years after 9/11 and more than a dozen years after the initial 1993 attempt to bring down the World Trade Center by thousands of pounds of explosives in a rental van, there is hardly any defense against *a single terrorist* driving a van filled with explosives into any one of the tens of thousands of soft targets found in the United States.

"Senior federal officials," concluded a recent report by the *Washington Post*, "acknowledge that the country has virtually no defense against a terrorist barreling down the street with a truck bomb." Such a low-tech, low-cost destructive weapon will work against the most powerful nation in the history of the world. "If a person doesn't care about dying [and the 9/11 terrorists clearly showed that they did not care about their own deaths]," said Michael E. Bouchard, assistant director of the federal Bureau of Alcohol, Tobacco, Firearms, and Explosives (ATF), "they can pull right up to a building, push a button, and the building would go" (Hsu and Horwitz 2004, A1).

In 2005, more than 5 million tons of the chemical used by the car/truck bombers, ammonium nitrate fertilizer, were sold in the United States without any requirements placed on the sale of this material. The private sector—the farm and chemical lobbyists maintain that such regulation would burden law-abiding citizens—has adamantly and successfully opposed such regulations. There is no way to control the use, sale, or rental of more than 100 million vans and trucks in use in the country in 2005. (Further compounding the dilemma is the fact that more than 1 million cars and vans are stolen each year in the United States.)

Security officials and experts have few options. Short of turning busy and important commercial or government areas of cities into pedestrian zones, or surrounding all buildings with concrete blocs in the effort to distance the structure from a would-be truck bomber, experts agree that, paradoxically, the more open the society, the easier it is for a terrorist to successfully blow up a target by driving up and detonating the explosives.

It is remarkably easy to enter the United States, legally or illegally. All nineteen 9/11 Al Qaeda suicide terrorists had officially issued U.S. visas. A few entered on student visas that lapsed while they were plotting the 9/11 attacks. Four of them received pilot certificates from an agency of the federal government, the Federal Aeronautics Administration.

The 9/11 National Commission's *Staff Report on 9/11 and Terrorist Travel* tells the shocking tale of the ease with which these nineteen terrorists were able to enter the United States between 1999 and 2001:

- Three of the nineteen were known by intelligence authorities to be Al Qaeda terrorists, but this information was not added to the watch lists used by immigration, border, customs, and State Department officials.

- The nineteen used 364 aliases, including different spellings of their names.
- Those from Saudi Arabia (fifteen in all) carried passports containing a "possible extremist" indicator. The indicator was not analyzed by the CIA, FBI, or border agents for its significance.
- Two of the nineteen were carrying passports that were clearly "manipulated in a fraudulent manner." They were not questioned.
- Beginning in 1999, the nineteen applied for twenty-three visas and were granted twenty-two.
- Thirteen presented passports less than three weeks old when they applied for visas, "but the new passports caused no heightened scrutiny of their visa applications."
- Two hijackers "lied on their visa applications in detectable ways, but were not further questioned about those lies."
- Two of the nineteen were "interviewed for reasons unrelated to terrorism." All had their applications approved and passports stamped with a U.S. visa. "Consular officials were not trained to detect terrorists in a visa interview."
- The nineteen entered the U.S. thirty-four times over twenty-one months, through nine airports. They were turned away only once during this period. "The culture at the airports was one of travel facilitation and law enforcement, with the exception of programs to interdict drug couriers and known criminals."

These activities were only entry matters. They occurred between April 1999 and August 2001, a time when "approximately 20 million people applied for visas, and more than 10 million people came into the United States through 220 airports of entry." Once inside the United States, all nineteen terrorists were able to get time extensions for their stay—as tourists, pilot trainees, businessmen, or students. They were able to acquire driver's licenses and other identification cards needed for the planning and execution of their 9/11 terror attacks (Zelikow 2004, 3–7, passim).

When the 9/11 terrorists entered the United States in the two and one-half years immediately preceding the attacks, they were nineteen of more than 500 million people who cross at hundreds of legal U.S. entry points annually. They were also just nineteen of the more than 350 million non-U.S. citizens who enter the United States each year. As the 9/11 Commission's final report noted in 2004, after 9/11 "the challenge for national security in an age of terrorism is to prevent the very few people who may pose overwhelming risks from entering or remaining in the U.S. undetected" (9/11 Commission 2004, 383).

Beyond the 500 million travelers that came to the United States in 2004, over 150 million cars, 13 million trucks, and nearly 3 million rail freight cars did so as well. They traveled over more than 600,000 bridges and on 4 million miles of paved highways, and flew into 14,000 small airports. Annually almost 100,000 vessels enter the United States at more than 3,700 terminals and more than 361 ports of entry. And there are over 16 million maritime containers annually moving or waiting to move on vessels, trucks, or trains within or bound for the United States. (In the first decade of the twenty-first century, more than 90 percent of the world's general cargo is moved in maritime containers) (Flynn 2004, 55-67, passim).

Almost one million passenger aircraft—domestic and international—landed in the United States in 2001. In that same year, almost 500,000 recreational boats sailed the waters and into the many harbors of the United States (Flynn 2002, 62). Federal border authorities at the time of 9/11 were charged with monitoring compliance with more than 400 laws and three dozen international treaties, statutes, and agreements on behalf of forty federal agencies. There is the reality of more than 7,000 miles of land borders and more than 95,000 miles of shoreline "which provide ample opportunities to walk, swim, or sail into the nation. Official estimates place the number of illegal migrants living in America at over 7 million" (Flynn 2002, 12).

In the United States, there are over 260,000 natural gas wells and 1.3 million miles of pipeline "that terrorists can blow up" (Flynn 2002, 12–13).

(Recall how the Iraqi insurgents, beginning in 2003, continually blew up oil pipelines in southern Iraq to categorically disrupt the flow of oil to commercial markets.) There are also over 15,000 chemical plants across the United States.

Survey after survey showed that [these plants] were probably the most vulnerable pieces of infrastructure in the nation. According to the Environmental Protection Agency (EPA), more than 100 of these plants could each endanger up to a million lives with poisonous clouds of ammonia, chlorine, or carbon disulfide that could be released into the atmosphere over densely populated areas by a terror attack. The military ranked a strike against the chemical industry as second only to biological warfare (and ahead of nuclear devices) in the total number of mass casualties it would produce. (Brzezinski 2004, 187)

Prior to the 9/11 attacks, however, terrorism was not on anyone's front burner in the world of law enforcement and information gathering. And "border security was not seen as a national security matter" (9/11 Commission 2004, 384). In 2001, for example, half of the inspection stations on the U.S./Canada border were unmanned because of staffing shortages. Port inspectors, too few of them and without the technology they needed to do their jobs competently, were only able to casually check no more than 4–5 percent of the 11 million maritime containers that entered the United States that year (Flynn 2004, 34–45, passim).

On September 10, 2001, it was believed—and planned for by policy makers in the Defense Department and the White House—that potential enemy attacks on the United States would come in the form of an *external* attack by America's traditional nation-state foes or by "rogue" nations such as North Korea, Iran, and Iraq. The attack would be an external one, delivered by intercontinental ballistic missiles fired from underground bunkers in the enemy's homeland, or by nuclear submarines or high-altitude bombers. Chapter 1 will show that such external threats of attack have been part of U.S. history since the nation's birth in 1789—with the exception of the country's bloodiest war, the American Civil War, 1861–1865.

The idea of an asymmetrical war—one between the United States and some foreign, tiny subnational band such as Al Qaeda's nineteen terrorists—was beyond the radar of most intelligence organizations' visions and dreams. This was so even though, since the 1980s, the world's communities had experienced asymmetrical acts of terrorist groups in Europe, the Middle East, South America, and Asia—and in the United States in the

1990s. Recall the domestic terrorist actions by Timothy McVeigh (the destruction of the federal Murrah Building in Oklahoma City, Oklahoma, in 1995) and the "Unabomber," Ted Kaczynski, among other domestic acts of terrorism by solitary "crazies," bandits, and survivalist or religious fundamentalists.

There had also taken place in the 1970s and 1980s a host of hijackings of commercial airliners by radicals, Islamic *jihadists*, and others. However, with heightened security at the airports, these hijacking events skittered off the front pages until Libyan terrorists in 1988 placed explosives on Pan Am Flight 109, blowing up the 747 jumbo jet and killing almost 300 innocent persons over Lockerbie, Scotland.

The last hijacking of an American airliner occurred in 1986. Until the horrifying reality of 9/11, the very idea that nineteen men, noncitizens living, working, and studying how to fly jet aircraft in the United States, would commandeer four fully fueled commercial jets and crash them into the Twin Towers in New York City and into the Pentagon in Virginia lay beyond the imagination of the intelligence bureaucracy.

With the exception of a small handful of FBI field agents who, after spotting Islamic visitors to the United States attending flight schools, voiced fears about such persons hijacking jet planes and using them as missiles, no one else in the nation's fifteen national intelligence agencies dreamed of that possibility or, equally disturbing, took any action on those sightings by the FBI field agents. As Richard A. Posner wrote, the 9/11 Commission's final report points to something banal and deeply disturbing:

> *that it is almost impossible to take effective action to prevent something that hasn't occurred previously.* Once the 9/11 attacks did occur, measures were taken that have reduced the likelihood of a recurrence. But before the attacks, it was psychologically and politically impossible to take these measures. The government knew that Al Qaeda had attacked U.S. facilities [abroad: USS *Cole,* the U.S. embassies in Africa] and would do so again. But the idea that it would do so by infiltrating operatives into this country to learn to fly commercial aircraft and then crash such aircraft into buildings was so *grotesque* that anyone who had proposed that we take costly measures to prevent such an event would have been considered a

candidate for commitment. (Posner 2004, 9; emphasis added)

From 1789 until 9/11, then, "geography was America's biggest security asset," (Flynn 2004, ix), and domestic terrorism against U.S. citizens was a far-fetched possibility, a very rare event in America's history. Domestic security against such terrorists, in essence, was a minor part of U.S. foreign and military policy ever since the end of World War II. Though there was a period of extreme xenophobic fear (1945–1972) of communists living in the United States and plotting the overthrow of the U.S. government by force and violence, by the 1960s the fear of *domestic* insecurity had abated dramatically.

Because of the comfortable topographic reality of the United States—two oceans separating the nation from enemy attacks, and friendly neighbors to the north and south—before the attacks of September 11, 2001, no federal agency made any effort to carefully analyze the travel strategies of members of well-known Islamic terrorist organizations. The idea that these known terrorists would travel to the United States with evil intentions was beyond the imagination of intelligence operatives responsible for analyzing the behavior and intentions of these groups. Although novelists such as Tom Clancy—see, for example, *Teeth of the Tiger*—wrote stories about radical terrorists who traveled to the United States for the purpose of wreaking havoc on the civilian population, that scenario simply was not going to happen in real time.

The national foreign intelligence community distinguished Clancy's fiction from their "real" assessments and rejected such a possibility. Therefore there were no efforts—strategic, tactical, financial, personnel—taken to carefully screen the tens of millions of foreigners who regularly entered the United States. And no effort was made by federal agents to use existing international and national data bases to screen America's visitors.

With the possible exception of U.S. airport security, strengthened in response to hijackings and terrorist violence in airports themselves, the national infrastructure was absolutely vulnerable to acts of terrorism. Every segment was an easy target: "water and food supplies; refineries, energy grids, and pipelines; bridges, tunnels, trains, trucks, and maritime cargo containers; the cyber backbone that underpins the information age in which we live" (Flynn 2004, ix).

At the time of the 9/11 attacks, the United States was home to more than 15,000 chemical plants and refineries that stored large quantities of hazardous biological and chemical materials on their property. Reflect for a moment: What if one of the four planes that flew into buildings on 9/11 had, instead, crashed into a chemical facility? How many tens of thousands of civilians would have died due to exposure to the chemicals released by the explosion? Flynn notes solemnly, "Much of what is critical to our way of life [was, in 2001, and, in 2005] remains unprotected" (Flynn 2004, ix–x).

And so nineteen of the twenty Al Qaeda cell members tasked with the 9/11 terror mission easily entered the country. The "twentieth terrorist," Zacarias Moussaoui, a French national, was stopped by an alert customs official and arrested. He was unable to participate in the 9/11 attacks. At present, he has been indicted, in federal custody, awaiting trial for his part in the 9/11 criminal conspiracy. Sadly, the 9/11 Commission's final report subsequently found that fifteen of the nineteen terrorists "were potentially vulnerable to interception by border authorities" (9/11 Commission 2004, 384). Furthermore, the report noted that had there been "a more effective use of information *in our own data bases,* another 3 hijackers could have been identified" (9/11 Commission 2004, 386).

The 9/11 infamy changed all thinking about domestic security. Until that tragic day, "Washington's singular preoccupation when it came time to protecting the U.S. homeland was *national missile defense.*" On the morning of September 11, 2001, there were only 300 border patrol agents and one analyst for the 4,000-mile land and water border with Canada (Flynn 2002, 60).

Less than one month after the attacks, on October 8, 2001, President George W. Bush issued Executive Order 13288, "Establishing the Office of Homeland Security and the Homeland Security Council." The primary function of the office and the council, stated in "Section 2: Mission" of the executive order, was to "develop and coordinate the implementation of a comprehensive national strategy to secure the U.S. from terrorist threats or attacks. The [office] shall perform the functions necessary to carry out this mission." The Office of Homeland Security (OHS) director and advisor to the president, Pennsylvania Governor Tom Ridge, was appointed by Bush in November 2001 to implement the office's important functions and missions. The OHS mission (and that of its successor organization, the DHS) is threefold. In order of priority, it is to:

1. prevent terrorist attacks within the United States
2. reduce America's vulnerability to terrorism
3. minimize the damage and recover from attacks that do occur

(Office of Homeland Security 2002, 7–8)

Initially the president was opposed to the creation of a cabinet-level Department of Homeland Security (DHS). Members of Congress, led by Senator Joseph Lieberman (D-CT), in contrast, clamored for the creation of such a permanent DHS, a move that required formal congressional approval. "The lack of a congressional mandate, they argued, left [OHS director] Ridge without an independent budget necessary to carry out his duties—and placed him beyond congressional accountability" (Conley 2002, 2).

However, on June 6, 2002, Bush flip-flopped—at the urging of Ridge, among others—and called for Congress to pass legislation creating an Executive Department of Homeland Security. In a televised address to the nation from the White House, Bush told the country that a major reorganization of the federal government was needed to improve domestic security: "Tonight, I ask the Congress to join me in creating a single permanent department with an overriding and urgent mission—securing the American homeland and protecting the American people. Thousands of trained killers are plotting to attack us. Employees of this new agency will come to work every morning knowing their most important job is to protect their fellow citizens."

Bush's televised address, as it turned out (not surprisingly), was "the first shot in a long drawn-out war of wrangling" over the contours of the proposed DHS (Ranum 2004, 32).

After six months of political fighting and stalemate, two weeks after the November 2002 midterm elections (wherein the Republicans regained control of both houses of Congress), Bush signed the legislation on November 25, 2002, creating the Department of Homeland Security. It is the first new executive-branch department to be created since the Department of Veterans Affairs was established in 1989 by the first President Bush.

As will be explored in chapter 2, the legislation led to the biggest reorganization of U.S. government since 1947, when the Department of Defense was established.

At least twenty-two federal agencies, in whole or in part, will be transferred into the DHS.

Of the DHS's 180,000 expected employees, more than 90 percent will handle border and transportation security—controlling who travels in the country and what they take with them. And more than 60 percent of its projected $37.5 billion budget for 2003 will go toward border, port, and airport security. (McLaughlin 2002, A1)

The legislation gave the new secretary of the DHS one year to accomplish the transfer of almost 200,000 employees from those aforementioned twenty-two federal agencies into one new large bureaucracy in one large office building. As will be fully explained in chapter 3, the legislative time frame was an impossible one to fulfill. All management experts, in and out of government, agreed that it would take many years to unify the DHS. Some pointed out that it took the Department of Defense decades to smooth out the dilemmas that arose when a handful of federal organizations were placed under the control of a single Secretary of Defense.

And in 2005, three years after passage of the law, there are many substantial problems that remain unresolved. From legislative oversight problems to the creation of a unitary, new Homeland Security culture; from the problem of budgetary and personnel management of such a huge bureaucracy to the problems of bureaucrat-citizen interaction, the leaders of the DHS still have a great deal to do to make it a bureaucracy capable of carrying out its mission.

Providing Homeland Security provides the reader with the brief history of U.S. foreign and domestic policy created to provide citizens with, as the Preamble to the U.S. Constitution states, "a common defense" and "domestic tranquility." The book will focus primarily, however, on the events of the 1990s and early 2000s, a time during which the threat to domestic tranquility became very real with the 1993 bombing of the World Trade Center in New York City, the destruction of the Murrah federal office building in 1995 in Oklahoma, and the monstrous events of 9/11. These events—especially 9/11, which occurred on President George W. Bush's "watch" as the commander-in-chief—provide the basis for the political and military policies that emerged.

Necessity, with political turf wars mixed in, led to the creation of the OHS and the DHS. The book will examine the politics of the passage of the legislation creating the Homeland Security Department. It will examine the structure of the new bureaucracy, the second largest one of its kind after the Department of Defense (which employs 3 million personnel). It will examine arguments in favor of the DHS as well as criticism that appeared while the proposed bill was being heard in Congress in the summer and fall of 2002. An examination of the problems that emerged, and the unanticipated consequences of the legislation, will follow, along with proposed solutions offered by management experts in and out of government service.

Providing Homeland Security will make available a host of reference resources, including:

- biographical information about the leading figures in this area
- a bibliography of print and Internet sources
- some major documents
- a detailed chronology, and the
- names and contact information about groups and federal, state, and local agencies involved with homeland security

These additional materials are presented so that the reader has adequate data about how a democratic republic deals with terrorism's threats while at the same time maintaining constitutional rights and liberties. As the reader will see, this balancing of the demands for a comprehensive homeland security program set against the rights, liberty, and decent treatment of the people being defended against terrorist strikes is the equivalent of walking a very high tightrope in a hurricane, a sort of constitutional razor's edge. The drama is unfolding as we talk and read about defending domestic tranquility in the age of asymmetric warfare.

References

Brzezinski, Matthew. 2004. *Fortress America: On the Frontlines of Homeland Security*. New York: Bantam.

Clancy, Tom. 2003. *Teeth of the Tiger*. New York: G. P. Putnams' Sons.

Conley, Richard S. 2002. "The War on Terrorism and Homeland Security: Presidential and Congressional Challenges." Paper presented at the conference Assessing the Presidency of President George W. Bush at Midpoint, University of Southern Mississippi, November 22.

Dimond, Diane. 2004. "Defending Our Skies Against the Elderly." *Newsweek,* August 30, 11.

Flynn, Steven. 2002. "America the Vulnerable." *Foreign Affairs* (January/February): 60–74.

———. 2004. *America the Vulnerable: How Our Government Is Failing to Protect Us from Terrorism.* New York: HarperCollins.

Hsu, Spencer S., and Sari Horwitz. 2004. "Impervious Shield Elusive Against Drive-by Terrorists." *Washington Post,* August 8, A1.

Kristov, Nicholas D. 2004. "An American Hiroshima." *New York Times,* August 11, A26.

Lappin, Elena. 2004. "Letter from a Deportee: Your Country Is Safe from Me." *New York Times Book Review,* July 4, 11.

McLaughlin, Abraham. 2002. "New U.S. Security Mantra: Keep Bad Guys Out." *Christian Science Monitor,* June 24, A1.

9/11 Commission. 2004. *The 9/11 Commission Report: Final Report of the National Commission on Terrorist Attacks upon the United States.* New York: Norton.

Office of Homeland Security. 2002. *Homeland Security: U.S. National Security Strategy.* Philadelphia: Pavillion.

Posner, Richard A. 2004. "The 9/11 Report: A Dissent." *New York Times Book Review,* August 29, 1, 9–11.

Ramirez, Anthony. 2004. "Off New Jersey, Coast Guard Seizes Container Ship, and a Million Lemons." *New York Times,* August 7, A16.

Ranum, Marcus J. 2004. *The Myth of Homeland Security.* New York: Wiley.

Strasser, Steven, ed. 2004. *The 9/11 Investigations: Staff Reports of the 9/11 Commission.* New York: Public Affairs Press.

Swarns, Rachel L. 2004. "Senator? Terrorist? A Watch List Stops Kennedy at Airport." *New York Times,* August 20, A1.

Zelikow, Philip, ed. 2004. *9/11 and Terrorist Travel: A Staff Report of the National Commission on Terrorist Attacks upon the United States.* Franklin, TN: Hillsboro.

Abbreviations

ATF	Bureau of Alcohol, Tobacco, Firearms, and Explosives
CAA	Civil Aeronautics Administration
CDC	Centers for Disease Control and Prevention
CIA	Central Intelligence Agency
COINTELPRO	Counter Intelligence Program (FBI)
DHHS	Department of Health and Human Services
DHS	Department of Homeland Security
DNI	Director of National Intelligence
DOA	Department of Agriculture (also USDA)
DOC	Department of Commerce
DOD	Department of Defense
DOE	Department of Energy
DOJ	Department of Justice
DOS	Department of State
DOT	Department of Transportation
EO	executive order
EPA	Environmental Protection Agency
FAA	Federal Aeronautics Administration
FBI	Federal Bureau of Investigation
FDA	Food and Drug Administration
FEMA	Federal Emergency Management Agency
FRS	Federal Reserve System
GAO	General Accounting Office
GSA	General Services Administration
HHS	Department of Health and Human Services
HSC	Homeland Security Council
INS	Immigration and Naturalization Service
NASA	National Aeronautics and Space Agency

NIAID	National Institute of Allergy and Infectious Diseases
NIH	National Institutes of Health
NLC	National League of Cities
NRC	Nuclear Regulatory Commission
NSA	National Security Agency
NSC	National Security Council
OHS	Office of Homeland Security
OMB	Office of Management and Budget
OPM	Office of Personnel Management
OSHA	Office of Safety and Health Administration
OTC	other than Canadians
OTM	other than Mexicans
SSA	Social Security Administration
TPO	Transition Planning Office
TSA	Transportation Security Administration
VA	Veterans Administration

1

A Brief History of Domestic Security

Through civil war and world war, through Red Scare and McCarthyism, our liberties have been challenged . . . but the Constitution has proved a resilient guardian of our political freedoms (Chang 2002, 19).

In a time of war, the survival of the nation comes first. Civil liberties are *not* sacrosanct. Liberty and the pursuit of happiness cannot be secured and protected without securing and protecting life first (Malkin 2004, xiv, xxxv).

Imagining terrorist scenarios was part of any public safety official's job description post-9/11 (Brzezinski 2004, 4).

Before 9/11 we saw a centralized government that was based on an organization designed to win the Cold War—an organization that resulted from the National Security Act of 1947 (Sieple 2002, 3).

To understand the Bush administration's call for the creation of an executive-branch Department of Homeland Security, one must first understand the dynamics behind the need for domestic security when the American colonies successfully revolted from British rule in 1776 and achieved independence in 1781. National security and defense, the ability to defend the nation from its enemies, is the hallmark of a viable, sovereign nation.

Achieving freedom from mighty Great Britain in the eighteenth century was certainly a signal event in history. It was then unheard of for a colony to rebel against the British crown and successfully achieve independence. But independence was not a necessary and sufficient condition for continued national existence. Independence had to lead to the creation of a viable governing structure, one that would, in part, provide the newborn nation with the capability to protect itself from further efforts by Great Britain and other preeminent, powerful European nations to subjugate the United States of America.

Beyond all other needs—and strategies of domestic governance—the new independent nation had to be able to defend itself, diplomatically and militarily, from other sovereign predators. It had to raise an army and a navy, it had to find the financial resources to support the troops and to make the necessary instruments of war, and it had to enter into foreign relations with the rest of the world in order to use diplomacy instead of canon to achieve national security.

By a stroke of unbelievable good fortune, the new nation had a number of brilliant statesmen, politicians, and philosophers working in the corridors of political power after the revolution. James Madison, Benjamin Franklin, James Monroe, Thomas Jefferson, John Jay, George Washington, John Marshall, and Alexander Hamilton were but a few of the best and the brightest men who played a major role in the creation of our constitutional system. In relatively short order, with haste forced upon them by the scary, anarchic dynamics of politics in the Articles of Confederation government, 1781–1789, a constitution was drafted in 1787, and, two years later, the first government began to function.

Some 215 years since the very first Congress and President George Washington took oaths of office to defend the sovereign nation, the United States is still under the sway of the U.S. Constitution. It has survived, the nation has survived, and liberty has survived because of the genius of the 1787 document. And a central aspect of that document, the nation's "fundamental law," is its grant of powers to the president and to the Congress in order to defend the nation from its enemies, domestic and foreign.

The nation's present asymmetrical war on terror, formally "declared" by President George W. Bush in September 2001 (although there was no declaration of war from the Congress), is the latest challenge to the United States and its people. In a time of war, there is the foundational challenge: the ability of the nation to balance the rights and freedoms of individuals against the need to take appropriate national actions to win the war against terrorists bent on destroying America. In 2001 the enemy was Osama bin Laden and his worldwide organization, Al Qaeda ("the base")—with "cells in over 60 nations, including the United States," (Byrd 2004, 83) and with almost 20,000 operatives (Fallows 2004, 84). However, there have been many earlier enemies and innumerable threats to the nation's sovereignty by them since the beginning of the republic in 1789.

Constitutional Foundations

When the men who wrote the Constitution in the summer of 1787 met, they knew they had to act immediately to create "a more perfect Union." After the American Revolution ended in 1781, the first national governmental structure was the Articles of Confederation. However, from the very beginning of the Articles government, critics saw a very weak political system, one that was a loose confederation of largely autonomous states with a central government that consisted of a single institution, the Continental Congress—an agency of government that had extremely limited powers.

The central legislature had no taxing authority and, with regard to foreign affairs and domestic security against the young nation's enemies, the Congress could raise troops only with the greatest difficulty. There was no standing army under the articles. If the Congress was successful in raising troops, they would come from the militias of the nine member states of the confederation. There was no executive agency to implement the few laws passed by the Congress. Nor was there a national judiciary established in the articles governance structure. For congressional legislation to have the effect of law among the states, *all* nine member states of the confederation had to agree on the appropriateness of the legislation.

By the time the delegates met in Philadelphia to "revise" the articles (the Philadelphia gathering was not the first time that critics of the governance structure attempted to meet to do something to improve the political system), there was a felt need on the part of some in attendance (those who believed in the importance of a strong national government) for a drastic change in the governance structure. What occurred in Philadelphia in the summer of

1787 was an amazing transformation from a confederation of sovereign states to a federal system of government, one in which the new creation, the tripartite national or central government, was granted significant powers in foreign affairs, diplomacy, and national defense (all at the expense of the states in the old confederation). Federalism, as incorporated into the document, provided for a strong central government to ensure tranquility at home and to provide the personnel and finances to protect the nation from foreign enemies. And the Constitution, as well, in Article Four as well as the Tenth Amendment, traced the general contours of power that remained in the hands of the states.

The men who toiled diligently and creatively in 1787 replaced the earlier governance arrangement with a very different—some thought radical—governing structure. The 1787 Constitution "was a reaction to the states' unhappy experiences in the decade following the Declaration of Independence" (Lieberman 1992, 6). The U.S. Constitution's first paragraph, the Preamble, succinctly stated the primary reasons for the creation of the fundamental law and the quite radical republican governance structure:

> "We the People of the United States, in Order to
> *form a more perfect Union,*
> *establish Justice,*
> *insure domestic Tranquility,*
> *provide for the common defence,*
> *promote the general Welfare,*
> *and secure the Blessings of Liberty to ourselves and our*
> *Posterity,*
> do ordain and establish this Constitution for the United States of America" (emphasis added).

These six purposes of the new central government had been absent in the government of the Articles of Confederation. Men who fought to achieve independence from the British monarchy now feared the polar opposite: "anarchy between states and despotism within." State legislatures were omnipotent and despotic. They took property, enacted ex post facto laws, impaired the obligations of contracts so that their citizens benefited, and "hindered the repayment of debts. Trade wars, which sometimes even led to armed conflict, threatened what fellow feeling remained from the revolutionary fervor" (Lieberman 1992, pp. 6ff).

The instrument of government that was then created, a federal system, was based on a notion of "humankind" held by most of the delegates attending the Constitutional Convention. This perception was best expressed by James Madison in his classic essay "Federalist 51," a part of the *Federalist Papers* written by Madison, John Jay, and Alexander Hamilton in the ratification campaign for the new Constitution during the fall and winter of 1787–1788.

> If men were angels, no government would be necessary.
>
> If angels were to govern men, neither external nor internal controls on government would be necessary.
>
> In framing a government which is to be administered by men over men, the great difficulty lies in this: you must first enable the government to control the governed; and in the next place oblige it to control itself.
>
> A dependence on the people is, no doubt, the primary control on the government, *but experience has taught mankind the necessity of auxiliary precautions.* (emphasis added)

In order to avoid either tyranny or anarchy, the powers of government must be separated in two general ways: (1) Separation of powers of the national government and the state governments, and (2) the separation of powers within each government, the national (central) government and state government, and between the legislative, the executive, and the judiciary. Legislatures legislated, presidents implemented the laws, and the judiciary's task was, when conflict arose over the actions of the legislators and/or the executive, to definitively interpret the law in order to resolve the conflict peacefully.

There was created, therefore, in the Constitution the central concept of *separated institutions sharing power*. For example, whereas the president was commander-in-chief of the army and the navy (Article II), it was Congress's responsibility and authority to raise funds for the army and navy and to declare war against the enemy (Article I, Section 8). This fundamental principle incorporated into the Constitution was the only way that a society could prevent the emergence of tyranny, whether it was the tyranny of the legislative majority, the tyranny of an all-powerful president, or the tyranny of the judiciary (labeled by Alexander Hamilton in another *Federalist Paper* as "the least dangerous branch" because it lacked neither the power of the purse nor the power of the sword). If powers are separated, if the institutions of government are forced to work together in order to meet the obligations enumerated in the Preamble, then tyranny cannot emerge.

Domestic Security Issues, 1789–2005

From the first decade of the republic to the present time, more than 215 years of American history indicate that some presidents have "imposed unconstitutional measures for [what they believed was for] the good of the nation" (Gottfried 2003, 55). John Adams, the man who succeeded George Washington as president, signed the infamous Alien and Sedition Acts of 1798, which, among other things, made it a crime to speak or write critically of the president's policies toward France at a time when the two nations were at odds, close to warring against each other, and when aliens from Europe were entering the United States. More than two dozen men, all of them political opponents (Jeffersonian Republicans) of the Federalists, were charged and convicted of violating the Sedition Act and were sent to prison for their comments.

Only after Thomas Jefferson became president in 1801 were the men pardoned and the Sedition Act allowed to lapse. James Madison, who entered the executive branch as secretary of state when Jefferson was elected president, said of the legislation: "It was a monster that must forever disgrace its parents [the Federalists]" (quoted in Gottfried 2003, 56).

The Alien Act of 1798 gave President Adams the power to seize, detain, and deport any noncitizen judged by the government to be "dangerous to the peace and safety of the United States." An alien so targeted had no right to an attorney, nor did the person have any right to present evidence on his/her behalf.

The Alien Act enables the president during a declared war to detain, expel, or constrain the freedom of any person over fourteen years of age of the country with which the United States is at war. It was initially used by President James Madison against the British in the War of 1812. President Woodrow Wilson invoked the act during World War I against Germans and Austro-Hungarians in the United States. The federal government arrested about 6,300 enemy aliens, placed 4,000 on parole, and held the remaining 2,300 in internment camps.

During World War II, President Franklin Roosevelt invoked the Alien Act against Japanese aliens the day Pearl Harbor was bombed. The following day it was applied against German and Italian aliens in the United States. Almost 1 million of the 5 million foreigners in the United States at the time were adversely affected by implementation of the act (Cole 2003, 92–93).

In 1861, faced with a Southern states rebellion that became the American Civil War, President Abraham Lincoln took aggressive steps to respond to the South's attempt to secede from the federal union. Usurping Congress's power to suspend the writ of habeas corpus (found in Article I, Section 9 of the U.S. Constitution), the president suspended the writ in Maryland, a hotbed of southern sympathizers. Chief Justice Taney, riding circuit in that state at the time, ruled against Lincoln, remarking that only Congress had the power to so act. Lincoln chose to ignore the judicial order, saying that "some temporary sacrifice of parts of the Constitution [was necessary] in order to maintain the Union and thus preserve the Constitution [and the sovereign people] as a whole" (quoted in Gottfried 2003, 57–58).

Lincoln also declared martial law in Missouri, Kentucky, Indiana, and parts of other battleground portions of the Confederacy. Under this order, military personnel ran the courts and carried out other local governmental services typically carried out by state and local government employees. Under martial law, almost 15,000 persons were held without trial. Lincoln also created military tribunals to try those persons charged with sabotage or spying for the enemy. (These people were not considered prisoners of war because of their actions behind battle lines.) One of those tried by a military tribunal in Indiana, Lamdin P. Milligan, a civilian, was sentenced to death. Used during the Revolutionary War and the Mexican War of 1846–1848 to prosecute enemy military personnel caught spying or attempting to incite fear behind enemy lines by committing acts of sabotage, military tribunals during the Civil War were the first to try civilians in areas where martial law was in effect. However, in 1866 the U.S. Supreme Court overturned the decision of the military court, saying that "except in war zones, the substitution of military tribunals for civilian courts is constitutionally permissible *only if authorized* by Congress" (emphasis added).

Even before the United States entered World War I (1914–1918), President Woodrow Wilson in his 1915 State of the Union message attacked unidentified foreigners who had entered the United States, stating that "such creatures of passion, disloyalty and anarchy must be crushed." Congress passed the Espionage

Act of 1917, and Wilson signed it into law. The act made it a crime for anyone to "willfully utter, print, write, or publish any disloyal, profane, scurrilous, or abusive language" about the United States, or to "cause or attempt to cause, or incite or attempt to incite, insubordination, disloyalty, mutiny, or refusal of duty, in the military or naval forces of the United States." In 1919 the U.S. Supreme Court in *Schenck v. United States* unanimously validated the statute. The Court said that when there is presented "a clear and present danger of bringing about the substantive evils that Congress has a right to prevent," the right to free speech must be set aside to protect the nation: "When a nation is at war many things that might be said in time of peace are such a hindrance to its [war] effort that their utterance will not be endured so long as men fight."

Before, during, and after World War I, the influx of immigrants from Eastern Europe and Russia into the United States, combined with the successful Communist Revolution in Russia (that began in 1917), led to a xenophobic fear that the United States was inundated with anarchists, socialists, and communists. The great fear on the part of a majority of Americans—politicians and the public—was that Bolshevism would spread from Russia through Europe and across the ocean. And these revolutionaries were already resident aliens in the United States.

During the war, the federal government arrested and the War Department interned more than 6,300 enemy aliens in three military prison barracks located in Georgia and Utah (Malkin 2004, xii). Thousands of other immigrants found themselves being investigated by the Department of Justice (DOJ) because of their "un-American" ideologies.

In June 1919, the home of the U.S. attorney general, A. Mitchell Palmer, was bombed by anarchists. Immediately thereafter, President Wilson had the DOJ "interrogate, arrest, and detain almost 10,000 resident aliens targeted because of their radical beliefs." The "Red Summer of 1919," also known as the "Palmer Raids," occurred in thirty major U.S. cities. These raids led to the beatings of thousands of aliens and to forced confessions used to convict them. The result was the incarceration of radical citizens and the deportation of more than 500 immigrants, "not one of whom was proved to pose a threat to the United States" (Hoyt 1969, 11–12).

During World War II (1939–1945), a number of actions were taken by President Roosevelt and the New Deal Congress to address the dangers the nation confronted from foreign enemies and their supporters (a number unknown by the government) living in the United States—citizens and resident aliens alike—even though such actions invaded their civil liberties. For example, in 1940 Congress passed and the president signed the Smith Act, which made it a crime to "knowingly or willfully advocate, abet, advise, or teach the duty, necessity, desirability, or propriety of overthrowing or destroying any government in the United States by force or violence [or to] organize . . . any . . . assembly of persons who teach, advocate, or encourage the overthrow or destruction of any government in the United States by force or violence."

The law was initially used against persons the government believed were "sleeper" agents of the enemy Axis nations—Germany, Italy, and Japan. After the war ended in 1945, the Smith Act was used through the 1970s by the DOJ and other governmental agencies as a tool against persons thought to be communist "sleeper" agents working for the nation's new enemies in the Cold War, the Soviet Union and its Eastern European bloc of nations.

After the "day of infamy," the sneak attack by the Japanese Imperial Navy against the U.S. naval installation at Pearl Harbor in the territory of Hawaii on December 7, 1941, the president and Congress, based on the advice of military commanders responsible for the protection of the homeland, issued executive orders, especially EO 9066, regarding the registration and internment of all resident "enemy" aliens in America.

These orders, issued in early 1942, led to the internment and incarceration of more than 110,000 Japanese resident aliens and Japanese Americans in almost one dozen relocation centers in U.S. western states. In 1943, in the case of *Korematsu v. United States,* a U.S. Supreme Court majority in a 6:3 opinion written by Justice Hugo L. Black upheld the constitutionality of the actions taken against the Japanese by both the president and the Congress.

There were also the Roosevelt executive orders that called for Italians and German resident aliens in the United States to register as "enemy aliens." Some 600,000 Italians (and a much lesser number of German immigrants) were registered and given Enemy Alien Identification cards. The orders also authorized the arrest and relocation to internment camps of the more dangerous persons. As a result, more than 10,000 Italian Americans were evacuated from their homes (on both the east and west coasts of the United States) and places of business, and sent to fifty internment camps around the country (DiStasi 2001, 3–4). All told, more than 31,000 "enemy" aliens from the three Axis nations—Germany, Italy, and Japan—were interned at these camps created by the DOJ—for the duration of the war. Half were Japanese enemy aliens.

In 1988, President Ronald Reagan formally apologized to Japanese Americans for the internment policy implemented during World War II. A few years later, President George H. W. Bush signed legislation providing financial remuneration for all those persons of Japanese ancestry—and their surviving family members—who were interned during the war.

In 1999 the U.S. Congress addressed the plight of Italian Americans during World War II. House Resolution 2442, "acknowledging that the United States violated the civil rights of Italian Americans during World War II," passed the House in 1999, the Senate in 2000, and was signed by President William J. Clinton in late 2000. However, "to date, no reparations have been demanded or paid to any Italian American interned and no reimbursement has ever been made to them for any property confiscated" (Scottolino 2004, 355).

Even so, many persons today, in the post-9/11 era, make the case for racial profiling and internment of "enemy aliens" in America's war on terror. They strongly believe that identification and internment of enemy aliens (in 2005 these are Muslims of Arabic ancestry) is necessary for homeland security.

> "Internment" is a precise legal term for the centuries-old, world-wide practice of detaining non-naturalized immigrants during wartime. Under the Alien Enemy Act of 1798 (which remains in place today), "whenever there shall be a declared war between the United States and any foreign nation or government, or any invasion or predatory incursion shall be perpetrated, attempted, or threatened against the territory of the United States, by any foreign nation or government [all males aged fourteen and older who are not naturalized are] liable to be apprehended, restrained, secured and removed, as alien enemies" (Malkin 2004, xi-xii).

In the early days of World War II, in 1942, eight German Nazi saboteurs (two were citizens of the United States) landed in New York and Florida in order to sabotage U.S. munitions plants. President Roosevelt, again on the advice of his subordinates in the DOJ, issued an executive order closing civilian federal courts to accused saboteurs and spies and authorizing a secret military tribunal to try them. The constitutionality of the tribunal was immediately attacked by the lawyers for the eight captured Nazis. Roosevelt was furious and, reminiscent of President Lincoln's response to Taney's Maryland order, said to his attorney general, Francis Biddle: "I won't hand them over to any U.S. Marshal armed with a writ of habeas corpus!" (quoted in Gottfried 2003, 61).

The U.S. Supreme Court in the summer 1942 "special term" case of *Ex Parte Quirin,* validated the use of a secret military tribunal. On August 8, 1942, the eight men were convicted. Six of them were sentenced to death; the punishment was carried out the day the sentences were announced.

In the half-century Cold War against the "evil empire" of Soviet communism, 1947–1991, the Smith Act was one of many tools used by the government to lessen the possibility of major domestic actions by communist agents and sleeper cells of communists hidden across the nation.

In 1948 the DOJ secretly adopted a program called "Portfolio." At its core was a plan for interning "dangerous persons" during emergencies, including war. Under the plan, "the president would suspend the writ of habeas corpus, and mass arrests would be made under a single 'master warrant' issued by the attorney general, bypassing the courts altogether. [The warrant] would also authorize widespread searches and seizures without probable cause." No appeals were allowed, other than one to the president. "By July 1950 the FBI had compiled a list of 11,930 persons (Communist Party members "or similar ideological groups") who would be subject to such detention in the event of a national emergency." At its peak in 1954, the FBI list contained the names of 26,174 persons. In the 1960s "the list included civil rights and anti-[Vietnam] war movement activists, including Dr. Martin Luther King, Jr." (Cole 2003, 101, 102).

At the same time, Congress—unaware of the DOJ's secret Portfolio program—passed the Internal Security Act of 1950. Title II of the act, valid through 1971, permitted emergency detention of dangerous persons in six detention centers authorized and funded by Congress in 1952. These camps were located in Arizona, California, Florida, Oklahoma, and Pennsylvania (Cole 2003, 101).

In its continuing effort to smash the communist terror network in the United States, the FBI created a secret intelligence program called COINTELPRO (Counter-Intelligence Program). Between 1956 and 1971, FBI agents and informants covertly spied on the U.S. Communist Party. According to a memo written in 1969 by powerful longtime director of the FBI, J. Edgar Hoover (1924–1972), the mission of COINTELPRO was "to expose, disrupt, misdirect, discredit, or otherwise neutralize activities" of individuals and organizations perceived as a threat to the U.S. government (Chang 2002, 30ff).

Its first action was taken in 1956 against the Communist Party. By 1961, COINTELPRO agents were at work in the Socialist Workers' Party in the United States. Within the next decade COINTELPRO infiltrated a number of organizations associated with the Anti–Vietnam War movement as well as the civil rights groups active during this decade in the effort to do away with racial and voting discrimination. By the time COINTELPRO came into public light in 1971, its targets included the Black Panthers and similar "black nationalist" organizations, the Ku Klux Klan and other white supremacist groups, women's movement organizations, and the antiwar "New Left" (Chang 2002, 30–31).

The Republican Party candidate for president in the 1964 election, U.S. Senator Barry Goldwater, uttered the following during his losing campaign to capture the White House: "Extremism in defense of liberty is no vice; moderation in the pursuit of justice is no virtue." President George W. Bush's attorney general, John Ashcroft, repeated that principle when, in a speech to U.S. attorneys in 2002, he said: "History instructs us that caution and complacency are not defenses of freedom. Caution and complacency are a capitulation before freedom's enemies—the terrorists" (quoted in Brzezinski 2004, 94).

When faced with attacks by armed enemy forces ready to destroy our national sovereignty, U.S. presidents have generally acted in aggressive—indeed in extremist—ways, to assure ultimate victory over our adversaries. Whether it was Lincoln facing the rebellious Southern states in a civil war, or Wilson facing the Central Powers in World War I, or Roosevelt facing the Axis in World War II, these chief executives took aggressive—many have argued unconstitutional—actions to protect the nation's sovereignty, its very existence. And, as some of the aforementioned events suggest, it follows that in time of great stress, overzealous federal agents go "over the top" in their actions to protect the nation. One example is sufficient: In November 1917, after the

United States entered World War I, Attorney General Thomas Gregory said: "May God have mercy on [the enemy aliens and the antiwar protestors] for they need expect none from an enraged people and an avenging Government" (quoted in Cole 2003, 111).

This, however, is the reality of life during wartime—even in a democratic republic. Generally, whether it was President Jefferson pardoning those imprisoned under the Sedition Act of 1798; the U.S. Supreme Court in the 1866 *Milligan* case, overruling President Lincoln's wartime martial law orders; or Presidents Reagan and Clinton apologizing for the harsh internment policies against "enemy aliens" during World War II, remediation actions have been adopted by the federal government after a war ends. This will continue to be the reality in the future when the United States responds to attacks by its foes.

The Al Qaeda Attacks of September 11, 2001

On the morning of September 11, 2001, a beautiful early autumn day, shortly before 9 A.M., two hijacked commercial airliners crashed into the twin towers of the World Trade Center in New York City. Thousands died when the two towers collapsed more than an hour after the jets, each loaded with more than 30,000 pounds of jet fuel, rammed into the structures at more than 300 miles per hour.

At about the same time, a third hijacked airliner smashed into one wing of the Pentagon, and a fourth airliner, probably bound for another target in the Washington, D.C., area, crashed in Somerset County, Pennsylvania, after passengers attempted to overpower the hijacker terrorists. As the nation found out later that day, nineteen Islamic terrorists, all members of Al Qaeda, had legally entered the United States in the preceding year and set about planning and training for their mission of terror and death.

As recalled by U.S. Supreme Court Associate Justice John P. Stevens:

> On [that day] agents of the Al Qaeda terrorist network hijacked four commercial airlines and used them as missiles to attack American targets. While one of the four

attacks was foiled by the heroism of the plane's passengers, the other three killed approximately 3,000 innocent civilians, destroyed hundreds of millions of dollars of property, and severely damaged the U.S. economy (*Rasul v. Bush,* 2004).

As soon as federal government officials realized what had happened, actions were taken to try to prevent further death and destruction by other terrorists—in the United States and abroad. The Federal Aeronautics Administration (FAA) suspended all air traffic in the United States and diverted international flights to Canada. Federal offices and public buildings in Washington, D.C., New York, and other large cities were immediately closed. U.S. Secretary of State Colin L. Powell instructed U.S. Embassy officials around the globe to close their facilities or suspend operations if they believed the threat level warranted such action. More than 25 percent of the embassies ceased operations for a short time.

President George W. Bush was in Florida at the time of the attacks. He flew to Louisiana and then to Nebraska before returning to Washington, D.C., in the early evening of September 11, 2001. Speaking to the nation that evening, Bush said that "the full resources of our intelligence and law enforcement communities" would be used to find the terrorists and to bring them to justice. "We will make no distinction between the terrorists who committed these acts and those who harbor them."

For President Bush, these terrorist attacks were "acts of war," and in his talk to the nation he declared that a war against terror had begun and that he would take all necessary actions to preserve the democracy and vanquish the terrorist enemy. He and his close advisors, especially Vice President Dick Cheney, viewed the attacks as acts of war by foreign aggressors, rather than heinous criminal actions.

The following day, September 12, 2001, Bush sent a letter to the Speaker of the U.S. House of Representatives. "Yesterday," he wrote, "evil and despicable acts of terror were perpetrated against our fellow citizens. Our way of life, indeed our very freedom, came under attack. Our first priority is to respond swiftly and surely. . . . Congress must act. [Pursuant to section 251 (b)(2)(a) of the Balanced Budget and Emergency Control Deficit Control Act of 1985], I ask the Congress to immediately pass and send to me the enclosed request for $20 billion in FY 2001 emergency appropriations to provide resources to address the terrorist attacks on the United States that occurred on September 11, 2001, and the consequences of such attacks."

That same day, Congress met in joint session and approved a joint resolution pledging support to President Bush in his efforts to find and pursue the terrorist organization that had committed the attacks. By then, intelligence sources had identified the terrorist group responsible for the attacks: the Al Qaeda organization, led by Saudi Arabian national Osama bin Laden. As President Bush told Congress one week later, "our war on terror begins with Al Qaeda. But it does not end there. It will not end until every terrorist group of global reach has been found, stopped, and defeated."

The attacks of September 11 were America's second "day of infamy," the first being Japan's surprise attack on Pearl Harbor on December 7, 1941. Unlike the 1941 sneak attack by the military forces of a nation state, the 9/11 attack was the coordinated action of a subnational band of terrorists, fifteen of them citizens of Saudi Arabia, against the most powerful superpower in the history of the world. "For perhaps the first time in the nation's history, Americans were feeling vulnerable. . . . There was a lingering sense of unease, of trepidation, that Al Qaeda could strike again—anywhere, at any time" (Brzezinski 2004, 13).

It was the nation's and the Bush administration's tragic introduction to the reality of asymmetrical warfare. Richard A. Clarke, the national counterterrorism director of the National Security Agency (NSA), had repeatedly warned Condoleeza Rice, President Bush's national security advisor, of the looming threat of Al Qaeda and other radical Islamic fundamentalist movements' plans (Clarke 2004). In addition, outgoing President Bill Clinton and his national security advisor, Sandy Berger, had advised the president-elect that the major threat against the United States was Osama bin Laden and his Al Qaeda terrorist movement (Clinton 2004).

However, President Bush chose to shift national security policy in more traditional directions. For example, new funding was appropriated for the continuation of the "Star Wars" missile defense program, a strategic policy introduced by President Ronald Reagan in his first term, 1981–1985, to defend against possible Soviet missile attacks against the United States. Only reluctantly, years after the 9/11 attacks, did President Bush indicate that his administration had made some "miscalculations" before and after the nation's second "day of infamy."

Immediate Responses by the Bush Administration

By the evening of September 11, President Bush and his foreign policy and national security advisors understood what had happened and realized that the United States was absolutely unprepared for any kind of defense against such a terrorist attack. After receiving authorization to act to defend the nation in this new, seemingly endless war on terror, the president took two decisive actions less than a month after the 9/11 terror.

One of the actions he and Attorney General Ashcroft took was to quickly draft and present to the Congress an antiterrorist act. Six weeks later, after a great deal of political infighting, the USA Patriot Act of 2001 was signed by President Bush. The antiterrorism omnibus statute was an effort to coordinate and to strengthen the intelligence gathering work of the FBI, the CIA, and the other thirteen national agencies responsible for acquiring information about "enemies" of the United States and to redirect the law enforcement actions of the DOJ, especially the FBI, so that tracking down and arresting the small bands of "sleeper cell" terrorists coming into the country and planning new attacks against the nation's infrastructure became the new number-one task of federal law enforcement.

The second action was the creation, by executive order of the president in early October 2001, of the Office of Homeland Security, with its director reporting directly to the president. The OHS would coordinate the dozens of agencies, from the U.S. Coast Guard and the U.S. Border Patrol, to the Immigration and Naturalization Service (INS) and the Federal Emergency Management Agency (FEMA), responsible for the protection of domestic security.

The 2001 USA Patriot Act

On October 26, 2001, Bush signed the USA Patriot Act into law (PL 107–56). Some of the president's words to the nation follow:

> The changes, effective today, will help counter a threat like no other our nation has ever faced. We've seen the enemy. . . . They have no conscience. The terrorists cannot be reasoned with. . . . But one thing is certain. These terrorists must be pursued, they must be defeated, and

they must be brought to justice. And that is the purpose of this legislation. . . . We're dealing with terrorists who operate by highly sophisticated methods and technologies, some of which were not even available when our existing laws were written. The bill before me takes account of the new realities and dangers posed by modern terrorists. It will help law enforcement to identify, to dismantle, to disrupt, and to punish terrorists before they strike. . . .

This government will enforce this law with all the urgency of a nation at war. The elected branches of our government, and both political parties, are united in our resolve to fight and stop and punish those who would do harm to the American people.

Summarized, the ten sections (Titles) of the USA Patriot Act cover the following national security matters:

Title I: Enhancing Domestic Security Against Terrorism. This section creates a counterterrorism fund and provides increased funding to the FBI for the enhancement of its technical support center. It also broadens the attorney general's authority to request assistance of the secretary of defense and the Department of Defense (DOD) in emergency situations involving weapons of mass destruction. Section 106 grants the president the power to confiscate and take possession of property when the United States is engaged in military activities as well as enabling courts to consider classified evidence, without making it public, in lawsuits that challenge the government's seizure of property.

Title II: Enhanced Surveillance Procedures. Title II provides federal agencies with authority to intercept wire, oral, and electronic communications relating to terrorism or relating to computer fraud and abuse offenses; share criminal investigation information; employ translators by the FBI; seize voice-mail messages pursuant to a warrant; issue subpoenas for records of electronic communications; delay notice of the execution of a warrant ("sneak and peek"), and to serve, *nation-wide,* search warrants for electronic surveillance. Additionally, the 1978 Foreign Intelligence Surveillance Act (FISA) was changed to enable closer wiretap and other electronic coverage by the FBI of suspected terrorists. The sharing, between federal agencies, of wiretap information and secret grand jury testimony regarding foreign intelligence and counterintelligence is also permitted by this section.

Title III: International Money Laundering Abatement and Anti-Terrorist Financing Act of 2001. Financing terrorist activities is a central problem the government had to end in order to limit the terrorists' war against the United States. This "money laundering" section provides governmental agencies, especially the U.S. Department of the Treasury, (Subtitle A) with powers to maintain long-term jurisdiction over foreign money matters, as well as to oversee correspondent activities and private banking accounts in order to deter money laundering. Subtitle B, the Bank Secrecy Act Amendments and Related Improvements, amended the act to make it easier for federal agencies to examine and report "suspicious activities" by securities brokers and dealers, and by "underground banking systems," and to create more pervasive anti–money laundering schemes. Subtitle C, "currency crimes and protection," is an effort to address the problem of bulk cash smuggling into or out of the United States by terrorist cells in their effort to wage terrorist war against U.S. citizens.

Title IV: Protecting the Borders. In order to protect the nation against the threat by terrorists who enter the country, this title triples the number of Border Patrol personnel and provides the Department of State (DOS) and the Immigration and Naturalization Service (INS) access to certain identifying information in the criminal history records of visa applicants and applicants for admission to the United States. Subtitle B enhances the powers of the INS and other federal agencies, including the Office of Homeland Security, to mandatory detentions of suspected terrorists, without providing them with due process rights. Foreign students are also monitored under this subtitle. The definition of *terrorist activity* was broadened to include all dangerous devices in addition to firearms and explosives. The attorney general is required to detain aliens whom he (or she) certifies as threats to national security.

Title V: Removing Obstacles to Investigating Terrorism. Under this title, the DOJ and the DOS are authorized to pay rewards to combat terrorism. In addition, the Secret Service's jurisdiction is extended to include terrorist investigations. Education and other records can be disclosed to federal agencies investigating terrorism and terrorist activities. The jurisdiction of the Secret Service is extended to investigate offenses against government computers, and the FBI can apply for an *ex parte* court order to obtain educational records that are relevant to an authorized investigation or prosecution of a grave felony or an act of domestic or international terrorism.

Title VI: Providing for Victims of Terrorism, Public Safety Officers, and Their Families. Among other things, this section adds amendments to the Victims of Crime Act of 1984 by establishing a crime victims fund, setting compensation guidelines, and providing assistance to crime victims and to victims of terrorist activities.

Title VII: Increased Information Sharing for Critical Infrastructure Protection. The section expands the regional information sharing system to facilitate federal, state, and local law enforcement responses related to terrorist attacks.

Title VIII: Strengthening the Criminal Laws Against Terrorism. This section of the Patriot Act defines domestic terrorism, terrorist attacks, cyber-terrorism, and other acts of violence against mass transportation systems. It also prohibits any person from harboring aliens or those engaged in sabotage against the United States. A separate offense created by this act punishes those persons harboring terrorists. This title also provides for extraterritorial jurisdiction to cover terrorist actions committed against United States facilities abroad. A person providing "material support" to individuals and organizations that commit terrorist crimes is another enhancement of the federal criminal code provided in this section. In addition, this section enables the U.S. government to seize the assets of all foreign terrorist organizations. Finally, the section underscores the severity of terrorist actions with harsh penalties for terrorist conspiracies.

Title IX: Improved Intelligence. This section of the Patriot Act expands the responsibilities of the director of the Central Intelligence Agency regarding foreign intelligence collected under the Foreign Intelligence Surveillance Act of 1978. The section, amending the National Security Act of 1947, requires the CIA director to assist the attorney general in the generation and dissemination of information regarding terrorism. It also creates the Foreign Terrorist Asset Tracking Center and the National Virtual Translation Center and provides for the training of governmental officials regarding identification and use of foreign intelligence.

Title X: Miscellaneous.   This section includes creation of an independent oversight review agency within the Department of Justice for the FBI as well as other definitions and clarification of terms used in the act.

In light of congressional concerns about the statute's language granting the FBI and other federal agencies the ability to seize data from persons under suspicion of aiding terrorism in violation of their civil liberties, the act contains sunset provisions (in effect as of December 31, 2005) for some—but not all—of the controversial wiretapping and foreign intelligence amendments in the legislation. Because of the efforts of Senator Patrick Leahy (D-VT), Speaker Dick Armey (R-TX), and other concerned legislators, the act also contains judicial safeguards for the monitoring of e-mail and grand jury disclosures.

When President Bush signed the Patriot Act, he declared that the purpose of the legislation was the pursuit, the defeat, and the bringing to justice of the terrorists who declared war on the United States. His message was a reflection of the new national security policy of the United States: *Preventive action* against America's enemies before they can strike against the United States.

> We have seen the horrors terrorists can inflict. [Law enforcement agencies—federal, state, and local—] deserve our full support and every means of help that we can provide. We're dealing with terrorists who operate by highly sophisticated methods and technologies, some of which were not even available when our existing laws were written. The bill before me takes account of the new realities and dangers posed by modern terrorists. *It will help law enforcement to identify, to dismantle, to disrupt, and to punish terrorists before they strike* (emphasis added).

U.S. Attorney General John Ashcroft, speaking a day before the signing of the Patriot Act, at the annual U.S. Mayors Conference, was even more direct—and more aggressive. On September 11, he said, "the wheel of history turned and the world will never be the same." He continued,

> A turning point was reached, as well, in the administration of justice. The fight against terrorism is now the first and overriding priority of the Department of Jus-

tice. But our war against terrorism is not merely or primarily a criminal justice endeavor—our battle is the defense of our nation and its citizens.

Ashcroft concluded that the Bush administration had, through the passage of the USA Patriot Act, "launched an extraordinary campaign against [terrorists]." He believed that the Justice Department was

> directed toward one overarching goal: to identify, disrupt, and dismantle the enemy. Let the terrorists among us be warned. . . . We will seek every prosecutorial advantage. We will use all our weapons within the law and under the Constitution to protect life and enhance security for America. The Bush Administration's new offensive against terrorism is the 2001 USA Patriot Act.

The legislation, said Ashcroft, "embodies two overarching principles: The first principle is airtight surveillance of terrorists." Once Bush signed the legislation, Ashcroft said,

> I will direct investigators and prosecutors to begin immediately seeking court orders to intercept communications related to an expanded list of crimes under the legislation. . . . Agents will be directed to take advantage of new, technologically neutral standards for intelligence gathering. . . . Investigators will be directed to pursue aggressively terrorists on the internet.

The second "overarching principle" that Ashcroft noted "enshrined in the legislation is speed in tracking down and intercepting terrorists." As soon as possible, said Ashcroft to the mayors, "law enforcement will begin to employ new tools that ease administrative burdens and delays in apprehending terrorists."

Finally, regarding the perennial and quintessential question of civil liberties versus domestic security, Ashcroft said:

> Some will ask whether a civilized nation—a nation of law and not of men—can use the law to defend itself from barbarians and remain civilized. Our answer, unequivocally, is 'yes.' Yes, we will defend civilization, and yes, we will preserve the rule of law because it makes us civilized. . . . Terrorists live in the shadows, under the cover of darkness. We will shine the light of justice on them.

Americans alive today and yet to be born and freedom-loving people everywhere will have new reason to hope because our enemies now have new reason to fear.

At the heart of the actions of the president and his advisors was an executive-branch understanding of justice, one that has been shared by U.S. chief executives since George Washington and John Adams. In time of danger to the nation—imminent or otherwise—the president acts on the basis of the concept of preventive justice. In so acting, the administration diminishes the constitutionally mandated concept of criminal justice. In replacing the notion of *due process* in the criminal justice process for the concept of *preventive justice,* secrecy replaces transparency, and secret administrative proceedings replace criminal proceedings. As a consequence, some of the sacred liberties outlined in the Constitution and the Bill of Rights are lost for the duration of the battles and war against the enemies of the nation. The bottom line for the president, whether it was President Lincoln, President Roosevelt, or, in 2001, President George W. Bush, was the preservation of the sovereign nation. U.S. Supreme Court Associate Justice Robert H. Jackson summed their position in a single sentence when, in 1952, he wrote: "While the Constitution protects against invasions of individual rights, it is not a suicide pact."

However, funding problems associated with providing domestic security, through implementation of the Patriot Act of 2001, were present from the very beginning. In 2005, due to the continuing—and escalating cost—of the war in Iraq, they are still problematic ones, with frightening adverse consequences for the nation.

Because of outlays for Iraq, the United States cannot spend $150 billion for other defensive purposes. [Many millions of] shipping containers enter American ports each year; only 2 per cent of them are physically inspected, because inspecting more would be too expensive. The DHS . . . is a vast grab-bag of federal agencies, from the Coast Guard to the Border Patrol to the former Immigration and Naturalization Service; ongoing operations in Iraq cost significantly more each month than all Homeland Security expenses combined. . . . An internal budget memo from the [Bush] Administration was leaked this past spring [2004]. It said that outlays for virtually all domestic programs, including homeland security, would have to be cut in 2005—and the federal budget deficit would still be more than $450 billion (Fallows 2004, 72–73).

Although there have been some successes, there have also been hasty and careless actions by the DOJ and other federal bureaucracies that led to dismissal of charges or acquittals of other alleged terrorists. Among the successes have been the guilty pleas by six Yemeni-American citizens living in Lackawanna, New York, on charges stemming from their attendance at Al Qaeda training camps; guilty pleas from a group of Muslims in Portland, Oregon, who sought to join the Taliban in Afghanistan; and the conviction of Richard Reid, a British citizen, for attempting to blow up a commercial jet with a bomb in his shoe.

There have also been embarrassing defeats for the federal government's investigators and prosecutors. The most recent event was the end of the story of the Detroit "sleeper cell" terrorists. The FBI apprehended four defendants in Detroit, Michigan, one week after 9/11. They were, the DOJ claimed, a terrorist sleeper cell, and they were charged with conspiring to launch attacks against a U.S. air base in Turkey. In June 2003, a federal jury found two of them guilty of aiding terrorists and found another guilty of document fraud. The fourth defendant was acquitted.

However, after a lengthy internal investigation by the DOJ, in which prosecutorial misconduct was discovered, that department agreed with defense lawyers that charges of material support for terrorism be dropped against the two men convicted of that crime. In September 2004, a federal judge threw out the convictions because, "among other things, [overzealous] prosecutors withheld a jailhouse letter discrediting the government's star witness and mischaracterized doodles in a sketchbook as drawings of likely terrorist targets" (*Los Angeles Times* 2004, A17).

In the four years following the 9/11 attacks, using the Patriot Act, the DOJ has charged more than 300 alleged sleeper cell terrorists with terrorist-related activities. There have been 179 convictions—however, many are for such relatively minor infractions as "document and credit card fraud and immigration violations" (Anderson 2004, 3A). There have been numerous foul-ups by the DOJ and the FBI in their efforts to locate and arrest members of terrorist sleeper cells in the United States. Other examples: Two leaders of a mosque in Albany, New York—allegedly members of a terrorist cell—were released on bail in late August 2004 "after a federal judge concluded the men were not as dangerous as federal prosecutors alleged." The evidence against them included a note-book seized at an Iraqi terrorist camp that the Justice Department said called one of the two defendants "commander." However, FBI translators later said "that the reference probably means 'brother'" (Anderson 2004, 3A).

Federal charges—giving material support to terrorists—against a Saudi college student attending school in Boise, Idaho, led to the computer major's acquittal in June 2004. He was accused of giving material support by creating an Internet network that prosecutors claimed "fostered Islamic extremism and helped them recruit. Said one juror: 'there was no clear-cut evidence that said he was a terrorist, so it was all on inference'" (Anderson 2004, 3A).

In Portland, Oregon, lawyer Brandon Mayfield was held for a number of days as a material witness "after the FBI mistakenly said his fingerprints matched one found on a plastic bag con-nected to the deadly terrorist bombings in Madrid. Closer in-spection proved the prints did not match" (Anderson 2004, 3A).

Governmental efforts to "nab 'sleeper cells' inside the United States . . . [don't] inspire much confidence about efforts to find real terrorists who may be lurking in the United States," argued the *Los Angeles Times* recently in an editorial blasting Attorney General Ashcroft and his associates who "too often have sleep-walked" (*Los Angeles Times* 2004). This problem, locating the lurking terrorists living in the United States *before they commit an act of terrorism,* is not a new one for federal law enforcement agencies. However, unlike past incidents where federal officers were able to penetrate communist cells or Klan cells (with infor-mants or with federal agents who went under cover), in the effort to ensure domestic security against the Islamic terrorists there has been an absolute lack of success in penetrating these organi-zations. Indeed, as will be noted in the next section, the Patriot Act was passed, in great part, in order to provide law enforce-ment agencies (i.e., the FBI) and intelligence gathering agencies (the CIA) with the sophisticated tools necessary to try to pierce the veil of the sleeper cells (Ball 2004).

Executive Order to Establish the Office of Homeland Security

Immediately after the 9/11 strikes, both Congress and the presi-dent looked at the state of homeland security, and both branches of government sought to quickly improve the nation's ability to prevent future acts of terrorism perpetrated by small bands of fanatic Islamic militants. The president, however, acting with dispatch (as he had done with the 2001 antiterrorism legislative proposal) issued Executive Order 13288 in early October, creating the Office of Homeland Security, and, weeks later, selected Pennsylvania governor Tom Ridge to serve as its first director (and presidential advisor for homeland security). Its mission: "Develop and coordinate the implementation of a comprehensive national strategy to secure [the United States] from terrorist threats or attacks, to reduce America's vulnerability to terrorism, and to minimize the damage and recover from attacks that do occur" (Homeland Security 2002, 7–8).

Although congressional leaders of both parties called for the creation of a permanent, cabinet-level Department of Homeland Security, in the immediate aftermath of 9/11 the president felt that such a major restructuring of the federal executive branch was not necessary. However, as the next chapter illustrates, there was a change in attitude about a dedicated department, and in June 2002, the political battles commenced over the structure and organization and powers of such a new executive department.

The 9/11 attacks forced all governmental officials to quickly reexamine the national security policy in place since 1947. U.S. foreign and national security policies were based on outdated Cold War realities. Before 9/11,

> The government [was] still organized according to what folks in Washington, D.C., called "stovepipes," according to the discreet and defined functions of sectors of government. National security was handled by the military . . . it was not something for domestic law enforcement to be involved in (Seiple 2002, 3).

The new *asymmetrical* warfare, typified by the 9/11 attacks, led to the still-continuing effort to change U.S. national security policy (reflected in the move toward a cabinet-level DHS). The "stovepipes," the separated agencies—the military, the CIA, the FBI, state and local law enforcement—had to dramatically increase their cooperation with each other. All these agencies were on the national security frontlines. There had to be a new organization that coordinated and synthesized the information that was, before 9/11, being collected by separate agencies—but not shared with each other. Chapter 2 looks at the political context out of which emerged the fifteenth cabinet-level department, the Department of Homeland Security.

References

Anderson, Curt. 2004. "Terror Prosecutors Record Uneven." *Burlington Free Press,* September 7, 3A.

Ball, Howard. 2004. *The U.S.A. Patriot Act: A Reference Handbook.* Santa Barbara, CA: ABC-CLIO.

Brzezinski, Matthew. 2004. *Fortress America: On the Frontlines of Homeland Security.* New York: Bantam.

Byrd, Robert C. 2004. *Losing America: Confronting a Reckless and Arrogant Presidency.* New York: W. W. Norton.

Chang, Nancy. 2002. *Silencing Political Dissent.* New York: Seven Stories.

Clarke, Richard A. 2004. *Against All Enemies: Inside America's War on Terror.* New York: Free Press.

Cole, David. 2003. *Enemy Aliens: Double Standards and Constitutional Freedoms in the War on Terrorism.* New York: New Press.

DiStasi, Lawrence. 2001. *Una Storia Segreta: The Secret History of the Italian American Evacuation and Internment During World War II.* Berkeley: Heyday.

Fallows, James. 2004. "Bush's Lost Year." *The Atlantic,* October, 68–84.

Gottfried, Ted. 2003. *Homeland Security Versus Constitutional Rights.* Brookfield, CT: Twenty First Century.

Hoyt, Edwin P. 1969. *The Palmer Raids, 1919–1920: An Attempt to Suppress Dissent.*

Lieberman, Jethro K. 1992. *The Evolving Constitution.* New York: Random House.

Los Angeles Times. 2004. "Bungling Justice." Editorial, September 5.

Malkin, Michelle. 2004. *In Defense of Internment: The Case for "Racial Profiling" in World War II and the War on Terror.* Washington, DC: Regnery.

Office of Homeland Security. 2002. *Homeland Security: National Security Strategy.* Philadelphia: Pavillion.

Seiple, Chris. 2002. "DHS: Security in Transition." Institute for Global Engagement. www.globalengagement.org.

2

Creating a Cabinet-Level Department of Homeland Security

It is well known in Washington that the Bush Administration was never overly enthusiastic about the idea of forming DHS, which was first floated by Democrats including Senator Joe Lieberman (Brzezinski 2004, 178).

This is an entirely solvable dispute if we have the will to do it.

—Senator Joseph Lieberman (D-CT),
quoted in Washington Post, *August 30, 2002, A6*

Although Democratic senators called for the creation of a permanent Department of Homeland Security as early as October 2001, with a cabinet-level secretary nominated by the president and confirmed by the Senate, initially President Bush and his senior White House advisors believed that a permanent bureaucracy was not needed. The "very notion [of a DHS] ran counter to the Republican mantra of fighting against 'big government'" (Brzezinski 2004, 178).

Instead, the initial response of the administration was to fashion an ad hoc Office of Homeland Security in the White House with its director also serving as an advisor to the president on all matters concerning domestic security. However, by the spring of 2002, eight months after 9/11, there was a reappraisal.

Bush Reverses Course: Calls for Creation of a Department of Homeland Security

By spring 2002 the Democrat-controlled Senate, in particular Senator Joseph Lieberman (D-CT), the chair of the Governmental Affairs Committee, working closely with moderate Republican Senator Arlan Specter (R-PA), "had drafted a proposal to create a cabinet-level agency responsible for homeland security, one subject to congressional oversight. The Bush administration furiously opposed the plan, arguing that homeland security was an executive function, one that could be adequately coordinated only in the White House" (Byrd 2004, 102).

OHS director Tom Ridge was ordered by the president not to speak to Lieberman's committee, and to stonewall other Senate requests for Ridge to testify. Ridge did this four times in 2002—three before the Senate Appropriations Committee and once before the House Appropriations Treasury Subcommittee.

The argument used by the Bush administration to justify Ridge's refusal to meet with Senators was presidential confidentiality. As a presidential advisor, Ridge and other advisors, wrote Nicholas Calio, assistant to the president for legislative affairs, "do not formally testify before Congress on policy matters." (quoted in Byrd 2004, 102).

Lieberman continued to push his draft proposal, and the press soon picked up on the concept. Soon Ari Fleischer, the presidential press secretary, was speaking against the proposed legislation, saying at one press conference that "a new cabinet post doesn't solve anything" (quoted in Byrd 2004, 104). Pressure grew to create such a top-level homeland security department with congressional oversight. During spring 2002, at least eight different proposals were floating around Congress, all calling for a cabinet-level DHS. The president and his political advisors "quickly decided to get on board the DHS train before it left them standing at the station, hat in hand" (Byrd 2004, 102–103).

Four White House staffers—Ridge; Andrew Card, the President's chief of staff; Alberto Gonzalez, the White House legal counsel; and Mitch Daniels, the director of the Office of Management and Budget (OMB)—drew up, without any congressional input whatsoever, the legislation introduced by the president on June 6, 2002. One of the major critics of the action was senior Democratic Senator Robert C. Byrd of West Virginia. He called their proposal a "massive reorganization of government, the largest since the birth of the Department of Defense and the CIA after World War II" (Byrd 2004, 105).

In his June 6 speech, Bush announced his intention to present to Congress a proposal authorizing the creation of the Department of Homeland Affairs. He knew of the eight proposals being considered in Congress, and by introducing his legislation before congressional committees could agree on one proposed bill, Bush had a decided advantage: Congress would have to respond to *his* initiative, not the other way around.

Essentially that was a major reason President Bush changed his view. Additionally, his advisors, including Ridge, pointed to two glaring weaknesses of the OHS: the absence of budgetary authority and the absence of a statutory mandate for the OHS. Ridge lacked substantive budgetary authority in two major ways: first, the executive order creating the OHS did not give Ridge that power; and second, it did not "enable Ridge to formally certify the budget proposals of other entities with homeland security responsibilities that he was to coordinate" (Cmar 2002, 35).

As has been noted, "budgetary control is the key to influencing policy, and centralization of responsibility is essential to improving policy" (Lindsay and Daalder 2003, 70). The OHS director did not have budgetary authority. Ridge's only power was the evanescent power to persuade, and that was, in hard-ball political Washington, a very slim reed with which to successfully oversee and direct the homeland security apparatus. Without budgetary authority over the agencies responsible for providing domestic, or homeland, security, Ridge was powerless to "compel agencies to cooperate with one another and with him" (Conley 2002, 8).

By the spring of 2002, Ridge's lack of budgetary authority or control had made his job increasingly indefensible. As a *New York Times* reporter wrote, "Instead of becoming the [czar] of domestic security, Tom Ridge has become a White House advisor with a shrinking mandate, overruled in White House councils and overshadowed by powerful Cabinet members reluctant to cede their turf or their share of the limelight" (Becker 2002, A1). Additionally, increased "congressional frustration and critiques of Ridge's lack of authority over the course of early 2002 were clearly factors in President Bush's gravitation toward the idea of creating a cabinet-level department" (Conley 2002, 15).

By late spring 2002 Ridge, along with others in the White House, concluded that a significant new direction was necessary and began pushing the president for a major reorganization of the many federal agencies involved in U.S. domestic security. He recommended that the new direction take the form of a cabinet-level federal executive department, with budgetary control and with formal relations—and oversight—with and by Congress. Such an entity would enable the White House to seriously address the many homeland security problems that surfaced after the OHS was created in October 2001.

And so, on June 6, 2002, President Bush called for a major reconstruction, a "huge merger," of the twenty-two federal departments and agencies—with over 180,000 federal employees—that were involved in a variety of domestic security matters (Byrd 2004, 107). In his televised message to the nation, Bush said: "Tonight, I ask the Congress to join me in creating a single permanent department with an overriding and urgent mission—securing the American homeland and protecting the American people." He continued,

> Thousands of trained killers are plotting to attack us. Employees of this new agency will come to work every morning knowing that their most important job is to protect their fellow citizens.
>
> By ending duplication and overlap, we will spend less on overhead, and more on protecting America.
>
> This reorganization will give the good people of our government their best opportunity to succeed, by organizing our resources in a way that is thorough and unified.

Bush said that the creation of a DHS "would make Americans safer because our nation would have:

- One department whose primary mission is to protect the American homeland
- One department to secure our borders, transportation sector, ports, and critical infrastructure
- One department to synthesize and analyze homeland security intelligence from multiple sources
- One department to coordinate communications with state and local governments, private industry, and the American people about threats and preparedness

- One department to coordinate our efforts to protect the American people against bioterrorism and other weapons of mass destruction
- One department to help train and equip for first responders
- One department to manage federal emergency response activities, and
- More security officers in the field working to stop terrorists and fewer resources in Washington managing duplicative and redundant activities that drain critical homeland security resources (Bush 2002, 1).

As presented to the Congress in early June 2002, the president's proposal called for the DHS to have four divisions:

Border and Transportation Security Division: To unify authority over major security operation relating to U.S. borders, territorial waters, and transportation systems: U.S. Coast Guard, Customs Service, INS and Border Patrol, Animal and Plant Health Inspection service of the Department of Agriculture, and the TSA, thereby allowing a single government entity to manage entry into the United States.

Emergency Preparedness and Response Division: To oversee federal governmental assistance in the domestic disaster-preparedness training of first responders, and to coordinate government's disaster response efforts.

Chemical, Biological, Radiological, and Nuclear Countermeasures Division (the final bill changed the name of this division to Science and Technology): To lead the governmental effort in preparing for and responding to the full range of terrorist threats involving weapons of mass destruction.

Information Analysis and Infrastructure Protection Division: To fuse and analyze intelligence and other information pertaining to threats to the homeland from multiple sources— including the FBI, CIA, NSA, INS, DEA, DOE, DOT, Customs, and data gleaned from other organizations.

(The bill that reached President Bush's desk in late November 2002 added another division, or "directorate," as they are formally labeled in the statute: the management division. See chapter 6 for a summary of the final bill signed by President Bush in November 2002.)

The immediate response from Democrats in the Senate was positive. For example, Senator Ted Kennedy (D-MA) said that the "reorganization is a positive step long awaited by many of us on Congress. We need to insure that this new office has the mandate and the tools to address our country's complex national security issues. We need a well organized, efficiently run office that works in coordination with existing law enforcement and intelligence agencies, not another bureaucracy" (quoted in King et al. 2002).

On closer look, however, the bill ran into opposition. The main point of contention was a provision in the bill that gave the president authority to peremptorily hire and fire workers in the new department. "Opponents, such as Senator Robert C. Byrd, Democrat from West Virginia, said that the provision would undercut protections enjoyed by other federal employees and weaken the civil service system" (Gottfried 2003, 18–19). Byrd believed that "Bush wanted a blanket waiver of all civil service laws in order to set up a new personnel system in the department. . . . The bill essentially gave the farm to the White House" (Byrd 2004, 108–109).

Senator Byrd and a small number of legislators were finally able to meet with Ridge and, briefly, the president a few days after the speech. It was a brief and desultory meeting from which Bush exited after making a few general comments about the DHS proposal. Recalled Byrd, who still remains a strident critic of President Bush:

> I was struck by the President's dismal performance. To say it was mediocre would be a gross exaggeration. He was disorganized, unprepared, and rambling.
>
> This fellow was all hat and no cattle, as they would say in Texas. It was obvious that he had no idea of what was in his DHS proposal, nor did he seem to care. . . .
>
> This president, this Bush number 43, was in a class by himself—ineptitude supreme. This meeting with Bush the Younger had topped anything I had seen, from [President Harry S] Truman on, for absolute tripe! (Byrd 2004, 107)

The open battles between the Republican White House and the Democratic Senate began in June 2002 and finally ended the following November after the results of the midterm congressional elections came in. The Republicans in the Senate regained the majority and, within weeks of the election, the now-minority Democratic Party stalwarts in the Senate capitulated and accepted the already passed House bill.

The essential battle, lost by the Democrats, was whether the president would retain the authority to hire, fire, or move around government workers in the DHS—all actions without congressional approval (Ranum 2004, 51–52).

Politics in the Creation of the DHS

The initial Bush DHS proposal sent to the Congress in June 2002 (HR 5710) was a 35-page document. It consisted of nine sections, or titles, and created four divisions (the aforementioned "directorates") in the new executive department. It gave the secretary of the DHS the power sought initially by President Bush: the ability to move personnel, including transfers and termination, in order to effectively deal with threats directed against the United States. The new management directorate in the final version of the DHS act signed by the president reflected this precedent-setting power of the secretary. (See Documents, chapter 6, for a full summary of the DHS Act of 2002.)

By November 25, 2002, the initial draft had transmogrified into a 485-page document. Its original nine titles had grown to seventeen. It contained a great many pieces of "pork" added by many members of Congress (see, for example, Titles VI and VIII). It was also padded with "tort reform" riders—unrelated to homeland security—that protect private industries from civil actions brought by plaintiffs allegedly injured by their products. Senator Leahy criticized these provisions in November 2002, just before the act was finalized:

> The bill provides liability protections for companies at the expense of consumers. I am extremely disappointed that the measure also contains sweeping liability protection for corporate makers of vaccines and any other products deemed to be "anti-terrorism technology" by the Secretary of Homeland Security. This unprecedented executive authority to unilaterally immunize corporations from accountability for their products is irresponsible and endangers the consumers and our

military service men and women. These provisions, for example, would apply to negligence, gross negligence, and even willful misconduct in producing vaccines, gas masks, airport screening machines and any other "antiterrorism technology" used by the general public. (Leahy 2002, 30–31).

The bill Bush signed contained these controversial riders because the GOP-controlled House of Representatives added them literally hours before passing the bill on November 12 and passing it on to the Senate the following day for final action in that congressional chamber. Senator Lieberman, always a political optimist, was forced by these last-minute changes to admit that he was "especially concerned" about the latest GOP version of the DHS Act because it contained "a number of special-interest provisions that are being sprung on the Senate without prior warning or consideration. This is really not the time for that," he concluded.

For the victorious Republicans, however, who had regained control of the Senate on November 5, it really was time for celebration. The Republicans had placed into the fast-moving legislation "a host of pet personal projects," Lieberman said (quoted in Mullins and Fulton 2002, 1).

Added by the House Republicans and accepted by the Senate conferees at the conference committee were provisions

> to eliminate or reduce a manufacturer's product liability, two of which related to vaccines. According to the new bill, a broad range of items, from drugs to life preservers, could escape liability lawsuits if the head of the homeland security department designated them as 'necessary for security purposes'. . . . Yet another provision in the bill would require liability claims against small pox vaccinations to go through the federal tort system [where] punitive damages would be banned. The new bill also would limit liabilities for airport screening companies and high-tech firms that develop equipment essential to ensure domestic tranquility (Mullins and Fulton 2002, 1–2).

The Eli Lilly drug company is but one example of such a rider inserted into the DHS bill. Lilly is the company that developed thimerosal, used in childhood vaccines that led to hundreds of cases of autism allegedly caused by the mercury-based preservative. As passed, "the bill removes all liability from the pharmaceutical industry and health officials for the injuries and death resulting from the drug" (Laurier 2002, 1).

(Another deal-breaking major problem was set aside until the recently created joint congressional 9/11 Intelligence Committee presented its final report. It involved the controversial question of whether the FBI and the CIA—the major law enforcement and intelligence gathering agencies of the federal government—would be included in the new DHS. These two major agencies would not be included in the DHS Act.)

From June 6 until the passing of the DHS Act in November 2002, the Bush administration insisted that the White House and the DHS be granted personnel management powers. Over that same period of time, Democratic legislators joined by a small handful of Republicans—with the encouragement of the powerful federal government employee unions—argued against granting the executive branch such powers, controls that ignored the principles and protocols of the federal civil service system itself.

The lines for the political battle in Washington, D.C., were stark. The White House reflected the core conservative Republican values, norms that instinctively rejected the very notion of "big government." And the creation of this new behemoth, the DHS, would be one of the very largest federal bureaucracies ever established, second in size to the Department of Defense. President Bush, however, had a strong group of allies in the U.S. House of Representatives, solidly controlled by senior conservative Republican legislators. (Indeed, after only two days of debate in the House in early July, the legislators gave Bush exactly what he wanted; see Miller 2002, A12).

The U.S. Senate, however, was a different story. When Senator James Jeffords, a Vermont Republican, renounced his ties with the Republican Party earlier in 2002 and became an "Independent" in the Senate (and began to attend the Democratic caucus), the razor-thin power base shifted to the Democrats by that single vote. As a consequence of Jefford's decision, in the Senate there were fifty Democrats, forty-nine Republicans, and one Independent.

And so, instead of working hand in hand with a solid Republican majority in both Houses of Congress to create the homeland security law, Bush's White House had to listen to the Senate Democrats and had to reach some sort of compromise with them if the DHS was to see the light of day. However, in the back of their minds—of both the Senate Democrats and the White House—was the reality of the looming November 2002 midterm elections and the possibility of the Republicans recapturing control of the Senate.

From the beginning, then, the lines were drawn in the sand. Director Ridge, speaking on behalf of the White House, declared "that the massive new department—the centerpiece of Bush's national anti-terror strategy—would not be effective without new management tools to recruit and reward top employees and the ability to move the workforce as needed." He continued,

> It's going to be tough enough grafting together 22 agencies and cultures and histories and technology and human resource challenges—but if you don't even have the tools to effect change, then one might suggest the status quo. If you're not really going to change the status quo, then why create a department that you can't effect the change within (quoted in Miller 2002, A6).

Bush and Ridge insisted from the outset a new personnel system needed to be created for the DHS, one that gave midmanagement leaders the ability to reward or to discipline workers in their agencies. At the same time, however, the Senate Democrats maintained that the existing federal civil service protections were appropriate for rewarding or disciplining employees. The first Senate draft of the DHS statute, prepared by Senator Lieberman's Governmental Affairs Committee and presented to the Senate, protected the existing civil service process and "voted to set new limits on Bush's ability to move employees out of unions for national security purposes." Debate began on the floor of the Senate on September 3, with a recess planned for October 11, 2002.

Bush's immediate response to the Lieberman bill was to threaten to veto it if it ever came to his desk. Republican senators responded sharply and critically to the Democratic proposal: "The [Lieberman] version of the DHS bill needs significant improvement before it gets to the President," said Ron Bonjean, a spokesman for Senate Minority Leader Trent Lott (R-MS) (quoted in Miller 2002, A6).

A week later President Bush, accompanied by Vice President Dick Cheney and DHS Secretary Ridge, met with six senators and told them that the president would veto DHS legislation that did not give him new powers and flexibility to manage the employees of the new antiterrorism force. By October, the Senate "remained at a stalemate on the homeland security bill." *(New York Times)*

Once again Bush threatened to veto legislation that did not give the executive branch the power to move workers in the DHS. "Workers' rights [remained] the biggest obstacle."(CNN 2002)

Bush supporters Phil Gramm (R-TX) and Zell Miller (D-GA) introduced an amendment to the Lieberman draft that would give the executive branch freedoms to hire, fire, train, and reassign the 180,000 workers in the DHS—[and] which also keeps intact Bush's ability to remove workers from unions for reasons of national security.

At the very same time, Democratic Senators John Breaux (D-LA) and Ben Nelson (D-NE), along with moderate Republican Senator Lincoln D. Chafee (R-RI), introduced an amendment that gave the president "the right to work with unions on personnel matters"; any disputes would go to a review board appointed by Bush. The President would still be able to remove homeland security workers from unions under the proposal, but only after showing that their job duties had changed to primarily involve intelligence or investigative work directly related to terrorist matters.

Senator Carl Levin (D-MI), chairman of the Senate Armed Services Committee, spoke about the Democrats' central problem with the bill introduced by the president:

> We want to secure the nation, and we want to do it by reorganizing where that's necessary. We think, as Democrats, that we can do it without watering down or changing the civil service laws. The president has all the authority he needs to hire and fire people in order to protect homeland security without amending those [civil service] laws. (CNN 2002)

His Republican colleague on the committee, Senator Fred Thompson (R-TN), disagreed with Levin. Thompson believed that the Senate should give the president "the benefit of the doubt. . . . We can't just have business as usual. We're inefficient. It takes too long to hire people and too long to fire bad employees. Appeals go on forever and ever and the Democrats wanted to preserve that system."

However, the deadlock continued up to and past the October 11 recess. Senator Lieberman, more optimistic than many of his colleagues, said: "This is an entirely solvable dispute if we have the will to do it" (Miller 2002, A12). At that point, Congress recessed for the November midterm elections.

The election results disheartened the Democrats, but the Republicans were overjoyed. They would once again be in control of the Senate in the new 108th Congress that would convene in January 2003. In the meantime, the lame-duck 107th Congress came back into session on November 12, and the moderates capitulated. The breakthrough came when the three key senators, Breaux, Nelson, and Chafee, along with the rest of the Democrats, "agreed with some apparent reluctance to a White House plan to resolve the dispute over worker rights."

The final deal was condemned by the American Federation of Government Employees, the large union of federal workers. The union's president, Bobby Harnage, said: "The American public needs to know that the president's so-called compromise . . . is a Trojan Horse. It has nothing to do with improving security. All it does is strip federal workers of the right to defend themselves in the workplace." Responding, Senator Breaux said: "This was the best we could get, knowing it would pass [anyway]" (quoted in Dewar 2002, A1).

With only days to get the bill through Congress and signed by the president before the end of the year, the House of Representatives passed (299 votes to 121) the legislation on November 13. Five days later the Senate voted 90–9 for the bill creating the DHS. President Bush signed the Department of Homeland Security Act on November 25, 2002.

The Department of Homeland Security Act

After Congress had finalized the DHS Act of 2002 on November 19, the president issued a statement to the nation. It said:

> The United States Congress has taken an historic and bold step forward to protect the American people by passing legislation to create the Department of Homeland Security. This landmark legislation, the most extensive reorganization of the Federal Government since the 1940s, will help our Nation meet the emerging threats of terrorism in the 21st Century.

This bill includes the major components of my proposal—providing for intelligence analysis and infrastructure protection, strengthening our borders, improving the use of science and technology to counter weapons of mass destruction, and creating a comprehensive response and recovery division.

I commend the employees who will move into this new department for their hard work and dedication to the war on terrorism. Setting up this new department will take time, but I know we will meet the challenge together.

I look forward to signing this important legislation.

Bush signed the act six days later, saying, "The continuing threat of terrorism, the threat of mass murder on our soil will be met by a unified, effective response." Bush cautioned, however, that setting up the new DHS was an "immense task," and that "the effort will take time and focus and steady resolve. Adjustments will be needed along the way, yet this is pressing business and the hard work of building a new Department begins today. . . . We're fighting a war against terror with all our resources and we're determined to win."

The major federal agencies responsible for a variety of domestic security matters, before DHS, were spread over nine federal departments. Furthermore, an important problem (discussed in chapter 3) was instantly created when the bill was signed by Bush: more than eighty congressional committees and subcommittees had oversight responsibility over these federal agencies.

The legislation transferred to DHS the following bureaucracies and their budgets, totaling $37 billion in FY 2004. (Their former homes are in parentheses.) They were assigned to one of the five main directorates of the DHS:

I. Border and Transportation Security Division:
- U.S. Coast Guard (DOT)
- Secret Service (Treasury Department)
- Transportation Security Administration (DOT)
- Office for Domestic Preparedness (DOJ)
- Federal Law Enforcement Training Center (DOT)
- Animal and Plant Health Inspection Service (DOA)
- Immigration and Customs Enforcement:
    U.S. Customs Service (DOT)
    Immigration and Naturalization Service (DOJ)

Federal Air Marshal Service (DOT; FAA; CAA) Federal
Protective Service (GSA)
- U.S. Customs and Border Protection:
Border Patrol (DOJ)
Customs Inspections (DOT)
Immigration Inspections (DOJ)
Agricultural Inspections (DOLA)

II. Emergency Preparedness and Response Division:
- Federal Emergency Management Agency (FEMA)
- National Disaster Medical System (DHHS)
- Domestic Emergency Support Teams (DOJ)
- National Domestic Preparedness Office (FBI)
- Nuclear Incident Response Team (DOE)

III. Science and Technology Division:
- CBRN Countermeasures Program (DOE)
- Environmental Measurements Laboratory (DOE)
- National Bio-Weapons Defense Analysis Center (DOD)
- Plum Island Animal Disease Center (DOA)

IV. Information Analysis and Infrastructure Protection:
- Energy Security and Assurance Program (DOE)
- Critical Infrastructure Assurance Office (DOC)
- National Infrastructure Protection Center (FBI)
- Federal Computer Incident Response Center (GSA)
- National Communications System (DOD)

V. Management:
As President Bush noted when he signed the legislation, "the bill
includes the major components of my proposal—providing for
intelligence analysis and infrastructure protection, strengthening
our borders, improving the use of science and technology to
counter weapons of mass destruction, and creating a comprehensive response and recovery division." He did not dwell on
the major changes in the personnel management system, nor did
he comment on the many riders attached to the final bill, ones
that immunized and/or rewarded companies and institutions involved in a variety of domestic security functions.

A cursory review (see chapter 6) of the final bill indicates
that for the most part, the DHS Act was a massive reorganization

and not a major expansion—some would argue an unconstitutional expansion—of federal government law enforcement and information-gathering policing powers, as was the case with the Patriot Act. While there was the necessity of adding new and potentially powerful administrative leadership positions, to be filled by the Bush administration, the DHS Act was essentially an effort to consolidate existing federal agencies into a single much larger one in order to more effectively protect Americans.

On January 24, 2003, the Department of Homeland Security officially came into existence. The president had submitted a Homeland Security Reorganization Plan to Congress when he signed the legislation; ninety days after the reorganization plan was submitted, on March 1, 2003, "day one" occurred: the beginning of the move of the twenty-two component parts of the DHS into the new department.

To assist in this monstrous move of agencies and personnel, a DHS Transition Planning Office (TPO) was established in late June 2002, headed by DHS Secretary Ridge, to work with Congress on the legislation and to coordinate planning for the new department. About fifty representatives from the tapped agencies, the Office of Personnel Management, the Office of Management and Budget, and the White House, were brought together to develop options that would allow the DHS to achieve new and enhanced capabilities in the most effective and timely manner.

The TPO was structured around several different teams that parallel the structure of the new department: Border and Transportation Security, Science and Technology, Emergency Preparedness and Response, Intelligence and Infrastructure Protection, United States Secret Service, Human Resources, Systems, Legal, Communications, and Budget.

The primary role of these teams during the transition process was to map out logistical options and reorganization details for the incoming DHS leadership who ultimately made the substantive policy decisions on these issues. The goal, to the greatest extent possible and from the very first days, was to make the reorganization a collaborative effort with the tapped agencies, employees, unions, Congress, state and local entities, and the private sector.

According to the reorganization planners, "the following are elements that we believe are important to ensuring a smooth and successful employee transition into the new Department of Homeland Security":

- A commitment to provide you with up-to-date information about the progress of the DHS transition team;
- Openness about the process and results;
- A pledge to build the new DHS culture upon the foundations of the cultures of the agencies moving into the new Department;
- A commitment to distribute paychecks on time and to ensure that services such as technical support, legal support, and human resources are not disrupted.

The transition timetable for moving the twenty-two agencies with their 180,000 employees was provided for in Title I of the DHS Act: the DHS secretary had one year from "day one" to bring all of the agencies into the new organization. On March 1, 2004, the date of the initial deadline, most if not all of the required federal agencies had been restructured into the DHS.

The DHS Reorganization Plan is subject to modification pursuant to Section 1502(d) of the DHS Act, which provides that

on the basis of consultations with appropriate congressional committees the President may modify or revise any part of the plan until that part of the plan becomes effective. Additional details concerning the process for establishing the Department will become available in the coming weeks and months, and the President will work closely with Congress to modify this plan consistent with the Act.

Unlike the still very controversial Patriot Act of 2001, the DHS Act was essentially a noncontroversial bill. Its passage did not trigger cries of "doomsday" by civil liberties organizations as was the case with the Patriot Act. The public wanted to see actions by government that would make events like the 9/11 attacks less likely. The American people clamored for "fixing" a national security system that had allowed nineteen terrorists (plus unknown numbers of others) to enter the United States, receive funds, plan their attacks, attend flight schools for training, and successfully carry out their suicide mission.

As will be seen in chapter 3, however, critics and outright opponents of the bill saw its enactment as providing the president with too much organizational power in the effort to maintain "homeland security." Some of the harsher opponents of the bill refer to the DHS as "America's Gestapo agency." They fear that "the new department would deliver an unprecedented amount of power to the president's doorstep, sweeping away crucial checks and balances between existing departments. . . . Everything a dictator would need unfettered access to in order to seize control of a country would be handed to President Bush and all future presidents on a silver platter" (Stanton 2002, 2).

However, this unrestrained kind of criticism of the DHS was secondary to the structural and organizational concerns raised by public administrators and organizational efficiency experts. Chapter 3 will examine the criticism, the problems, and the proposed solutions—by DHS leaders and the nongovernmental reviewers of the DHS.

References

Ball, Howard. 2002. *The USA Patriot Act of 2001.* Santa Barbara, CA: ABC-CLIO.

Becker, Elizabeth. 2002. "Big Visions for Security Post Shrink Amid Political Drama." *New York Times,* May 2, A1.

Brzezinski, Matthew. 2004. *Fortress America.* New York: Bantam.

Bush, George W. 2002. "The Department of Homeland Security." Speech, Washington, DC, June 6.

Byrd, Robert C. 2004. *Losing America: Confronting a Reckless and Arrogant Presidency.* New York: W. W. Norton.

Cmar, Thomas. 2002. "Office of Homeland Security." *Harvard Journal on Legislation* 39 (Summer).

CNN. 2002. "Labor Rights Issue Still a Stumbling Block." November 11. www.cnn.com.

Dewar, Helen. 2002. "Homeland Bill Gets Boost: 3 Key Senators Agree to White House Plan for Department." *Washington Post,* November 13, A1.

Gottfried, Ted. 2003. *Homeland Security Versus Constitutional Rights.* Brookfield, CT: Twenty-First Century.

King, John, Kelly Wallace, and Jeanne Meserve. 2002. "Bush Wants Broad 'Homeland Security' Overhaul." CNN, June 6. www.cnn.com.

Laurier, Joanne. 2002. "Bush Administration Moves to Suppress Documents on Vaccines." *WSWS: New And Analysis,* December 10. www.wsws.org.

Leahy, Patrick. 2002. *Statement of Senator Patrick Leahy on the Homeland Security Department Act.* Congressional Record. U.S. Senate. November 19, 2002.

Light, Paul C. 2002. "Assessing the Department of Homeland Security." *Testimony Before the U.S. Senate Committee on the Judiciary, Subcommittee on Technology, Terrorism, and Government Information.* 107th Congress. Washington, DC: Brookings Institution. Available at www.brookings.edu.

Lindsay, James, and Ivo Daalder. 2003. "Whose Job Is It? Organizing the Federal Government for Homeland Security." In James Lindsay, ed., *American Politics After September 11.* Cincinnati: Atomic Dog.

Miller, Bill. 2002. "Lieberman Warns of Homeland Bill Hurdles: Senator Aims to Guard Worker Protections." *Washington Post,* August 30, A6.

———. 2002. "Standoff on Homeland Security: Bill Stalled as Senators Can't Agree on Workers' Rights." *Washington Post,* September 26, A12.

Mullins, Brody, and April Fulton. 2002. "Controversial Provisions Could Delay Senate Homeland Vote." *Congress Daily: Daily Briefing,* November 14. www.GovExec.com.

Progressive Management. *21st Century Complete Guide to Homeland Security: Policy, Oversight, and the New Department.* Core Federal Government Information Series. 2-CD set. ISBN 1-59248-207-4. 2003.

Ranum, Marcus J. 2004. *The Myth of Homeland Security.* New York: Wiley.

Stanton, John. 2002. "Homeland Security Department: Another Production from the *Real* Shadow Government." *CounterPunch,* September 6. www.counterpunch.org.

3

Problems Facing the DHS and Proposed Solutions

The large increase in [homeland security] spending appears to have occurred without risk and cost benefit analysis, leading to a large amount of wasteful spending (de Rugy 2004, 1).

Congress wants to build this department on the cheap; it's like lashing together two mobile homes and putting them in the path of a hurricane.
                    —*Paul Light, quoted in* Seattle Times, *2004, A1*

If we imagine a 22-sided fort we only begin to get a sense of the requirements its connecting beams and support elements must meet. Select any 2 sections of the wall and you are sure to have 2 sets of systems that evolved out of entirely disparate interests, along entirely disparate lines (Badley 2004, 49).

Reading these words sometime in 2005, the reader must pause and realize that the DHS celebrated only its *second year* of existence in March of that year. If the Department of Defense's (DOD) reorganization history is used as a guide, then the DHS, with the "assistance" of Congress, major lobbyists, and the executive branch, will continue to fine-tune its structure and functions for decades to come. And, in the meantime, the question raised by critics is: *Are we safer now than the nation was on September 10, 2001?*

Since the DOD was created in 1947, there have been five major reorganization efforts, the last one occurring in 1989. The 1958 DOD Reorganization Act strengthened coordination between the armed services. In 1980 the Defense Officer Personnel Management Act was passed. In 1985 Congress passed and the president signed the Defense Procurement Improvement Act and the Goldwater/Nichols DOD Reorganization Act (because, even though forty years had passed since the creation of the DOD, coordination between the military branches was still problematic). And in 1989 the Base Closure and Realignment Act was passed and implemented shortly thereafter.

Considering the DOD's history (and the history of other major governmental reorganizations that occurred in Social Security, Education, and the Health and Human Services organizations), as Paul Light noted in testimony before the U.S. Senate's Committee on the Judiciary Subcommittee on Technology, Terrorism, and Government Information, the DHS is "a work in progress" (Light 2002, 1). This is reflected in the DHS Act itself, in which Title VII gives the DHS secretary the "authority" to "establish, consolidate, alter, or discontinue such organizational units within DHS as he may deem necessary or appropriate."

Some observers give the DHS's actions in its first two years a grade of B– or C+. Christian Becker, a Fellow at the Center for Strategic and International Studies, recently noted that "[DHS] has done a good job, given the difficulties of creating a whole new governmental agency in a short period of time" (quoted in James 2004, A1). In a report issued on March 1, 2004, the Century Foundation graded the DHS's activities in five areas: management, intelligence analysis and dissemination, immigration, aviation security, and coordination with state and local governments. "Overall, DHS received a grade of C+" (Sirota et al. 2004, 1). To many observers, the DHS has gotten off to a good start, given the immense task its leaders faced in March 2003: melding twenty-two federal agencies, with over 180,000 employees, into a unitary culture, one that had as its primary mission the protection of all U.S. citizens from acts of terror.

Other observers are much harsher in their criticism of the DHS Act of 2002. Senator Robert Byrd (D-WV) called the final version of the legislation "a swindle foisted on Americans by the Bush administration." On the Senate floor on November 14, 2002, Byrd condemned the legislation:

To tell the American people they are going to be safer when we pass this is a hoax. We ought to tell the people the truth. [This act] is not homeland security. . . . This bill does nothing—not a thing—to make our citizens more secure today or tomorrow. This bill does not even go into effect for up to 12 months. . . . The bill just moves [twenty-two federal agencies] around on an organizational chart. That is what it does—moves [them] around on an organizational chart . . . a plan to create a giant, huge bureaucracy (Byrd 2002, 3, 4).

Although there have been fairly harsh condemnations of the DHS Act of 2002, for the most part the observations have raised professional concerns about the structure of the new huge organization. Most of the critics believed it was important to restructure the many federal agencies responsible for providing homeland security for Americans. As Senator Patrick Leahy (D-VT) said: "Overall, I support the President's conclusion that several government functions should be reorganized to improve our effectiveness in combating terrorism and preserving our national security. . . . [Domestic security] functions are now dispersed among more than 100 different governmental organizations" (Leahy 2002, 1).

That said, however, Leahy and others raised concerns about the new DHS; apprehensions that focused on the huge reorganization problems facing the new administrators of the DHS as well as problems faced by those midlevel managers whose agencies address specific dimensions of domestic security: port security, border security, air travel, rail travel, shipping problems, and so on. Has the reorganization, underway only since March 2003, adversely affected domestic security while it is in this "break in" period of time?

The next section of this chapter looks at specific examples of alleged weaknesses—some structural, many financial, and others that exhibit troublesome signs in America's homeland security systems.

Problems Confronting Homeland Security

The glaring general problems are those that emerged when efforts were made, after March 1, 2003, to implement the massive reorganization of the nearly 200,000 federal bureaucrats working on homeland security. The reorganization and management problems that naturally emerge from such an action (creation of the DHS) are discussed first. Following that, the discussion will turn to specific problems associated with the efforts of a number of DHS agencies to improve homeland security.

DHS Problems

Secretary Tom Ridge's job "is a job made for failure," wrote one observer of the newly created DHS. The leader of DHS has to integrate diverse bureaucratic cultures, has to appear before many congressional committees, and definitely "needs a thick skin and sharp elbows." Ridge must create a new DHS culture to overcome—that is, replace—the twenty-two entities that comprise the DHS, each "with its own historical role and professional expertise. Such an effort can easily take 10–15 years, enough time for a large portion of the workforce to turn over" (Victor 2002, 1775 ff).

The Reorganization/Management Challenge Facing DHS. Recall Senator Byrd's criticism of the homeland security reorganization effort: "The bill just moves [the federal agencies] around on an organizational chart. That is what it does—moves [them] around on an organizational chart . . . a plan to create a giant, huge bureaucracy." Ironically, the White House *agreed* with Byrd's observations—until the president, in June 2002, changed his mind and called for the massive reorganization through the creation of the cabinet-level DHS.

For example, in May 2002, Governor Ridge, then the director of the OHS, said that if such a bill ever got to Bush's desk, "I would probably recommend that [Bush] veto it." Also in that month, Ari Fleischer, the president's press secretary, said: "You still would have agencies within the federal government that have to be coordinated. So the answer is: Creating a cabinet post doesn't solve anything" (both quotes in Leahy 2002, 5).

Byrd, other senators, and the White House itself prior to June 2002 believed that "simply moving agencies around among departments does not address the problems *inside* agencies like the FBI and the Immigration and Naturalization Service (INS)—problems like outdated computers, hostility to employees who report problems, lapses in intelligence sharing . . . along with what many have termed 'cultural problems'" (Leahy 2002, 6).

"Cultural problems" is a problem that arises whenever there is a major governmental reorganization. Under the DHS Act, almost 200,000 government employees, working in two dozen federal agencies for decades, now find themselves in the DHS but doing precisely the same jobs, reporting to the same congressional committees, functioning and being evaluated according to the norms, traditions, customs—in short, the "culture"—of their old agencies. The problem is compounded because the new department

> does not have a culture, does not have norms and standards for reporting. . . . These [employees] will be acting as if they have two masters, one being the DHS, the other being the agency they are accustomed to working for. As a result of this discrepancy, things might fall through the cracks. But this is only natural. It's part of the evolutionary process of such things, but it is something to watch out for (Seiple 2002, 5).

The resolution of the "culture" issue, for the DHS as it was for the DOD, may take decades. The troublesome question: Has the creation of DHS made the United States more vulnerable to terrorist attacks in the short term, the time during which the organizational duality is being overcome? Many security experts ruefully acknowledge that the United States has not yet overcome the bulk of the vulnerability problems that existed prior to 9/11.

One concerned critic of the reorganization effort, William Saletan, presented the worries of many quite clearly. President Bush in his June 6, 2002 speech indicated that if you put all the multipurpose agencies involved in domestic security into one huge DHS, "you end duplication and overlap." "Not so," argued Saletan:

> If Agency X in Department X deals with *problems X and Y,* and Agency Z in Department Z deals with *problems Y and Z,* it seems logical to tear Agency X and Agency Z out of their respective departments and put them in a *new Department Y committed to problem Y.* Poof—no more duplication when dealing with problem Y. But what about problems X and Z? Now all of the people in the two reshuffled agencies who were working on X and Z are stuck in a department devoted to Y (Saletan 2002, 1).

For example, writes Saletan, the U.S. Coast Guard has been folded into the new DHS. It has traditionally had "several missions, from search and rescue to maritime treaty enforcement. . . . The U.S. Customs Service, among other duties, collects tariffs and prevents smuggling. [It too is now a part of the DHS]." However, what about the personnel in the Coast Guard who do search and rescue or the customs people who collect tariffs? What about FEMA employees (FEMA is another federal agency placed into the new DHS) who deal with the extensive damage in Florida and other states brought on, not by terrorists, but by Hurricane Ivan's arrival in September 2004? "Do you want those people stuck in a department devoted single-mindedly to homeland security?" he asks (Saletan 2002, 1).

The DHS, in other words, contains agencies and bureaus that spend money for non–homeland security projects. In FY 2004, the DHS spent billions of dollars on programs offering food and shelter for the poor; disaster aid for farm states plagued by droughts, floods, and freezes; and hurricane disaster relief for Floridians. "This is likely the first step toward the slippery slope of the increased involvement of the DHS in non–homeland security activities," observed one concerned reviewer of the new department (de Rugy 2004, 8).

Paradoxically and troublesome to the experts is the fact that there are dozens of federal agencies involved in homeland security that are *not in the DHS*. An examination of the FY 2005 budget indicates that there are at least two dozen federal agencies that in FY 2005 received $20.2 billion "outside the DHS." (The DHS FY 2005 budget was $47 billion.) The following agencies are in the position of spending appropriated funds for homeland defense *even though they are not part of the DHS*:

Department of Agriculture
Department of Commerce
Department of Defense
Department of Energy
Department of Health and Human Services
Department of Justice
Department of State
Department of Transportation
Treasury Department
Army Corps of Engineers
National Aeronautics and Space Agency

National Science Foundation
Social Security Administration
Veterans Administration

Four of these agencies—the DOD, HHS, DOJ, and the DOE—account for over 80 percent of these outside-DHS homeland security appropriations. (Two agencies will receive about half of these funds: the DOD will spend over $8 billion, and the DOJ will spend $2.5 billion during FY 2005.)

These are troublesome figures because a number of these agencies have an atrocious management record regarding use of the funds allocated to them. The General Accounting Office (GAO) has issued reports that criticize NASA, the Army Corps of Engineers, and the DOE, among others, for mismanagement of funds. The GAO has written that the DOD's "financial management problems are pervasive, long-standing, and deeply rooted in virtually all business operations throughout the department. And DOC is found to need improvement in its financial management and control over its internal weaknesses while the [DOA] is often declared to 'lack financial accountability over billions of dollars of assets'" (de Rugy 2004, 7–8).

There is also very little homeland security coordination between the DHS and these outside-DHS agencies that are spending vital billions of dollars on homeland security projects. Further compounding the dilemma is the fact that the DHS has to rely on these agencies for intelligence-gathering information. As Veronique de Rugy concludes:

> With the money split between so many departments and programs—including those with troubling track records—the ability of DHS or Congress to conduct effective oversight decreases. The new department has authority over the parts of agencies subsumed under it but not over the many more that remain outside of its control (de Rugy 2004, 8).

According to some experts, the general rule of thumb when engaged in a governmental reorganization is that the process should bring together agencies that share at least 50 percent of the same mission. "That is certainly the case for the Customs Service, INS, Border Patrol, and TSA [Transportation Security Administration], all of which serve a common commitment to homeland security," says Paul Light. However, "That is not the case for many of the other agencies on the transfer list, including the Agriculture Department's Animal and Plant Health Inspection System, the Coast Guard, and FEMA (Light 2002, 3).

These problems are some of the ones that will linger long after the creation of the huge DHS. It may take decades for Congress and the executive branch to resolve these reorganization glitches. Chris Seiple, like so many others concerned about this problem, has said that that the "bad news [about the creation of the DHS] is [this]: It will take a long time to consolidate these different components of the federal government; it should be done, but it will take a long time. And if you don't have a plan for education and training, i.e., the creation of a new culture within the new bureaucracy, you could make the situation worse" (Seiple 2002, 3).

The bottom line: does the massive reorganization make "the country secure enough?" (Sirota 2004, 1). As Representative Jim Turner (D-TX), the ranking minority member of the U.S. House of Representatives Select Committee on Homeland Security, asked: "Are we as safe as we need to be?" (quoted in Sirota 2004, 1).

As already noted, the general consensus is that Americans are not as safe as we ought to be and, in many instances, not as safe as the nation was on September 10, 2001.

Budget and Funding Problems.   Senator Byrd said bluntly: "The DHS needs money" (Byrd 2002, 116). Senator Joseph Lieberman (D-CT), one of the first legislators to call for the creation of a DHS, in 2004 said, in disgust, that President Bush's proposed budget for the DHS in FY 2005 was $14 billion less than was needed for the department. "President Bush," said Lieberman, "seems to have checked 'homeland security' off on his to-do list, persuaded that the public won't notice the difference between building a robust, new homeland security effort and merely rearranging the piecemeal efforts we had before." He and other Democrats in the Congress point out that such small budget increases in the DHS (a 10 percent increase over the 2004 budget) have created huge "security gaps" in intelligence, infrastructure, cyberspace, and other areas. For example, Lieberman pointed out that there are fewer than 100 inspectors assigned to overseas ports to inspect millions of cargo containers headed for the United States annually (quoted in *Seattle Times* 2004, 2).

Senator Byrd, a very outspoken critic of President Bush, has chronicled Bush's blocking of additional funding for the DHS: In mid-November 2001, Bush opposed the inclusion of $15 billion for homeland security because such funding "will only expand the size of government," he warned. As Byrd observed, "all Senate Republicans voted to block the funding."

In December 2001, the 2001 defense appropriations bill was sent to the floor of the Senate for a vote. It contained $13.1 billion for homeland security. Ultimately, due to White House pressure, the final bill reduced the HS budget by almost $5 billion.

In June 2002, the Senate passed (71 votes to 22) a supplemental appropriations bill that contained $8.3 billion for homeland security. The president threatened to veto the legislation because of the "excessive" funding for homeland security.

In August 2002, Bush refused to spend an emergency designation of $2.5 billion for homeland security by the Congress. "I made my opposition clear," he said later. "We were pretty plain-spoken. I understand Congress' position, and today they're going to learn mine. We'll spend none of it." (quoted in Byrd, 2002, 112)

In October 2002, the Congress adjourned without appropriating any funds for homeland security projects that were to be implemented to improve security at seaports, airports, border security, and nuclear facilities. The president's press secretary, Ari Fleischer, said: "There's a new sheriff in town, and he's dedicated to fiscal discipline."(Byrd 2002, 112)

On December 2, 2002, the DOJ announced that it would not release funds for state and local law enforcement agencies for first responders.

On January 15, 2003, months after the president signed the DHS Act of 2002, Senate Republicans—in control of that body since the November 2002 elections—"whipped into line by Bush," defeated an amendment that would have added $5 billion to the department. The funds were to be used for enhancing security at ports, airports, borders, and chemical and nuclear plants. Senator Byrd's effort to reduce the funding to $2 billion in order to get *some* funding to these areas was defeated in the Senate.

In April 2003, $9 billion for homeland security was defeated in the Senate. And in July 2003, Byrd tried to add $1.75 billion to appropriations for security programs. His efforts were unsuccessful. Again in July and September 2003, amendments that would have increased homeland security funding were defeated on party line voting (Byrd 2002, 112–115, passim).

Byrd wrote about President Bush:

> Nobody can convince me that this White House is seri-
> ous about homeland security. I have broken my pick,
> threatened, cajoled, pleaded, and lost sleep countless
> nights because I know how underfunded these security
> programs are. . . . With the possible exception of airline
> security, very little has been done, three years after we
> were attacked, to address glaring deficiencies and pro-
> tect obvious targets of terrorist attack. (Byrd 2002, 115)

Another paradox is the fundamental reality that whatever
funds are appropriated to the DHS and the other non-DHS agencies that engage in homeland security are committed to these organizations on the basis of pork-barrel politics as usual, not on
the findings of a rational risk- and cost-benefit analysis of homeland security funding. Are homeland security funds within DHS
well-spent? The answer, for a number of reasons discussed here
and elsewhere in this chapter, is a ringing "no." According to the
chairman of the U.S. House Select Committee on Homeland Security, Chris Cox (R-CA), the DHS spends the way Congress generally spends the revenues collected by the federal government—
carelessly! Cox reported that

> In keeping with the way Washington spreads federal
> taxpayers' money to the states—whether for highways,
> education, or emergency preparedness—DHS follows in
> part a formula set by Congress that provides every state
> with a guaranteed minimum amount to the states re-
> gardless of risk or need. (Cox, quoted in de Rugy 2004, 9)

De Rugy concludes that the "theory that money should be
spent smoothly across states has not been supported by reasoned
analysis during the public policy debate" (de Rugy 2004, 10).

The funding problem for DHS has been further and dramatically compounded by the huge Bush tax cuts instituted during his
first term, as well as the expenses incurred by the United States
after it invaded Iraq in March 2003 (almost $200 billion through the
end of fiscal year 2004). From a $3 trillion *surplus* in 2001, the
United States government (and its citizens) found itself looking at
an almost $3 trillion *deficit* in 2005. As a consequence, Congress
(with both houses controlled by Republicans) has been reluctant to
generously fund domestic programs, including the DHS.

Ironically, since 2001, there have been a wide variety of serious cuts—amounting to billions of dollars—in domestic pro-

grams for the aged, the poor, schools, veterans' assistance, and those in need of medical care and in domestic entitlement programs. Without proper funding for the DHS, the reorganization effort is essentially rearranging deck chairs on the *Titanic*. Without proper funding, and without a reasonable spending model that maximizes the use of these federal funds, large holes remain in homeland security, thereby making the United States vulnerable to terrorist attacks.

Too Many Congressional Committees. The funding problem facing DHS ties into another problem that has emerged since the creation of the fifteenth cabinet-level federal executive department: the reality of a multitude of congressional committees that have budgetary and oversight responsibilities over the twenty-two agencies that comprise the DHS. Presently there are eighty-eight committees and subcommittees that handle DHS nominations, budget, oversight, and new DHS legislation. Clearly, say observers, there needs to be a qualitative and "significant revamping of the committee processes in Congress to streamline appropriations, authorization, and oversight" (Conley 2002, 17).

A big challenge for the DHS secretary (Tom Ridge was replaced in early 2005 by Michael Chertoff) is to convince Congress that the Byzantine congressional committee structure over aspects of domestic security has to go, replaced by a single oversight and appropriations committee in each house. "You can't create a new department if all the elements of the old departments keep going back to their old bosses," said John Hanre, a former deputy secretary in the DOD. And Newt Gingrich, the former Republican Speaker of the House of Representatives, asked: "It is absurd how many places a Secretary of DHS has to report to. . . . How do you get a coherent policy, and how do you get a coherent budget [under these circumstances]?" (both quoted in Cohen et al. 2003, 17).

When the DHS was introduced by President Bush and Secretary Ridge in June 2002, Ridge said of the congressional labyrinth: "I believe that they'll work their way through that maze of committees and subcommittees, and end up providing the kind of leadership we need at the congressional level" (quoted in Cohen et al. 2003, 21). But without a major revamping of the committee structure in Congress, it is impossible to have focused and directed congressional oversight. Without such necessary congressional oversight and assessment—and criticism and modification—of the DHS, there is no way that Congress can help guide homeland security policy. And, as of early 2005, there was still no action taken by the Congress to end the serpentine ways of legislative oversight.

The Intelligence "Information Sharing" Dilemma. "Information must be fully shared, so we can follow every lead," said President Bush in his June 6, 2002, address to the nation about his decision to ask Congress to create a cabinet-level DHS. "The reason to create this department is not to increase the size of government, but to increase its focus and effectiveness." However, even after 9/11, the nation's intelligence gatherers—especially the FBI, the CIA, the National Security Agency (NSA), and the DOD—are still "largely untouched" by the DHS. None of them has been moved to the DHS, and their $30 billion intelligence budgets remain with them still. As one severe critic of the DHS wrote, "The DHS organizations are both blind and paralyzed because [DHS] does not have an intelligence gathering and analyzing department [and] must rely on the CIA and FBI" (Ranum 2004, 60).

Furthermore, how can intelligence be shared between federal agencies in and outside of the DHS when the bureaucracies can't communicate because their computer systems are not compatible with each other? One example of this problem is symptomatic of the largely unfixed communications problem existing in the federal government's intelligence-gathering operations. The U.S. Border Patrol, now a part of the DHS, uses an electronic fingerprint-identification system. The system enables officers "to determine how many times an alien has been caught sneaking into the U.S." However, the Border Patrol system has only a small amount of data in its system about the possible criminal past of these illegal aliens.

> The FBI maintains a separate electronic fingerprint-identification system that covers everyone ever charged with a crime. *In true bureaucratic fashion, the two computer systems do not talk to each other* (emphasis added).
>
> In the 1990s the two agencies were directed to integrate their systems. They are still working at it. The most optimistic completion date is 2008. Until then, illegals picked up at the border may have any number of criminal charges pending, but the arresting officers will never know (Barlett and Steele 2004, 62).

There is a major *disconnect* between the intelligence gatherers and the new DHS. Intelligence-gatherers, policy makers, and field operators are still separate from and jealous of their competitors (Victor 2002, 1779). The DHS does not generate its own intelligence about terrorists and radical terrorist groups such as Al Qaeda; it is "heavily dependent on the analytical capabilities and resources of America's intelligence community, [one] known for its reluctance to share information with others" (Badley 2004, 1–2).

Gathering and sharing intelligence between federal, state, and local agencies is still very problematic. The 9/11 Commission's final report spent a great deal of time on this continuing dilemma and has made recommendations that the intelligence gathering agencies find very uncomfortable.

Because of this political/bureaucratic infighting—real hardball tactics employed by all—the DHS does not have the ability to compete with the major intelligence-gathering and law enforcement agencies. Although the Coast Guard, Secret Service, INS, Border Patrol, and Customs—all part of the DHS—provide intelligence-gathering components, all these *combined* cannot compare to the capability of the major intelligence gatherers outside the DHS. There must be better information sharing and the end to the "stovepipe" phenomenon for the DHS to be an effective domestic security agency of the federal government.

From a number of organizations came an insistent demand, after 9/11 and after the surfacing of major intelligence gaffes surrounding the presidential rationale to go to war in Iraq in March 2003, for improvement in the nation's intelligence-gathering processes. Both the 9/11 National Commission and the very influential organization of 9/11 families recommended (in the 9/11 Commission's final report) and demanded (through testimony before congressional committees) major changes in the structure and functions of the intelligence-gathering agencies.

In a lame-duck session after the November 2004 presidential election, Congress reluctantly agreed to a restructuring of the intelligence community and to the creation of a director of National Intelligence (DNI) who would have budgetary control over much of the $40-odd billion national intelligence budget. (At the present time, the Pentagon controls most—80 percent—of the intelligence budget.) Major turf battles are expected once the president nominates the DNI and that person's major deputies.

The bill also created a National Counterterrorism Center, which will, it is anticipated, function as a clearing house for terrorist threats; a National Counterproliferation Center, "which will oversee the government's efforts to halt the spread of chemical, biological, and nuclear weapons and the technology to make them;" and a Board "to police against abuses of civil liberties and privacy" (Shenon 2004, A1).

In early December 2004, President Bush signed the intelligence restructure bill into law. Whether the CIA and the other fourteen intelligence-gathering agencies (many under the authority of the Secretary of Defense and the military establishment) will work more cooperatively than they have in the past is still a matter for conjecture. The success of the new restructuring will depend in great part on the assertiveness of the new head, the director of National Intelligence, and on President Bush "making it clear over the next several months that the DNI has his support." Said the co-chair of the 9/11 National Commission, Thomas H. Kean: "This person [DNI] must have the real confidence of the president or he is not going to be able to do this job" (quoted in Shenon 2004, A1).

Less than one week after President Bush signed the controversial bill, stories were leaked to the major newspapers about the Pentagon's plans to "fight for intelligence," to expand even further its role in intelligence gathering, especially in those areas of intelligence-gathering that traditionally have been the province of the CIA. For the Defense Department, this military expansion "includ[ed] [combat] missions aimed at terrorist groups and those involved in weapons proliferation" (Jehl and Schmitt 2004, A1).

Whereas the restructuring bill will continue the turf war that has been fought for decades between the CIA and military intelligence agencies, the irony is that the bill has not strengthened the DHS's own intelligence analysis division. After the smoke of intelligence-gathering restructuring dies down, the DHS will still be in the frustrating position of having to receive intelligence information from the DNI and his (or her) office. The result? The DHS, charged with protecting the homeland from terrorist strikes, will still have to rely on the generosity of intelligence-gathering agencies totally outside the control of the secretary of the DHS.

Maritime Cargo Container and Port Security. Cargo containers brought into U.S. ports remain a serious area of homeland security concern. More than 15 million containers arrive annually from overseas.

One large container ship contains 8,000 of these huge containers—
"potential Trojan Horses" (Nye 2004, 32). As already noted there
are approximately 100 U.S. inspectors trying to check the containers shipped to the United States from overseas ports. Before September 11, 2001, less than 2 percent of these containers were inspected upon arrival. In 2004–2005, only about 5–6 percent of the
millions of containers were examined by DHS personnel. Today
there are huge machines that can screen these containers; however,
in 2004 only 135 were actually in place and being used by DHS inspectors at U.S. ports, of which there are over 360 harbors that receive these containers (Nye 2004, 32).

In 2004 M. R. Dinsmore, the chief executive of the Port of
Seattle, met with Secretary Ridge in Seattle, Washington. Ridge
told Dinsmore and other Port of Seattle officials that he slept better at night because "our country is better prepared than before
to defend against a terrorist attack." Dinsmore turned to Ridge
and said: "I'm glad you're sleeping better, Mr. Secretary, because
I'm not" (Dinsmore 2004, 26).

He told Ridge that *every day*, the nation's 361 river and seaports receive 21,000 containers. Annually, there are 50,000 visits
from 8,100 foreign flag vessels.

> Imagine what would happen if a biological, chemical or
> some other kind of weapon arrived in one of our har-
> bors. Every U.S. port would be affected as authorities
> worked to determine the extent and the source of the
> threat. Global trade could practically be shut down.
> And we don't have the systems in place to get the ports
> up and running again. . . . Reviewing the threats to our
> transportation network, I have to conclude that when it
> comes to maritime security, we haven't done nearly
> enough (Dinsmore 2004, 26).

Whereas almost $7 billion was spent on air transport secu-
rity in 2004, "it is a very different story at our nation's seaports."
A fraction of the money spent for aircraft security is spent on port
security, which is a "far more complex problem." There is no
comprehensive plan for seaport security. There are no common
standards and protocols for DHS officials to use working to secure the nation's ports. Finally, there is very little funding for security screening devices. Dinsmore and other port officials are
critical of Ridge's suggestion for additional funding: generate
funds from the private sector, not the federal government. All the

"demonstration" projects implementing new technology and protocols work fine, claims Dinsmore, "and they are available. We need to act on maritime security now [with an influx of federal funding] so we can *all* sleep better at night" (Dinsmore 2004, 26).

Airport Security. More than 90 percent of the more than 186,000 DHS employees (as of December 2004, up from 170,000 "expected" employees identified in November 2002) handle border and transportation (air and sea) security—and more than 60 percent of the FY 2004 budget of more than $37 billion was spent on border, port, and airport security. The largest of the DHS agencies in this area is the Transportation Security Administration (TSA).

In 2004 there were over 45,000 employees in the TSA. The agency, which was created prior to the DHS, "is one of the growth areas" in the new department (Nye 2004, 32). On November 19, 2001, President Bush signed the comprehensive (more than 21,000 words long) Aviation and Transportation Security Act. The act created the TSA and laid out its general purposes: "providing civil aviation security; related research and development activities; and security responsibilities over other modes of transportation that are exercised by the Department of Transportation."

The act called for the TSA to (1) "assume civil aviation security functions and responsibilities" within three months (by February 19, 2002), and (2) "implement an aviation security program for charter air carriers." It called for the TSA to establish by November 19, 2002, "a program for screening passengers and property at airports, carried out by the screening personnel" (sections of the act quoted in Dunham 2002, 65).

When in June 2002, President Bush introduced his plan for the creation of a DHS, the TSA was part of the reorganization plan. It was one of the twenty-two federal agencies transferred into the new cabinet-level executive department with the passing of the DHS Act. From its inception, TSA administrators focused most of their attention on screening commercial airline passengers. According to critics of the TSA (see, for example, 2004 Democratic presidential candidate Senator John Kerry's repeated criticism of the agency's focus on passenger screening rather than cargo screening), the agency responsible for airline security searches gray-haired little old ladies "while only 2% of cargo on passenger planes is screened" (quoted in Nye 2004, 32).

And if the screening focus of the TSA inspectors is off target, there are at least two other airport security dilemmas that have surfaced since 2002. Many TSA inspectors have been arrested for stealing money, jewelry, and other personal items from the checked bags of passengers. Across the nation, from Philadelphia to Detroit, from Fort Lauderdale to New Orleans, TSA inspectors have been caught stealing items from bags that required inspection by the TSA staff (Bovard 2004, A23).

One reason for this crime wave is that the more than $5 billion spent since 2002 by the TSA for electronic bomb-detector machinery has been used to purchase unreliable equipment. When the TSA was still an agency in the Department of Transportation, the DOT secretary, Norman Y. Mineta, "told Congress that the machines have a false-positive rate of 35%—and if a bag tests positive, it must be searched by hand. To do this, agents routinely examine baggage in closed areas, far from prying eyes." A second reason for this problem is that the TSA "has done an abysmal job of managing its work force. In June 2003, the agency admitted that it had failed to screen its own screeners and fired more than 1,200 employees after they failed criminal background checks or other internal investigations" (Bovard 2004, A23).

To further compound the problem, Clark Kent Irvin, the DHS's inspector general, found that the TSA inspectors do a poor job inspecting airline passengers and their baggage. In April 2004, Irvin told a congressional committee that TSA inspectors performed poorly in a number of covert tests conducted by his office. And the 9/11 Commission's final report, published in summer 2004, warned that "major vulnerabilities" still exist in aviation security against terrorist attacks (quoted in Bovard 2004, A23).

Another problem that has surfaced recently is the dilemma of "mission creep" in aviation security programs. For example, the TSA employed a computer-based system intended for spotting possible terrorists before they could board airplanes. However, "its use was expanded to serve broader police purposes unrelated to passenger profiling, according to internal documents of the TSA."

The DHS canceled that program this summer, without ever using it, after opponents argued that it intruded too much on people's privacy. A TSA spokesman acknowledged . . . that the program's mission had become so broad that the department could not build the political consensus to see it through. (Bovard, 2004, A23)

What had started off as a program identifying possible terrorists or those who are seen as "a threat to aviation safety, civil aviation, or national security" had turned into a program that could be used to profile persons involved in cases of violent crime or in cases where there was an outstanding warrant for the person's arrest. The TSA could then provide that passenger information to "appropriate federal, state, local, international, or foreign agencies or authorities." As a consequence, the program had to be withdrawn, and TSA planners went back to the drawing board to reinvent the process—without "mission creep" (Wald and Schwartz 2004, A25).

There is, finally, a problem in the TSA and DHS that was discussed earlier in this chapter: the absence of a DHS effort to consolidate twelve separate systems and multiple terrorist watch lists. Nine federal agencies inside and outside the DHS, including the TSA, CIA, FBI, State Department, Customs, and Border Patrol Protection's Interagency Border Inspection System, collect and create separate terrorist watch-lists. There is the problem of sharing information with all involved—including airlines personnel—in checking passengers and foreigners entering the United States through seaports, airports, cars, and trains.

DHS Inspector General Ervin in an October 2004 report, "DHS Challenges in Consolidating Terrorist Watch List Information," wrote that "in the absence of central oversight and a strategic approach to watch list consolidation, problems with uncoordinated interagency planning, budgeting, staffing, requirements definition, and policy management problems persist" (Department of Homeland Security Inspector General's Report 2004, 2).

The problem continues to be dealt with on an "ad hoc basis, posing a risk to the successful accomplishment of the goal," the report concluded. Through October 2004, commercial airline personnel screened all passengers against a list of potential terrorist suspects, but not a consolidated list. Consequently, there have been a number of embarrassing errors made by these personnel.

For example, United Airlines personnel allowed Yusuf Islam, on a government no-fly list, formerly known as the popular music star Cat Stevens, to board a London–New York Boeing 747 carrying 248 other passengers. After take-off, the TSA realized what had occurred, ordered the jet to land in Bangor, Maine,

and removed Mr. Islam. Secretary Ridge b.
had the ability to act on the information l
fense, United said that the information prov
match that supplied by Mr. Islam. "The syste
as a no-fly passenger" (quoted in Wald 2004, ⁄

In fall 2004, TSA officials reported that
dozens of incidents where no-fly-list passengers
way because of mix-ups between agencies and \   ..nd
the exponential growth of these no-fly lists.

> The situation is overstretching law-enforcement person-
> nel, who must scramble to respond to each incident. The
> no-fly list now has 20,000 names, and up to 300 new
> ones are added daily. There are dead people and people
> in prison on the list. At least 1,000 names are duplicates.
> Checking the unwieldy list has caused airline computer
> systems to crash (Donnelly 2004, 18).

However, because this problem has had transparency, adjustments have been made by Congress and the DHS to improve the
watch-list screening protocols. Under the new system, "the airlines will provide the DHS with passenger lists and government
officials will check those names against more expansive [but not
coordinated] watch lists." The start-up date for this new program, called Secure Flight, was November 2004 (Swarns 2004,
A1). (This programmatic change implements one of the recommendations made by the 9/11 Commission, issued in July 2004,
which called for governmental takeover of implementation of the
no-fly security lists.)

Border Patrol Security.   "The big, big core of [the DHS] is border
patrol [i.e., Coast Guard, Customs, INS, TSA, Border Patrol, visa-
granting authority]," said Elaine Kamarck, who worked in Democratic Vice President Al Gore's "Reinventing Government"
project in the 1990s. "Everything else is trivial" (quoted in
McLaughlin 2002, A1). *Every day* in 2004, for example, U.S. Customs officers processed more than 50,000 trucks and containers—
and 500 ocean-going ships. "In a single day, more than 4,000 illegal aliens will walk across the busiest unlawful gateway into the
U.S., the 375-mile border between Arizona and Mexico. . . . The
total number of illegal aliens flooding into the U.S. in 2004 will
total 3 million, . . . roughly three times the number of immigrants
who will come to the U.S. by legal means." It is estimated that in

05, more than 15 million illegal aliens were living and working—and possibly plotting a terrorist attack—in the United States (Barlett and Steele 2004, 51, 52).

Further adding to this illegal-alien security dynamic is the fact that more than 110,000 of the illegals crossing into the United States are labeled by the Border Patrol as "other than Mexicans, or OTM. These OTM included, in 2004, aliens from Afghanistan, Bulgaria, Russia, China, Egypt, Iran, and Iraq. Given the tightened controls on legal visitors at airports, the U.S.-VISIT policy, for example, the "mass movement of illegals offers the perfect cover for terrorists seeking to enter the U.S." (Barlett and Steele 2004, 52)

Asa Hutchinson, the undersecretary for border security at DHS, confirmed this homeland security dilemma. Recently he said to the press that "there is concern that as we tighten the security of our ports of entry through our biometric checks that there will be more opportunity or more effort made by terrorists to enter our country through our vast land borders" (Swarns 2004, A1).

And yet, as is known, only a small portion of the human and manufactured products traffic is properly inspected. And stretches of the 9,500 miles of U.S. border are totally unprotected or protected by only a fraction of the personnel needed to do a competent security job. The number of U.S. Border Patrol officers working on the 1,951-mile U.S.-Mexican border was 8,600 in 2000. In 2005, the number had increased only slightly, to 9,900 personnel.

There are other security problems that arise from the private sector, including giant merchandisers like Wal-Mart and automobile companies like General Motors. They require on-time delivery of their goods—much of which comes to the United States from other countries—and are fearful of the delays that will occur when more funds are spent in buttressing border, airport, and port security.

Prior to 9/11, border agents were committed to ensuring the smooth flow of commerce through all entry ports in order to facilitate delivery of goods to private-sector businesses. "Having a slowdown at ports of entry," said Bill Reinsch, president of the private National Foreign Trade Council, in Washington, D.C., "would be a huge problem and—because of just-in-time delivery—could mean shutting down assembly lines." There is also a risk, he said, of creating "a deeper recession than we have now [in 2002]" (quoted in McLaughlin 2002, A1).

Tightening the borders will exacerbate another problem: strict enforcement of immigration laws will conflict with businesses' need for cheap labor from Mexico and South America. According to a recent investigative report, "Corporate America thrives on illegals. . . . For corporate America (which sends recruitment personnel into Mexico to line up workers), employing illegal aliens at wages so low few citizens could afford to take the jobs is great for profits and stockholders" (Barlett and Steele 2004, 58). Few corporations are penalized for these business practices. Although Congress in 1986 passed the Immigration and Reform Act, which provided for $10,000 fines for every illegal alien hired as well as possible prison terms for repeat offenders, the law is honored in the breech. It has never been enforced since passage almost two decades ago.

These very visible border security problems have affected the morale of the thousands of border patrol personnel. In a study published in August 2004 by the Peter Hart Research Associates organization,

> more than 60% of Border Patrol agents and immigration officers surveyed said the DHS could do more to stop potential terrorists from entering the country, and more than a third said they were not satisfied that they had the tools and training to do so. . . . [The survey] found them sharply divided on whether the country was safer now than before the 9/11 attacks: 53% said it was, but 44% said it was no safer or was less safe. . . . The survey found low morale to be pervasive (Swarns 2004, A1).

A final, potentially troublesome issue is the fact that in August 2004, the DHS announced that effective immediately, it "planned to give border patrol agents sweeping new powers to deport illegal aliens from the frontiers with Mexico and Canada without providing them the opportunity to make their case before an immigration judge" (Swarns 2004, A1).

The change was proposed because of the persistence of a chronic immigration problem: the backlog of illegal immigrants' cases waiting to be heard by immigration judges. Prior to the DHS change in protocol, a border patrol officer brought an undocumented immigrant to the immigration courts. There the immigration judge made decisions regarding the status of the illegal alien that would ultimately determine whether he or she would remain in the United States or be deported.

Critics called the former system "sluggish and cumbersome," stating that illegals had to wait months, and even years, before being deported. Under the new protocols, illegals would be deported within eight days. The new DHS rule applies to illegal immigrants caught within 100 miles of the border who are not Mexicans or Canadians. It applies only to the OTM and OTC ("other than Canadians") held by border patrol agents—about 50,000 per year.

The new rule is problematic for two reasons: (1) There are too few border patrol agents, and this new responsibility may not be used fairly because border patrol agents are not properly trained to make these decisions about undocumented aliens. (2) Critics of the rule change, representing civil liberties organizations, argue that for many undocumented aliens, entering the United States is a matter of life or death. Being sent back to the country the person fled could result in torture or death. "We're very concerned that we may see the mistaken deportations of refugees, citizens and other legitimate visitors. For refugees, it could be a . . . death sentence," said Eleanor Acer, director of the asylum program of Human Rights First (quoted in Swarns 2004, A1).

Private-Sector Security Problems

The United States, concluded two researchers in November 2004, "remains woefully unprepared to protect the public against terrorists wielding biological agents despite dramatic increases in biodefense spending by the Bush administration and considerable progress on many fronts" (Mintz and Warrick 2004, A1).

"There's no area of homeland security in which the administration has made more progress than bioterrorism," said Richard A. Falkenrath, formerly President Bush's deputy homeland security advisor, "and none where we have further to go" (quoted in Mintz and Warrick 2004, A1).

The nonmilitary private industrial sector—in particular, the chemical, biological, radiological, and nuclear industrial complexes—is the most feared type of terrorist attack and provides the greatest challenge for those involved in homeland security. "Current and future enemies will find the opportunity irresistible to assault nonmilitary elements of U.S. power that arise from our growing dependence on sophisticated networks to move people, food, cargo, energy, and information at higher volumes and greater velocities" (Flynn 2004, 5).

More than 85 percent of potential U.S. targets for terrorists—chemical plants, nuclear power plants, and so on—are held in private hands. Consequently, their lobbyists in Washington work hard to limit the extent of governmental regulation of these industries.

And, because of the need to maximize profits and the accompanying lobbying efforts in Washington, D.C., by these various industries to minimize government regulation, the private sector generally remains the most vulnerable terrorist target. This is seen quite clearly when observing the chemical industry in the United States.

Extremely dangerous chemical tanks, located in 15,000 chemical plant facilities across the United States, are very easy targets for terrorists. When ruptured by accident or by design, the chemicals released from these tanks will kill millions of persons. However, because this industry has excellent ties with the Republican Party in the White House and with Republican legislators and staffers in both houses of Congress, it is almost invulnerable to regulatory edicts from the federal government requiring the industry to better secure its facilities.

Indeed, as it is the EPA that is responsible for regulating the industry, the DHS can only make recommendations and give advice to the owners about tightening security at their vulnerable-to-terrorists chemical facilities. This is also true with other major private-sector industries not subject to DHS requirements and regulations. For example, the NRC is responsible for regulating the safety and security of the nuclear power plant industry. If that regulatory agency does not do a good job of forcing the industry to secure its nuclear power plants, if the NRC relies on voluntary security actions by the industry instead, the DHS cannot do very much to change the scenario, no matter how dangerous the consequences are for domestic security (see, generally, Hirsch 2003).

> While President Bush continues to make terrorism and domestic security the centerpiece of his [2004 presidential] campaign, he has made little mention of one of the most urgent threats to our safety: the risk that terrorists could cause thousands, even millions, of deaths by sabotaging one of the 15,000 chemical plants across the United States (Hind and Halperin 2004, A27).

In understanding the threat of a chemical plant catastrophe, recall the 1984 Union Carbide insecticide plant event in Bhopal,

India. That *accidental* rupture of pipes led to the deaths of 20,000 and injuries to over 200,000 persons. Imagine what horrors a terrorist could initiate if a person entered a New Jersey chemical plant, just across from lower Manhattan, and set off a time bomb. The explosion would set free into the atmosphere deadly chemical poisons that would, in a matter of minutes, drift onto the New York City denizens, killing many tens of thousands almost instantly.

> A study by the Army surgeon general found that up to 2.4 *million* people could be killed or wounded by a terrorist attack on a single chemical plant. In February 2003, the government's National Infrastructure Protection Center (NIPC) warned that chemical plants in the United States could be Al Qaeda targets. Investigations by the *Pittsburgh Tribune-Review* and the CBS program *60 Minutes* have highlighted lax or nonexistent security at chemical plants, with gates unlocked or wide open and chemical tanks unguarded (Hind and Halperin 2004, A27).

Since 9/11, the EPA has identified 123 chemical plants where an accident or a terrorist attack could threaten more than a million persons at each site. It also identified 7,600 plants that threatened more than 1,000 people at each site. The EPA, using the Clean Air Act, has tried to improve the safety of these plants by compelling the plants to increase security and to use less hazardous chemicals.

The EPA has also regularly informed DHS officials that chemical plants "could endanger up to a million lives with poisonous clouds of ammonia, chlorine, or carbon disulfide that terrorists could release over densely populated areas" (Nye 2004, 32). When asked about this security problem, DHS officials have said that "regulating is not our role." The Department of Homeland Security "merely" advised the chemical plants in the United States "on what their vulnerabilities are" (DHS quotes from Nye 2004, 32).

The DHS does not have legislative authority to do anything but suggest that chemical plants bulk up their security. It relies solely "on voluntary efforts by the industry." However, "without enforceable requirements, chemical firms will remain reluctant to put sufficient safeguards in place, for fear that their competitors will scrimp on security and thus be able to undercut them on price" (Hind and Halperin 2004, A27).

Another vulnerable homeland security issue closely related to the minimal security matter is that reality that when such an attack occurs, "the great majority of U.S. hospitals and state and local public health agencies would be completely overwhelmed trying to carry out mass vaccinations or distribute antidotes after a large biological attack." In addition, the NIH, "which has the lead role in researching biological warfare vaccines and antidotes, remains largely wedded to its traditional role of doing basic research and producing enough new drugs." Furthermore, in 2005, "because of scientific complexities, no technology exists to detect a biological attack as it occurs" (Mintz and Warrick 2004, A1, 8).

Unless there are tough chemical industry-wide regulatory requirements by the DHS and federal regulatory agencies such as the EPA, the chemical industry will remain extremely vulnerable to the possibility of terrorist attacks. Unless there are Biowatch programs developed across the breadth of the United States, especially in its largest cities, there will be no warning of such an attack until after victims turn up in hospitals with the symptoms of small pox, anthrax, plague, tularemia, botulism, or some other deadly bacteriologic disease. (Biowatch is a pilot program where technicians remove filters from air-checking units in thirty cities once a day and carry them to labs to detect whether biological agents are in the city's air.)

A closely related homeland security problem related to the chemical industry is the transportation of these hazardous materials in pressurized rail tank cars that do not meet national safety standards. On January 6, 2005, a train crash in South Carolina illustrated the dilemma. The crash caused rail tank cars containing deadly chlorine to rupture, thereby releasing the deadly chemical into the air. Almost one dozen persons were killed and hundreds hospitalized or treated because of their exposure to the chemical. This event, unfortunately, is not unusual; similar incidents have occurred in Texas, North Dakota, and other states (Bogdanich and Drew 2005, A1).

Shortly after 9/11, the FBI, after seizing photos of rail tank cars taken by Al Qaeda suspects, warned the rail transportation industry that Al Qaeda "might be planning to attack trains in the United States, possibly causing derailments or blowing up tank cars laden with hazardous materials." The Federal Railroad Administration sent investigators to visit railyards in Las Vegas, Nevada, after receiving a credible terrorist threat. The inspector visited at least three yards and found that all three were open, no security personnel were present, and there would have been absolutely no difficulty setting explosives on the rail tank cars.

Furthermore, it was revealed that more than half of the 60,000 rail tank cars in the United States (those manufactured prior to 1989) were subject to catastrophic explosions because they were built before the current industry standard calling for a special heat treatment to make the steel stronger and less brittle took effect. Michael E. Lyden, the vice president for storage and transport at the Chlorine Institute, indicated that the leading chemical companies were "working in a cooperative manner to improve the pressure vessels." Very little has been done to remove the older rail tank cars from use. U.S. Representative Edward J. Markey (D-MA), who has tried to pass tougher legislation to address this segment of the chemical industry security problem, said: "Whether it's an accident or Al Qaeda, these hazardous materials are very vulnerable and pose a great risk to densely populated areas" (quoted in Bogdanich and Drew 2005, A1).

A final observation: federal agencies responsible for dealing with the safety and security of these private-sector industries, and of dealing with the threat of bioterrorism (the CDC, FDA, EPA, NIAID), like the DHS itself, "have all seen budget decreases and the graying of the staffs" (Flynn 2004, 43–44). Without the necessary—and constant—vigilance by the private sector and appropriation of funds to the DHS and other federal agencies, there will remain in place a very vulnerable industry, one subject to deliberate attacks on its plants and on the rail tanks cars carrying these toxic deadly chemicals across America.

State and Local Government "First Responders" Problems

Karen Anderson, president of the National League of Cities in 2002, was very critical of the DHS. "The [DHS] doesn't get the resources to our cities and towns. While the [2003 authorization was] $38 billion for [DHS], it did not authorize the $3.5 billion for our first responders—our local police, local firefighters, and our emergency medical personnel—for our cities and towns. And that's a great loss" (NewsHour 2002, 3).

This is still the major problem confronting homeland security at the state and local levels. If in 2002 and 2003 presidential actions defeated efforts to fund local communities, by 2004 the problem had flip-flopped. Funds were freed up and sent to states that did not need the money. For example, Alaska officials were given $2 million to spend on homeland security when the state had asked for that amount to purchase a small jet plane. DHS rejected that proposal but wrote that it would be "happy to entertain" further proposals for spending the $2 million.

> Alaska's good fortune highlights what many critics say is a serious failing in the way America is fighting the battle against terrorism at home. While there is consensus that the threat of an attack should supercede politics as usual, the billions of federal dollars for terrorism preparedness are [now] being doled out to states in much the same way as money for schools, bridges, and other routine federal projects (Murphy 2004, A1).

The formula used to distribute the homeland security funds to first responders is one that spreads the money rather than distributing the funds where they are needed the most. A provision in the 2001 Patriot Act guarantees each state at least 0.075 percent of the total in terrorism preparedness grants for states and local communities, "locking up nearly 40% of the [homeland security] money, according to a study by the U.S. House of Representatives Committee on Homeland Security. The rest of the grants for states have been allocated on a state's percentage of the national population" (Murphy 2004, A1).

Because congressional politics reflects the federal political system, even in serious matters such as homeland security, the results can be problematic. For example, Alaska's money from the DHS came to $92 for each Alaska resident; New York's per capita for the same time was $32 per resident; California, $22; and Texas and Florida, $21 per resident, according to a recent Congressional Research Service report.

More than $8 billion was allocated in 2003 and 2004 for state and local first responders, including in Juneau, Alaska. That town has received, through October 2004, almost $1 million in security grants, even though it is a tourist city of 31,000 residents and "shuts down when the last cruise ship leaves in September." The local emergency programs manager, Michael Patterson, said: "I don't have to go looking for grants, they are coming to me." To date, he has purchased a robot for deactivating bombs, decontamination equipment, night-vision goggles, pharmaceutical supplies, and a back-up emergency radio system. Juneau's police chief said, simply: "I don't need more stuff anymore, I need more people" (both quoted in Murphy 2004, A1).

Tom Ridge, asked to comment about this "general revenue sharing" program, said that "[President Bush and I] would like to see more of the dollars go toward areas where the population density is greater, where there is more critical infrastructure, and where the threat seems to be higher" (quoted in Murphy 2004, A1).

From an absolute scarcity of funds for first responders, the nation has gone to a funding scheme for homeland security first responders that is simply not justifiable: It is a formula not based on risk assessment or cost-benefit analysis but on a pork-barrel methodology.

Alaska, Wyoming, North Dakota, South Dakota, and Vermont are the states that have received the largest per capita local responder funds. All five states have, together, a population of 3.2 million residents, roughly one-third the size of Los Angeles County, California! Each has a single U.S. representative in the Congress.

The total lack of risk-based funding "coupled with the absence of federal terrorism preparedness standards or goals to guide expenditure of funds at the state and local levels has resulted already in some questionable uses of terrorism preparedness grants" (deRugy 2004, 17).

Some of the misused federal funds include the following very questionable grants:

- A decontamination unit in storage in Washington state because the state does not have a HAZMAT (hazardous materials) team to use it
- Purchase of radios that are incompatible with county radios
- Purchase of defibrillators by a county in Tennessee to have on hand for a basketball tournament
- A volunteer fire department in a Virginia county received $350,000 to purchase a custom-made fireboat
- $100,000 spent on training courses in a Michigan county that no one attended
- $1.5 million spent by a North Dakota county to buy more biochemical suits than police officers
- Washington, D.C., used its homeland security funds to fund leather jackets for its police force, for a computer-

ized car towing system to help combat fraud by private towing companies, and for a popular summer jobs program

As Veronique de Rugy observed, these examples "are not isolated cases of unfortunate uses of homeland security funds" (deRugy 2004, 11).

This funding dilemma for local responders seems to be an intractable one. Observers believe that there is no quick fix to this dilemma. Richard Ben-Veniste, a member of the 9/11 Commission, said that "members of Congress privately told us that there was no way that they could achieve [funding] reforms on their own, without some external force making the argument. The notion of those with authority ceding authority is more or less equivalent to the notion of water running uphill" (quoted in Murphy 2004, A1).

Some Proposed Solutions

A review of the problems confronting homeland security leaders highlights a small number of problems that seem to appear across the board: *underfunding*, a general revenue sharing approach to the distribution of scarce funds rather than a rational risk management methodology, underfunding, underfunding, and, finally, underfunding. With regard to solving these homeland security problems, the solution *in part* is appropriating the necessary funds to do the job of protecting against terrorism properly. The *larger* problem is

> figuring out which attacks are worth worrying about and spending money on and which are better left ignored. It is spending more resources on the serious attacks—defined as being very likely or if successful having devastating effects—and spending less on the trivial ones. It is taking a finite security budget and making the best use of it. *In other words, homeland security should be about wise choices, not just increased spending.* (de Rugy 2004, 13; emphasis added)

A great many homeland security problems can be solved if the national government can find additional funds to, for example, buy the necessary equipment that will enable agency computer systems to speak to each other. Additional funds appropriated to the DHS will enable the government to hire the additional personnel to screen cargo containers in foreign ports, to purchase the very expensive equipment desperately needed to screen cargo entering the holds of commercial jet aircraft, or to screen the containers entering U.S. rivers and seaports.

Beyond finding the necessary funds needed to provide adequate domestic security against terrorists, the 9/11 Commission final report recommended that such additional financial assistance not be based on a simple general revenue sharing: Disbursement of funds must be based "strictly on an assessment of risks and vulnerabilities; [DHS financial assistance] should not remain a program for general revenue sharing. . . . Congress should not use this money as a pork barrel" (9/11 Commission 2004, 396).

The 9/11 Commission also addressed the problem confronted by the new leadership of the DHS: having to report to more than eighty congressional committees and subcommittees in order to discuss and receive support for budgetary matters, policy matters, and personnel matters. The 9/11 Commission's recommendation was to the point: "Congressional oversight for intelligence [and DHS matters generally] is now dysfunctional. . . . Congress should create a single, principal point of oversight and review for homeland security" (9/11 Commission 2004, 420–421).

Of course, resolving the problems associated with underfunding—personnel and equipment—as well as those that emerge because there is no rational cost-benefit analysis of DHS spending, is tied in with the general financial condition of the United States. As noted, because of the 2002 tax cuts, the largest in U.S. history, and because of the billions of dollars spent on the war in Iraq (close to $200 billion by the end of 2004, without an end in sight to these expenditures), domestic program budgets have been cut from education and child-care programs, from veterans' hospitals and urban renewal programs, and, naturally, from homeland security budgets. Without the necessary funds for DHS, the critics will be correct: all the creation of DHS led to was a huge shuffling of agencies and the people working in them.

Another basic solution to another set of problems that naturally emerge with almost every major governmental reorganization—large or small—is *time,* time, and time. "Time" is the period spent by the new organization's leadership to replace old cultures and old ways of doing business with a new culture and new protocols. As pointed out earlier in this chapter and in chapter 6, over time—with acute, professional leadership and with a well-developed strategic plan for the new entity—this set of problems can be rectified. However, as already noted, the immediate dilemma for America's citizens and government leaders is whether over the time necessary to accomplish these organizational goals—oftentimes decades—the nation will be less secure, and more vulnerable to terrorist attacks.

Still another solution to problems facing the DHS is finding the right men and women to lead the reorganization effort. In addition, these new leaders need to be provided with the *power and authority* to make the necessary changes in homeland security protocols that will dramatically improve domestic security. For example, there is the problem of "territoriality" in the fifteen agencies that make up the national government's intelligence community. Prior to 9/11, because of the "natural" bureaucratic need to protect "their turf," there was little or no transmission of law enforcement and intelligence information between the CIA, the DOD, the NSA, and other intelligence-gathering operations. "Not connecting the dots" was a major fault in intelligence gathering prior to 9/11 that led to that fateful, terrible day of infamy in U.S. history.

Furthermore, there still exists the tradition of "stovepiping," the generation of information in one specific sector by one of the dedicated intelligence agencies without any transmission of the important data to a central intelligence organization for coordinated analysis of all this information. This critical problem has been addressed by the 9/11 Commission. Its final report, published in July 2004, called for the creation of a National Intelligence Director (NID) who would lead and direct the federal government's intelligence apparatus—and who would have control over the budgets (and personnel) of these fifteen federal intelligence organizations. Specifically, the commissioners called for a "seamless integration" of all the intelligence agencies under the leadership of this new NID, who should have two main areas of responsibility:

1. Oversee the national intelligence centers on specific subjects of interest across the U.S. government, and
2. Manage the national intelligence program and oversee the agencies that contribute to it (9/11 Commission 2004, 399–400, 411).

The latter recommendation has caused the greatest consternation within the fifteen separate intelligence communities and among the top leadership of these agencies. In a conversation with a group of private satellite builders, three "spymasters" in the Bush administration disagreed with the 9/11 Commission's recommendations for the creation of the office of NID.

The three men, George Tenet, the former director of the CIA; Lt. General Michael V. Hayden, director of the NSA; and Lt. General James R. Clapper Jr., director of the National Geospatial-Intelligence Agency (NGIA), argued that "the way to defend the United States against terrorist attacks was not to reshuffle the top management but to improve cooperation among rank-and-file analysts, spies, investigators, and military officers" (Lipton 2004, A1).

Though Tenet confessed that "we [CIA] were inconsistent, and [that] we need to make improvements in the way American intelligence works," he did not see the need for a new change in top management. For General Clapper, what was needed to improve the intelligence-gathering and analysis processes was "knowledgeable professionals from each of our silos (agencies) sitting at each other's elbows," not a new layer of bureaucratic management (both quoted in Lipton 2004, A1).

While Congress in fall 2004 was continuing discussion of the 9/11 recommendation, many were hopeful that there would be extended debate on how the nation can solve the dilemma of silos/stovepipe reality and the absence of cooperation within the intelligence community (see, for example, Martin 2004, 26).

Flynn has written that the biggest challenge facing homeland security leaders "lies with identifying how to formally *engage the broader civil society and the private sector,* not just the federal government, in a national effort to make America a less attractive terrorist target" (Flynn 2004, 144; emphasis added).

The government takes professional care in securing military and air bases across the nation. However, these possible terrorist targets (air bases, military storage facilities, military bases, the Pentagon, and other regional military headquarters) only account for about 10 to 12 percent of the total number of targets in the United States that terrorists can attack. Moreover, terrorists want to attack much more vulnerable private sites; places that, if struck properly, can cause millions of deaths and injuries and wreak havoc immediately—because of the lack of first responders and hospital personnel—as well as long-term destruction of an industry.

There must be an attentive public that (1) is not confused with the DHS color-coded terrorist alert system, (2) takes seriously the need to understand the terrorist threat, and (3) is given substantive information about domestic security matters rather than the ludicrous messages that initially came out of DHS asking people to stock up on plastic sheets and duct tape.

The private sector, accounting for more than 85 percent of the very vulnerable targets for terrorists, must seriously address—with the "encouragement" of the DHS and other federal agencies such as the EPA and DOT—the need to adequately protect their properties from insertion by terrorists, even if it means increased industry-wide expenditures for security at the thousands of presently exposed chemical plants, fertilizer factories, nuclear power plants and other energy facilities, transportation companies, financial centers, communications centers (including the plethora of cyber-electronic institutions), and so on. The 9/11 Commission's recommendation regarding this problem called upon DHS leaders to induce the private sector to carry out the needed changes in security at their sites:

> The [DHS] is also responsible for working with the private sector to ensure preparedness. This is entirely appropriate, for the private sector controls 85% of the critical infrastructure in the nation. Indeed, unless the terrorist's target is a military or other secure governmental facility, the "first" first responders will almost certainly be civilians. Homeland security and national preparedness therefore often begins with the private sector (9/11 Commission 2004, 397–398).

Beyond time, funding, and other solutions, at the core of finding answers to the problems of developing an *effective* homeland security is the human dimension: finding solutions requires the presence of men and women who, as leaders, act "quick[ly], imaginative[ly], and [with great] agility" to defend the United States against the threat of new terrorist attacks (9/11 Commission 2004, 399).

References

Badley, Thomas J. 2004. *Homeland Security, 2004–2005*. Guilford, CT: McGraw-Hill/Dushkin.

Barlett, Donald L., and James B. Steele. 2004. "Who Left the Door Open?" *Time,* September 20, pp. 51–66.

Bogdanich, Walt, and Christopher Drew. 2005. "Deadly Leak Underscores Concerns About Rail Safety." *New York Times,* January 9, A1.

Bovard, James. 2004. "Bag It." *New York Times,* August 18.

Byrd, Robert C. 2002. "Homeland Security Act of 2002." *Congressional Record,* November 14. www.truthout.org.

Cohen, Richard E., Siobhan Gorman, and Sydney J. Freedberg Jr. 2003. "The Ultimate Turf War." *National Journal,* January 4, pp. 16–23.

Conley, Richard S. 2002. "The War on Terrorism and Homeland Security." Paper presented at the conference Assessing the Presidency of President George W. Bush at Midpoint, University of Southern Mississippi, November 22.

Department of Homeland Security Inspector General's Report. 2004. "DHS Challenges in Consolidating Terrorist Watch List Information." October 4. www.fcw.com.

de Rugy, Veronique. 2004. "What Does Homeland Security Buy?" *American Enterprise Institute for Public Policy Research* (November 3): 10–21.

Dinsmore, M. R. 2004. "Make Our Ports Safer." *Washington Post,* September 27–October 3, national edition, 26.

Donnally, Sally B. 2004. "Should the No-Fly List Be Grounded?" *Time,* October 18, 18.

Dunham, Steve. 2002. "Transportation Security Administration Faces Huge Challenges." *Journal of Homeland Security* (February): 65–75.

Editorial. 2004. "Homeland Security Dept. Marks Fractious First Year." *Seattle Times,* March 1, sec. A. www.seattletimes.nwsource.com.

Flynn, Stephen. 2004. *America the Vulnerable: How Our Government Is Failing to Protect Us from Terrorism.* New York: HarperCollins.

Hind, Rind, and David Halperin. 2004. "Lots of Chemicals, Little Reaction." *New York Times,* September 22.

Hirsch, Daniel. 2003. "The NRC: What, Me Worry?" *Bulletin of the Atomic Scientists* (January/February): 39–44.

James, Frank. 2004. "Homeland Security Department Gets Mixed Grades After First Year." *Macon* (GA) *Telegram,* February 29, A1.

Jehl, Douglas, and Eric Schmitt. 2004. "Pentagon Seeks to Expand Role in Intelligence-Gathering." *New York Times,* December 19, A1.

Leahy, Patrick. 2002. "The Homeland Security Department Act." Office of Senator Leahy, Washington, DC., November 19. www.leahy.senate.gov.

Light, Paul. 2002. *Assessing the Department of Homeland Security.* Washington, DC: Brookings Institute. www.brook.edu.

———. 2004. "Homeland Security Department Marks a Fractious First Year." *Seattle Times,* March 1, A1.

Lipton, Eric. 2004. "Spy Chiefs Say Cooperation Should Begin at Bottom." *New York Times,* October 14, A1.

Malkin, Michelle. 2002. *Invasion: How America Still Welcomes Terrorists, Criminals, and Other Foreign Menaces to Our Shores.* Washington, DC: Regnery.

Martin, Kate. 2004. "Irresponsible Intelligence Reform." *Washington Post,* October 4–10, national weekly edition, 26.

McLaughlin, Abraham. 2002. "Emerging Plans for Homeland Security Department Focus on Border and Transportation Issues." *Christian Science Monitor,* June 24, A1. www.csmonitor.com.

Mintz, John, and Joby Warrick. 2004. "U.S. Unprepared Despite Progress, Experts Say." *Washington Post,* November 8, A01.

Murphy, Dean E. 2004. "Security Grants Still Streaming to Rural States." *New York Times,* October 12, A1.

NewsHour. 2002. "Securing Our Homeland." *PBS Online NewsHour,* November 20. www.pbs.org/newshour.

9/11 Commission Report. 2004. *Final Report of the National Commission on Terrorist Attacks upon the United States.* New York: Norton.

Nye, Joseph S., Jr. 2004. "Watch Out." *Washington Post,* September 27–October 3, national weekly edition, 32.

Ranum, Marcus J. 2004. *The Myth of Homeland Security.* New York: Wiley.

Saletan, William. 2002. "Ballot Box: Reorganizing Government: Does Bush's DHS Make Sense?" *Slate,* June 7. www.slate.msn.com.

Shenon, Philip. 2004. "New Phase Begins in Push to Reorganize Intelligence." *New York Times,* December 20, A1.

Seiple, Chris. 2002. "DHS: Security in Transition." *Institute for Global Engagement* (November). www.globalengagement.org.

Sirota, David, Christy Harvey, and Judd Legum. 2004. "Homeland Security: Dangerous Holes." *Center for American Progress* (March 4). www.americanprogress.org.

Swarns, Rachel L. 2004. "U.S. to Give Border Patrol Agents the Power to Deport Illegal Aliens." *New York Times,* August 11, A1.

———. 2004. "Government to Take Over Watch-List Screening." *New York Times.* August 17, A1.

————. 2004. "Study Finds Most Border Officers Feel Security Ought to Be Better." *New York Times.* August 24, A1.

Victor, Kirk. 2002. "The Experiment Begins." *National Journal,* June 15, 1775–1787.

Wald, Matthew L. 2004. "Accusations on Detention of Ex-Singer." *New York Times,* September 23, A1.

Wald, Matthew L., and John Schwartz. 2004. "Screening Plans Went Beyond Terrorism." *New York Times,* September 19, A25.

4

Chronology

2001

August 16   Zacarias Moussaoui, the "twentieth 9/11 hi-
               jacker," is detained by U.S. Customs officials be-
               cause of passport violation; he subsequently is
               charged by federal authorities with involvement
               in the terrorist attacks of September 11, 2001. As
               of 2005, his criminal trial had not begun in fed-
               eral court.

September 11   Four commercial airliners are hijacked in the
               early morning; two strike the World Trade Cen-
               ter towers in New York City; one strikes the Pen-
               tagon; and the fourth plane crashes in a field in
               Pennsylvania before reaching its target in Wash-
               ington, D.C.

September 14   A presidential executive order is issued ordering
               Ready Reserves of Armed Forces to Active Duty.

September 18   Anthrax letters are mailed to a newspaper and to
               Tom Brokaw of NBC News.

September 24   President Bush signs an executive order freezing
               all Bin Laden and Al Qaeda funds in the United
               States.

October 1   First anthrax-letter death occurs in Florida.

October 7	U.S. jets strike terrorist camps in Afghanistan.
October 8	President Bush issues an executive order creating the Office of Homeland Security (OHS) and Homeland Security Council.
October 8	Tom Ridge is appointed director of the OHS.
October 9	An anthrax letter is received by Senate majority leader Tom Daschle (D-SD).
October 22	OHS Director Ridge meets with officials to discuss the anthrax danger.
October 26	President Bush signs the USA Patriot Act of 2002.
October 29	OHS Director Ridge issues first "security alert" to the American public.
October 29	President Bush issues Homeland Security Presidential Directive #2: Combating Terrorism through Immigration Policies.
November 13	President Bush, declaring an "extraordinary emergency," issues a military order, *Detention, Treatment, and Trial of Certain Non-Citizens in the War Against Terror,* authorizing the Department of Defense to establish protocols for the detention and establishment of secret military tribunals to try enemy combatants and terrorists.
November 16	An anthrax letter is received by Senator Pat Leahy (D-VT).
December	American citizen John Walker Lindh is found among Taliban prisoners captured in Afghanistan.
December 14	A presidential executive order declares Afghanistan a Combat Zone.

2002

January 11   The Department of Justice releases information on 725 alien detainees confined by the federal government.

January 25   President Bush increases his budget request for border security.

February   The Bush administration announces that Taliban prisoners will be treated as POWs according to the Geneva Conventions of 1949 and 1977; Al Qaeda prisoners will be classified as "enemy combatants" and will not be afforded the protections of the Geneva Conventions.

February 5   President Bush increases funding for bioterrorism defense by 310 percent.

March   U.S. military forces are active in the Philippines, Yemen, and the Republic of Georgia, battling Al Qaeda terrorists in those nations.

March 12   The color-coded Homeland Security Advisory System Terrorism Alert System is announced in Homeland Security Presidential Directive #3. Five threat conditions:

                            Low = Green
                            Guarded = Blue
                            Elevated = Yellow
                            High = Orange
                            Severe = Red

March 28   The DOJ announces that it will seek the death penalty in the trial of Moussaoui.

June 6   President Bush presents a message to Congress regarding his belief that the OHS should be terminated, replaced by a cabinet-level Department of Homeland Security.

June 7	President Bush meets with congressional leaders on the Department of Homeland Security Act proposed by his administration.
June 18	A DHS presidential proposal is delivered to Congress.
July 16	President Bush issues the *National Strategy for Homeland Security.*
September	One year after 9/11, more than 450 enemy combatants are held at Guantanamo, Cuba.
September	President Bush issues a new *National Security Strategy of the United States of America.*
September 28	President Bush pushes for passage of the DHS Act of 2002.
November 5	Midterm congressional elections. Republicans regain control of the U.S. Senate and maintain control of the U.S. House of Representatives.
November 22	The president and Congress create the National Commission on Terrorist Attacks Upon the United States, PL 107–306 (generally referred to as the "9/11 Commission").
November 26	President Bush signs PL 107–296, the Department of Homeland Security Act of 2002.
November 26	President Bush announces that Tom Ridge is the administration's nominee for the position of secretary of the DHS.

2003

January 17	Secretary of DHS–designate Tom Ridge testifies before the U.S. Senate Committee on Government Affairs.

January 22   The Senate Confirms Tom Ridge as secretary of DHS.

January 24   Tom Ridge is sworn in as the first secretary of the DHS.

April 29   End of the first 100 days of the DHS.

April 30   The DHS announces funding for state and local "first responders."

May 16   The DHS admits that it had been asked—and it consented—to find Texas Democratic legislators who left the state and hid in Oklahoma to avoid closure on the hotly contested state reapportionment battles.

May 28   School children in Akron, Ohio, will be fingerprinted by DHS personnel so they can be identified in school lunch lines.

June 15   All persons named "David Nelson" find themselves unable to fly because the name appears on DHS "no-fly" lists.

June 18   President Bush issues guidelines banning racial profiling by DHS personnel, "except in cases of terrorism and national security."

September 16   The New Terrorist Screening Center is established by President Bush.

September 18   JetBlue Airways admits that in 2002 it shared its list of 5 million passengers with a Defense Department contractor that was testing a passenger-screening system for the TSA.

November 3   Secretary Ridge announces $2.2 billion in funding for "first responders."

November 22   The DHS plans to drop its program requiring most Arab and Muslim men to register with the

U.S. government. DHS sources say that the program was "expensive, inefficient, and useless."

December 19   A federal appeals court orders President Bush to release Jose Padilla, a U.S. citizen arrested in Chicago in 2002 and, since then, held in navy brigs as an enemy combatant.

2004

January 4   A new DHS security program called U.S. Visitor and Immigrant Status Indicator Technology system (US-VISIT) is launched to photograph every foreign visitor who needs a visa to enter the United States. (On October 1, 2004, the program is extended to visitors from all twenty-seven nations whose citizens do not need visas if their stay is ninety days or less.)

January 28   The DHS unveils its National Cyber Alert System to better secure private and governmental computer systems.

February 6   The FBI Joint Terrorism Task Force subpoenas Drake University in Des Moines, Iowa, to hand over records concerning an antiwar conference on campus by the university and the National Lawyers Guild.

February 27   The DHS issues its first set of Radiation and Nuclear Detection Equipment Standards.

April 3   The DHS announces that visitors from the United Kingdom, France, Germany, Spain, Australia, and twenty-one other nations will be photographed and fingerprinted when they enter the United States, effective October 1, 2004.

May 20   The DHS issues its first security directives for passenger rail operations.

May 22   Police in Boston, Massachusetts, confirm that they will begin stopping passengers on the Boston "T" for identity checks as part of a new national rail security plan initiated by the DHS.

May 24   The DHS awards a $15 billion contract for a massive electronic-surveillance and data-mining system to attempt to track foreign visitors in the United States.

June 21   Secretary Ridge announces creation of a Nationwide Port Security Program.

July   The "9/11 Commission" final report is published.

July 6   Secretary Ridge announces the Homeland Security National Center for Food Protection and Defense.

July 8   DHS Secretary Tom Ridge warns Americans that Al Qaeda might be planning a terrorist attack in November to disrupt the presidential election of 2004.

July 21   The Project Bio-Shield Act of 2004 is signed by President Bush. It creates defenses against three catastrophes by (1) storing vaccines for small pox and other diseases, (2) providing funds for research and development of new medicines, and (3) developing new deployment protocols in event of an emergency.

July 30   The U.S. Census Bureau admits that its data and population statistics on Arab Americans, broken down by zip code, have been given to the DHS.

August 1   Secretary Ridge increases the Threat Level to "Orange" for financial center areas in New York, New Jersey, and Washington, D.C.

August 27   Presidential Executive Order Strengthening
                Sharing of Terrorism Information to Protect
                Americans is announced.

August 27   Presidential Executive Order Strengthening
                Management of the Intelligence Community is
                announced.

September 21   The ten-point Biometric Identification System
                becomes operational at all U.S. Border Patrol sta-
                tions.

September 27   The DHS launches the Office of Interoperability
                and Compatibility (OIC) to oversee the wide
                range of public safety programs and efforts that
                were spread across many of the twenty-two fed-
                eral agencies that make up the DHS.

October 1   A DHS policy shift regarding incoming travelers
                to the United States from twenty-seven industri-
                alized nations takes effect. All visitors who come
                to the country for up to ninety days without a
                visa must be fingerprinted and photographed.

November 30   Secretary Ridge announces his departure from
                the DHS as soon as a successor is confirmed by
                the Senate but no later than February 2005.

December 2   President Bush announces nomination of
                Bernard B. Kerik, a former New York City police
                commissioner who was in office on 9/11, as sec-
                retary of Homeland Security to replace Tom
                Ridge.

December 9   DHS Secretary-designate Bernard Kerik with-
                draws his name from consideration because of
                personal problems.

December 10   The DHS begins use of a British-created (World-
                Check, Ltd.) wide-ranging computer base sys-
                tem that allows investigators to match financial
                transaction against a watch-list of 250,000 people

and firms with suspected ties to terrorist financing, drug trafficking, money laundering, and other financial crimes.

December 13   President Bush signs a bill to restructure the intelligence community and create the job of National Intelligence Director.

2005

January 10   Outgoing DHS Secretary Ridge suggests that the United States should begin to issue U.S. passports that include a full set of the bearer's fingerprints.

January 11   President Bush nominates U.S. Court of Appeals Judge Michael Chertoff to become secretary of the DHS.

January 29   Michael Chertoff is confirmed by the U.S. Senate.

July 8   Terrorist bombs explode on two subway trains and a double decker bus in London; DHS Secretary Chertoff elevates threat level to Yellow.

5

Biographical Profiles

Top Leadership in the U.S. Department of Homeland Security

All information in this section is taken from press releases of the DHS, found on the public domain website www.dhs.gov., and, in the case of the new secretary, from the *New York Times*, the *Washington Post*, and the *Christian Science Monitor*.

Michael Chertoff, Secretary, DHS, 2005

President George W. Bush nominated U.S. Court of Appeals Judge Michael Chertoff to be the secretary of the Department of Homeland Security on January 11, 2005, about one month after the Kerik nomination went south. In 1983 Chertoff was a federal prosecutor working with then-U.S. Attorney Rudolph W. Giuliani in New York. President George W. H. Bush in 1990 appointed him U.S. attorney for New Jersey, a position he held until 1994. After that job, he entered private practice. Later in the decade, Chertoff served as the U.S. Senate Republicans' chief counsel for the Clinton-era Whitewater investigation. At the time of the 9/11 attacks, Chertoff was the head of the DOJ's Criminal Division.

Chertoff played a major role in the DOJ's successful effort to quickly draft and submit to Congress, in the weeks after 9/11, a bill giving additional powers to domestic law enforcement and foreign intelligence-gathering agencies. Passed in late October 2001, it is known as the Patriot Act. As head of the DOJ Criminal

Division, Chertoff argued the government's case in the appeal brought by the "twentieth 9/11 terrorist," Zacarias Moussaoui.

In 2003 President Bush nominated Chertoff to fill a vacancy on the 3rd Circuit U.S. Court of Appeals, and the Senate quickly confirmed him by a vote of 88–1. (The sole dissenting vote came from the Junior Democratic Party Senator from New York, Hillary Rodham Clinton.)

The 51-year-old nominee attended Harvard University and Harvard Law School. After law school, he served as a law clerk for the late Associate Justice William J. Brennan in the 1979 term of the Court. Chertoff is married, and he and wife Meryl have two children.

When confirmed by the Senate, Chertoff will leave a life-tenure federal judgeship for the daunting political and management chore of trying to pull together the various federal agencies now joined in the DHS into one cohesive federal executive branch agency.

James Loy, Deputy Secretary

On December 4, 2003, Admiral James Loy was sworn in as the deputy secretary of the Department of Homeland Security.

Loy graduated from the U.S. Coast Guard Academy in 1964 and holds two master's degrees, one from Wesleyan University and the other from the University of Rhode Island. In 2003 he received the Honorary Degree in Science from the Webb Institute. He also attended the Industrial College of the Armed Forces and interned at the John F. Kennedy School of Government at Harvard University. His commendations are numerous, including the Department of Transportation Distinguished Service Medal, four Coast Guard Distinguished Service Medals, the Defense Superior Service Medal, the Bronze Star with Combat "V," and the Combat Action Ribbon.

A career seagoing officer, Admiral Loy has served tours aboard six Coast Guard cutters, including command of a patrol boat in combat during the Vietnam War and command of major cutters in both the Atlantic and Pacific Oceans.

Loy served as the Coast Guard chief of staff from 1996 to 1998, during which time he redesigned the headquarters management structure and overhauled the Coast Guard planning and budgeting process to focus more sharply on performance and results. From 1994 to 1996 he was commander of the Coast Guard's Atlantic Area, leading U.S. forces during the mass Haitian and Cuban migrations of 1994, and leading Coast Guard forces participating in Operation Restore Democracy.

As commandant of the U.S. Coast Guard from May 1998 to May 2002, Loy focused on restoring readiness and shaping the future. Although both themes involved many initiatives, the most visible expressions of restoring readiness were rebuilding the Coast Guard's workforce to authorized levels, improving retention, and managing operational tempo. He oversaw the Integrated Deepwater System acquisition project, which is modernizing the ships, aircraft, and sensors that the Coast Guard uses to perform its many open ocean missions.

Loy retired from the U.S. Coast Guard as its commandant on May 30, 2002. Transportation Secretary Norman Y. Mineta immediately appointed him to the newly created post of deputy undersecretary for Transportation Security and chief operating officer of the Transportation Security Administration.

Asa Hutchinson, Undersecretary for Border and Transportation Security

On January 23, 2003, former Drug Enforcement Administration head Asa Hutchinson was confirmed as undersecretary for Border and Transportation Security. As such, Hutchinson leads a directorate of more than 110,000 employees and is responsible for coordinating the enforcement activities of U.S. borders and transportation and immigration systems. He heads the effort to reform border inspections through the use of biometric technology and continues to oversee the reorganization of border agencies into a unified inspection force.

Hutchinson practiced law in rural Arkansas for twenty-one years and tried over 100 jury trials. During that time, he was appointed by President Ronald Reagan as U.S. attorney for the Western District of Arkansas. At the age of thirty-one, he was then the youngest U.S. attorney in the nation.

Hutchinson served as a U.S. Representative from Arkansas from 1997 to 2001. While in Congress, he served on the Select Committee on Intelligence and the House Judiciary Committee. After being reelected to his third term, he was appointed administrator of the Drug Enforcement Administration (DEA), where he combined tough law enforcement initiatives with advocating increased investment in treatment and education programs.

Michael Brown, Undersecretary for Emergency Preparedness and Response

Michael Brown was confirmed as the first undersecretary for Emergency Preparedness and Response (EP&R). He will coordinate federal disaster relief activities, including implementation of the Federal Response Plan, which authorizes the response and recovery operations of twenty-six federal agencies and departments as well as the American Red Cross. He will also oversee the National Flood Insurance Program and the U.S. Fire Administration, and initiate proactive mitigation activities. Additionally as undersecretary, Brown will help the secretary of the DHS ensure the effectiveness of emergency responders, and direct the Strategic National Stockpile, the National Disaster Medical System, and the Nuclear Incident Response Team.

A native of Oklahoma, Brown holds a BA in public administration/political science from Central State University, Oklahoma. He received his JD from Oklahoma City University's School of Law and was for a time an adjunct professor of law for the Oklahoma City University.

Brown practiced law in Colorado and Oklahoma, where he served as a bar examiner on ethics and professional responsibility for the Oklahoma Supreme Court and as a hearing examiner for the Colorado Supreme Court. He had been appointed as a special prosecutor in police disciplinary matters. His background in state and local government also includes serving as an assistant city manager with emergency services oversight and as a city councilman.

Brown previously served as the Federal Emergency Management Agency's deputy director and the agency's general counsel. Shortly after the September 11 terrorist attacks, he served on the president's Consequence Management Principal's Committee, which acted as the White House's policy coordination group for the federal domestic response to the attacks. Later, President Bush asked him to head the Consequence Management Working Group to identify and resolve key issues regarding the federal response plan. In August 2002, Bush appointed him to the Transition Planning Office for the new Department of Homeland

Security, serving as the transition leader for the EP&R Division. Brown currently chairs the National Citizen Corps Council, part of the president's USA Freedom Corps volunteer initiative.

Frank Libutti, Undersecretary for Information Analysis and Infrastructure Protection

Frank Libutti was confirmed by unanimous vote of the Senate in June 2003 as undersecretary for Information Analysis and Infrastructure Protection.

Libutti had a long and distinguished career in the U.S. Marine Corps, retiring in October 2001 as a lieutenant general. He served as an infantry platoon commander in Vietnam. His last assignment before retiring from the Marine Corps was as the commanding general of U.S. Marine Forces Pacific and commanding general of Marine Forces Central Command. His many personal awards include the Defense Distinguished Service Medal, Silver Star Medal, Legion of Merit (with gold star), Purple Heart (with two stars), Navy and Marine Corps Commendation Medal, and the Combat Action Ribbon. He was also presented with the Order of the Rising Gold Sun and Silver Star by the Emperor of Japan for service dedicated to the security of Japan and the mutual cooperation between Japan and the United States.

Following his retirement from the USMC, Libutti served as special assistant for Homeland Security at the Department of Defense. He also was the New York City Police Department's deputy commissioner of counterterrorism. His mission was to plan and direct the NYPD's efforts in preventing, responding to, and investigating acts of terrorism in the City of New York. He served in this capacity from January 2002 to May 2003.

Janet Hale, Undersecretary for Management

Janet Hale was confirmed as undersecretary for Management on March 6, 2003.

Hale holds a BS in education and a master's degree in public administration from the John F. Kennedy School of Government at Harvard University. She has held the positions of associate administrator for Finance for the House of Representatives and associate director for Economics and Government at the Office of Management and Budget, responsible for budget and policy development, regulatory reform, and financial management for the departments of Treasury, Transportation, Commerce, Justice, and twenty-five smaller agencies. She has also served as the assistant secretary for Budget and Programs at the Department of Transportation, acting assistant secretary of Housing at the Department of Housing and Urban Development, vice president with the U.S. Telephone Association, and executive vice president for the University of Pennsylvania. Prior to her nomination and confirmation as undersecretary, she served as the assistant secretary for Budget, Technology, and Finance for the U.S. Department of Health and Human Services (HHS), and as chief financial officer and chief information officer.

Charles E. McQueary, Undersecretary for Science and Technology

Charles E. McQueary was appointed by President Bush as undersecretary for Science and Technology of the Department of Homeland Security and confirmed by the U.S. Senate in March 2003. As such, he leads the department's research and development arm, utilizing our nation's scientific and technological resources to provide federal, state, and local officials with the technology and capabilities to protect the homeland.

McQueary holds both a PhD in engineering mechanics and an MS in mechanical engineering from the University of Texas, Austin. Prior to joining the DHS, McQueary served as president of General Dynamics Advanced Technology systems, in Greensboro, North Carolina. Earlier in his career, he served as president and vice president of business units for AT&T and Lucent Technologies, and as a director for AT&T Bell Laboratories.

Andrew B. Maner, Chief Financial Officer

Andrew Maner was appointed the chief financial officer (CFO) for the Department of Homeland Security in January 2004. As the CFO, he is responsible for all budget, finance and accounting, strategic planning and evaluation, GAO liaison, bankcard programs, and financial systems for the DHS. He is also responsible for the ongoing integration of all those functions within the new department.

Maner is a graduate of Purdue University (BA) and the J. L. Kellogg School of Management (MBA). He served as a vice president at ICG Commerce, where he led the company's capital raising and partnership efforts and later its central region sales and operations. He was also a partner with Aligne, Inc., and held positions at the Chicago Board of Trade and in the Financial Institutions Group at A. T. Kearney.

Maner served in the administration of George H. W. Bush in the White House Press Office and later accompanied the former president to Houston, Texas, to serve as his director of Press and Political Affairs. He later served as special assistant to the United Nations envoy to Somalia in Mogadishu, where he assisted with political, military, financial, and trade development efforts.

Prior to his present appointment, Maner was the chief of staff to Commissioner Robert C. Bonner at U.S. Customs and Border Protection (CBP). In that capacity he was the commissioner's principal operating officer on enforcement, trade, finance, budget, transition, and management issues. He also served as the director of the CBP's Transition Management Office (TMO), which led the CBP's complex operations and mission support merger between portions of the former U.S. Customs, U.S. Immigration and Naturalization Service, Agricultural Plant Health Inspection Service, and the U.S. Border Patrol.

Admiral Thomas H. Collins, Commandant, United States Coast Guard

Admiral Thomas H. Collins assumed the duties of commandant of the U.S. Coast Guard on May 30, 2002.

Collins graduated from the Coast Guard Academy in 1968 and later served as a faculty member within its Humanities Department. He earned a Master of Arts degree in liberal studies from Wesleyan University and an MBA from the University of New Haven.

From 1998 to 2000 he served as commander of the Pacific Area and Eleventh Coast Guard District, where he developed the successful Coast Guard response to the increase in illegal drug and migrant smuggling traffic in the Eastern Pacific. His other flag assignments include serving as commander of the Fourteenth Coast Guard District in Honolulu, Hawaii, and chief of the

Office of Acquisition at Coast Guard Headquarters, where he managed the acquisition of twelve major systems worth nearly $3 billion and laid the foundation for the Integrated Deepwater System project, which will modernize the ships, aircraft, and sensors that the Coast Guard uses to perform its many open ocean missions. Collins served as the Coast Guard's vice commandant from 2000 to 2002, during which time he created the Innovation Council, spearheaded service-wide process improvement initiatives, and directed system enhancements such as the Coast Guard Acquisition Executive.

W. Ralph Basham, Director, United States Secret Service

Basham's career with the Secret Service began in 1970 when he was appointed as a special agent in the Washington Field Office. Subsequent assignments included duty in a number of Washington, D.C., based divisions, as well as the Cleveland (OH) and Louisville (KY) Field Offices. He served as special agent in charge of the Cleveland Field Office, the Washington Field Office, and the Vice Presidential Protective Division. Basham also was the deputy assistant director of the Office of Training and assistant director of the Office of Administration.

In January 1998, Basham was appointed director of the Federal Law Enforcement Training Center (FLETC). The center, located in Glynco, Georgia, and Artesia, New Mexico, provides training for nearly all of the nation's federal law enforcement officers, including Secret Service recruits. FLETC also serves the state, local, and federal law enforcement communities with training programs tailored to their specific needs.

Clark Kent Ervin, Inspector General, 2003–2004

Clark Kent Ervin became the inspector general of the U.S. Department of Homeland Security on December 26, 2003, pursuant to a recess appointment by President Bush. Ervin had served as acting inspector general of DHS since his January 10, 2003, nomination was sent to the U.S. Senate. Prior to his service at DHS, he served as the inspector general of the U.S. Department of State and the Broadcasting Board of Governors.

Ervin holds a BA in government from Harvard University and a JD from Harvard Law School. He studied politics, philosophy, and economics at Oxford University as a Rhodes Scholar, returning to his native Houston, Texas, to practice law.

He served in the administration of President George H. W. Bush from 1989 to 1991 as associate director of policy in the Office of National Service. From 1995 until 1999 he served as the assistant secretary of state of Texas. From 1999 until April 2001 he served as deputy attorney general, general counsel, and director of administration in the office of then Texas attorney general and now U.S. Senator John Cornyn.

Eduardo Aguirre Jr., Director of the Bureau of Citizenship and Immigration Services

Eduardo Aguirre Jr., director of the Bureau of Citizenship and Immigration Services (BCIS), was appointed by President Bush to this key leadership position in the Department of Homeland Security in February 2003.

Roger Mackin, United States Interdiction Coordinator and DHS Counternarcotics Officer (CNO)

In March 2003, DHS Secretary Tom Ridge appointed Roger Mackin to be the United States Interdiction Coordinator (USIC) and the DHS Counternarcotics Officer (CNO).

As the USIC, Mackin acts on behalf of the president and the director of the Office of National Drug Control Policy to ensure that the interdiction efforts of the United States are consistent with the objectives of the National Drug Control Strategy. He coordinates with department and agency heads, U.S. ambassadors and military commanders, interagency working groups, task forces, and coordinating centers having interdiction responsibilities. He reviews the assets committed by federal agencies to drug interdiction to ensure that they are sufficient and their use is properly integrated and optimized.

As the CNO, Mackin has the primary responsibility for coordinating policy and operations within the DHS and between the department and other federal agencies with respect to illegal drug trafficking and its terrorist-related ramifications. Mackin is also to facilitate the tracking and severing of connections between drug trafficking and terrorism.

Mackin served as an operations officer for 27 years in the Central Intelligence Agency, managing intelligence collection, special operations, counterintelligence, and counternarcotics programs. Earlier in his career he led CIA efforts against heroin-producing organizations in Southeast Asia.

Mackin had a parallel career in the military, retiring from the U.S. Air Force Reserve in 1991 as a lieutenant colonel after 31 years of active and reserve assignments, including five years in the Vietnam War.

Daniel W. Sutherland, Officer for Civil Rights and Civil Liberties

On April 16, 2003, President Bush appointed Daniel W. Sutherland to be the officer for civil rights and civil liberties at the U.S. Department of Homeland Security. In this position, Sutherland will provide legal and policy advice to the secretary and the senior officers of the DHS on a full range of civil rights and civil liberties issues.

C. Suzanne "Sue" Mencer, Director of the Office for Domestic Preparedness

C. Suzanne "Sue" Mencer was nominated by President George W. Bush, and subsequently confirmed by the United States Senate on September 16, 2003, as director of the Office for Domestic Preparedness (ODP), U.S. Department of Homeland Security.

As ODP director, Mencer directs federal government initiatives to help states, local jurisdictions, regional authorities, and tribal governments build their capacity to prepare for, prevent, and respond to acts of terrorism. She is responsible for administering more than twenty-five programs and initiatives to equip, train, exercise, and assist state and local first responders, and for managing a budget of over $4 billion.

Mencer is a graduate of the John F. Kennedy School of Government's State and Local Executive Program at Harvard University. She received a bachelor's degree from Ohio State University and completed graduate courses at the University of South Florida.

Mencer is a twenty-year veteran of the Federal Bureau of Investigation (FBI), serving from 1978 to 1998. She began her FBI career as a special agent in Mobile, Alabama, and later served in New York City. From 1985 to 1990 she was a supervisory special agent at FBI Headquarters in Washington, D.C., where she was responsible for national security investigations. In 1990 she transferred to the FBI's Denver, Colorado, office, where she started and supervised the Joint Terrorism Task Force and headed investigations involving civil rights, foreign counterintelligence, economic espionage, and international and domestic terrorism. During this period, Mencer chaired the Interagency Threat Analysis Group for the Summit of Eight in 1997 and the Intelligence and Threat Analysis Committee of the Denver Consortium of the White House Commission on Aviation Safety and Security. In addition, she served on the security committee for the trials of Timothy McVeigh and Terry Nichols, who were convicted of the Murrah Federal Building bombing in Oklahoma City.

Prior to her current appointment, Mencer was executive director of the Colorado Department of Public Safety, where she was responsible for overseeing the Colorado State Patrol, the Colorado Bureau of Investigation, the Division of Criminal Justice, and the Office of Preparedness, Security, and Fire Safety. She served on the Governor's Columbine Review Commission, reviewing law enforcement's response to the tragedy at Columbine High School in Littleton, Colorado, and was a consultant for the Institute for Intergovernmental Research, where she provided antiterrorism training to law enforcement officers throughout the country.

Prakash I. Khatri, Citizenship and Immigration Services Ombudsman

Prakash I. Khatri was appointed by Secretary Tom Ridge in July 2003 to serve as the first Citizenship and Immigration Services (CIS) ombudsman at the Department of Homeland Security. He will identify areas in which individuals have problems dealing with the CIS, assist individuals and employers in resolving service or case-related difficulties, and propose changes in the CIS administrative practices to mitigate identified problems. In addition, Khatri will provide policy, planning, and program advice to the DHS secretary, deputy secretary, and other key officials regarding immigration matters.

Khatri spent fourteen years in private practice specializing in immigration law. He was admitted to the Florida State Bar in

1984, and, at the age of twenty-two, was the youngest attorney in the state bar's history. He was among the first thirty-five members of the Florida Bar to pass the Immigration and Nationality Board Certification examination. He subsequently served on the Florida Bar Immigration and Nationality Board Certification Committee, where he developed and evaluated board certification exams.

As manager of Immigration and Visa Processing for Walt Disney World in Florida, Khatri traveled to U.S. consular posts throughout the world. He developed and implemented an automated high-volume visa processing system and other innovations that reduced unnecessary paperwork and improved efficiencies related to handling employee visa applications at the Disney theme parks.

Susan K. Neely, Assistant Secretary for Public Affairs

On January 30, 2003 DHS Secretary Tom Ridge announced the appointment of Susan K. Neely to be assistant secretary for Public Affairs. She oversees both external and internal communications for the department, its twenty-two component agencies, and nearly 180,000 employees.

A graduate of the University of Iowa in journalism and French civilization, Neely holds a master's degree in public administration from Drake University. The Iowa native has held senior positions on the staffs of Governor Terry Branstad (IA), U.S. Representative Sid Morrison (WA), and U.S. Representative Jim Leach (IA). In the private sector, she was an executive at the Association of American Medical Colleges and the Health Insurance Association of America. She founded the Washington, D.C., office for the advertising and public relations firm CMF&Z, a subsidiary of Young & Rubicam.

Prior to her current position, Neely helped establish the Office of Homeland Security, serving as special assistant to the president and senior director of communications.

Nuala O'Connor Kelly, Chief Privacy Officer

Nuala O'Connor Kelly was appointed chief privacy officer of the Department of Homeland Security by Secretary Ridge on April

16, 2003. In this capacity, she is responsible for privacy compliance across the department. Her responsibilities include assuring that the technologies used by the department to protect the United States sustain, and do not erode, privacy protections relating to the use, collection, and disclosure of personal and department information. The Privacy Office has oversight of all privacy policy matters, including compliance with the Privacy Act of 1974, the Freedom of Information Act of 1966 (as amended), and the completion of Privacy Impact Assessments on all new programs, as required by the E-Government Act of 2002 and Section 222 of the Homeland Security Act. The Privacy Office also evaluates legislative and regulatory proposals involving collection, use, and disclosure of personal and department information by the federal government.

O'Connor Kelly received her AB from Princeton University, a master's of education from Harvard University, and JD from Georgetown University Law Center. She has practiced law with the firms Sidley & Austin, Hudson Cook, and Venable, Baetjer, Howard & Civiletti in Washington, D.C. She is a member of the bar in Washington, D.C., and Maryland.

O'Connor Kelly served as vice president of data protection and chief privacy officer for emerging technologies for the online media services company DoubleClick. She helped found the company's first data protection department and was responsible for the creation of privacy and data protection policies and procedures throughout the company and for the company's clients and partners. She also served as the company's first deputy general counsel for privacy.

Before joining the Department of Homeland Security, O'Connor Kelly served as chief privacy officer for the U.S. Department of Commerce. While at the DOC, O'Connor Kelly also served as chief counsel for technology, and as deputy director of the Office of Policy and Strategic Planning.

Duncan Campbell, Chief of Staff

Duncan Campbell was appointed chief of staff for Tom Ridge, secretary of the Department of Homeland Security, in October 2003. In this capacity, he is involved in managing the department's policy, planning, and operations. Prior to his newest position, Campbell served as deputy chief of staff for operations at DHS, where he led the department's external affairs outreach by coordinating the public affairs, state and local, private sector, and legislative affairs efforts.

Campbell is a graduate of Cornell University, where he received his degree in government and history. He served as executive director of the Republican Governors Association and as Pennsylvania's state director for the Bush-Cheney 2000 Campaign. He served on then–Pennsylvania governor Tom Ridge's staff as deputy chief of staff and director of the Governor's Office of Labor-Management Cooperation.

From October 2001 until his current appointment, Campbell was director of intergovernmental affairs for the Office of Homeland Security, where he served as the primary liaison to state and local public officials.

Steven I. Cooper, Chief Information Officer

Steven Cooper was appointed by President Bush to be the first chief information officer (CIO) of the Department of Homeland Security in February 2003. He and his team have responsibility for the information technology assets supporting the nearly 190,000 federal employees of the twenty-two agencies now comprising the new department.

Cooper holds a BA degree from Ohio Wesleyan University. He served in the Naval Air Reserve during the Vietnam War. He spent more than twenty years in the private sector as an information technology professional, most recently as CIO of corporate staffs and executive director of strategic information delivery for Corning, Inc. Previously he served as director of information technology for Eli Lilly & Company. He held senior-level technical and management positions with CSC, MAXIMA, and CACI prior to forming his own consulting organization, Strategic Information Concepts.

Cooper was appointed in March 2002 as a special assistant to the president for Homeland Security and served as senior director for information integration in the Office of Homeland Security. In this role, he launched the development of the National Enterprise Architecture for Homeland Security to address information integration within the federal government and the sharing of homeland security information with state, local, and relevant private-sector entities. With James Flyzik, senior advisor to the Homeland Security Director and former CIO of the Treasury Department, he provided the input for information sharing and systems to the National Strategy for Homeland Security.

Jack L. Johnson Jr., Chief Security Officer

On December 12, 2003, Secretary Tom Ridge appointed Jack L. Johnson Jr. as the chief security officer (CSO) for the Department of Homeland Security. Prior to this appointment, Johnson had been serving (since January 2003) as a detailee from the U.S. Secret Service, where he was a deputy assistant director.

Reporting directly to the deputy secretary, Johnson directs all security-related activities as they relate to the twenty-two agencies and over 180,000 employees that now comprise the DHS. The CSO develops security-related policy and procedures and provides direct support to the chief information officer in the area of security policies and procedures as they relate to the IT environment within the DHS.

Johnson received a BS from the University of Maryland and a masters in forensic science from George Washington University. He has done additional post-graduate study at the University of Virginia and Johns Hopkins School of Management.

From 1975 to 1979 he served in the U.S. Army as a criminal investigator at installations in California, Maryland, and Korea. He was a police officer and detective for the Fairfax County (VA) Police Department before joining the Secret Service.

Robert C. Bonner, Commissioner of Customs and Border Protection

The Bureau of Customs and Border Protection (CBP) within the Department of Homeland Security is comprised of 35,000 federal employees, which includes 17,000 inspectors and canine enforcement officers from the APHIS-Agricultural Quarantine Inspection program, INS inspection services, and the Customs Service, and 10,000 Border Patrol Agents.

Prior to his role as commissioner of the CBP, Robert C. Bonner served as commissioner of the U.S. Customs Service beginning on September 24, 2001.

Bonner is a graduate of the University of Maryland and the Georgetown School of Law. After clerking for a U.S. district judge, he served for three years on active duty in the U.S. Navy Judge Advocate General's Corps. Bonner then spent four and one-half years as an assistant U.S. attorney in Los Angeles, California, before turning to private practice in 1975. His law firm focused on business crime matters, governmental investigatory and regulatory actions, complex civil cases, and alternative dispute resolution.

In 1984 Bonner returned to public service after he was appointed by President Ronald Reagan to be the U.S. attorney for the Central District of California. He was subsequently appointed by former President George H. W. Bush in 1989 to serve as U.S. District Judge for the U.S. District Court for the Central District of California. Former President Bush went on to appoint him as administrator of the Drug Enforcement Agency in 1990.

Michael J. Garcia, Assistant Secretary, U.S. Immigration and Customs Enforcement

On March 11, 2003, President Bush announced his intention to nominate Michael J. Garcia as assistant secretary for the U.S. Immigration and Customs Enforcement, Department of Homeland Security. Garcia served as acting commissioner of the Immigration and Naturalization Service from December 2002 to February 2003, and as assistant secretary of commerce for Export Enforcement from August 2001 to November 2002.

A career federal prosecutor, Garcia was previously with the Department of Justice's Office of the U.S. Attorney for the Southern District of New York. He participated in the prosecution of four defendants for conspiring with Osama bin Laden, leader of al Qaeda, a worldwide terrorist organization, and seventeen others to kill American nationals abroad with the bombing of two U.S. embassies in East Africa. The four defendants were convicted on all counts in May 2001.

Garcia joined the U.S. Attorney's Office in 1992 and participated in the successful prosecution of four defendants in the first World Trade Center bombing trial. He also participated in the successful prosecution of Ramzi Ahmed Yousef and two others on charges of planning forty-eight hours of "terror in the sky" in a conspiracy to plant bombs aboard twelve American passenger airlines in Asia. He was awarded the U.S. Attorney General's

Award for Exceptional Service, the Department of Justice's highest award, in 1994 and 1997 for those cases. In 2002 Garcia was awarded the Attorney General's Award for Distinguished Service for his work on the embassy bombing case.

Alfonso Martinez-Fonts Jr., Special Assistant to the Secretary for the Private Sector

On January 30, 2003, Alfonso "Al" Martinez-Fonts Jr. was sworn in as the special assistant to the secretary for the Office of the Private Sector in the Department of Homeland Security. In this capacity he is charged with providing the U.S. private sector with a direct line of communication to the DHS. He and the Office of the Private Sector work directly with individual business and through trade associations and other nongovernmental organizations to foster dialogue between the private sector and the department.

Born in Havana, Cuba, Martinez-Fonts received his undergraduate degree in political science from Villanova University and his MBA in finance from Long Island University. He began a thirty-year career with Chemical Bank (a JP Morgan Chase predecessor organization) as a management trainee and worked his way through the organization as a lending officer in the metropolitan and international divisions.

He has lived and traveled extensively overseas, including managing Chemical Bank's offices in Manila, Philippines (1976–1979), and Mexico City, Mexico (1982–1988). While stationed in New York he was a regional manager of Chemical Bank's business in Argentina, Chile, Uruguay, Paraguay, and Bolivia (1980–1982). In April 2002, he retired as chairman and chief executive officer of JP Morgan Chase Bank in El Paso, Texas.

Robert P. Liscouski, Assistant Secretary for Infrastructure Protection

Robert Liscouski assumed the post of assistant secretary of homeland security for Infrastructure Protection in March 2003. He is responsible for the department's efforts to identify critical infrastructures and propose protective measures to keep them safe from terrorist attacks.

Liscouski received his BS degree in criminal justice from John Jay College of Criminal Justice in New York, and his masters of public administration from the Kennedy School of Government, Harvard University. He worked for eleven years with the Diplomatic Security Service of the U.S. Department of State and five years as a homicide and narcotics investigator in Bergen County, New Jersey.

Liscouski was a vice president for the Law Enforcement Division of ORION Scientific Systems, developing and integrating software for the civilian intelligence community. He was also the founder and CEO of PoliTech Research, Inc., a firm providing open-source research and business intelligence services to Fortune 500 firms. Prior to returning to government service, he was the director of information assurance for the Coca-Cola Company.

Liscouski was a member of the Director of Central Intelligence Science Board, comprised of industry representatives providing consultation and analysis on scientific, technical, and engineering matters to the Director of Central Intelligence (DCI) and to the senior leadership of the Intelligence Community.

C. Stewart Verdery Jr., Assistant Secretary for Border and Transportation Security Policy and Planning

Assistant Secretary Verdery serves as the first DHS assistant secretary for Border and Transportation Security (BTS) Policy and Planning, directing the BTS Office of Policy and Planning and advising the BTS undersecretary and DHS secretary on policies related to immigration and visa issuance, cargo and international commerce, international trade, transportation security, counternarcotics, and federal law-enforcement training. Verdery was nominated by President Bush on April 10, 2003, and confirmed by the U.S. Senate on June 19, 2003.

Verdery graduated cum laude with honors in history from Williams College and holds a law degree from the University of Virginia School of Law. He was an associate at the Washington office of the law firm Baker & Hostetler, concentrating on antitrust and litigation, from 1993 to 1995.

Verdery served as counsel to two Senate committees and to Senator John Warner (R-VA), then worked for Senator Orrin

Hatch (R-UT), chairman of the Senate Judiciary Committee. He was general counsel to U.S. Senate Assistant Republican Leader Don Nickles (R-OK) from October 1998 until March 2002. As a member of the Republican leadership staff team, Verdery played a major role in the Congress on such policy issues as crime and law enforcement, commerce, judicial nominations, constitutional law, campaign finance, and telecommunications. During the Clinton impeachment trial, he served as a lead attorney to the Senate leadership in devising and implementing trial procedures. As part of his leadership duties, Verdery handled lead staff duties for the Senate Republican High Tech Task Force, the Republican leadership's outreach arm to the technology community.

In addition to his government service, Verdery was the senior legislative counsel for the government affairs and public policy office representing Vivendi Universal in Washington, D.C., from 2002 to 2003. In this capacity, Verdery was a lead strategist for the corporation in lobbying of Congress and the executive branch, focusing on technology, telecommunications, and intellectual property issues on behalf of the company's business units.

William H. Parrish, Acting Associate Director for Homeland Security, Terrorist Threat Integration Center

On May 1, 2003, the Terrorist Threat Integration Center was established under the Director of Central Intelligence. William Parrish was then nominated by Secretary Ridge as the associate director for homeland security.

Parrish, a retired U.S. Marine Corps colonel, serves as senior advisor to the secretary of the Department of Homeland Security for combating terrorism and serves as the senior Homeland Security representative to the Terrorist Threat Integration Center. Prior to assuming this position, Parrish served on the secretary's staff, where he was the lead planner of Operation Liberty Shield, a comprehensive national security operation that was executed within the fifty states and six U.S. territories during the U.S. military's Operation Iraqi Freedom.

Parrish received his undergraduate degree in criminal justice from Central Missouri State University and then attended the Naval War College, earning a masters degree in international strategic studies. He also holds a masters in management from Salve Regina University.

He served as commanding officer of the U.S. Marine Corps Security Forces, a unit comprised of nearly 4,000 marines charged with providing antiterrorism security to U.S. government installations around the world and to U.S. Navy ships in port and at sea. In this assignment he was responsible for expanding the capabilities of Fleet Antiterrorism Security Teams (FAST) in support of antiterrorism operations worldwide. Colonel Parrish also served as director of operations and plans for the Atlantic and U.S. Marine Corps Forces South.

Following his retirement from the Marine Corps, Parrish went to work for the U.S. Customs Service, where in October 2001 he established the Office of Anti-Terrorism. He directed and managed the Office of Anti-Terrorism's efforts to coordinate all policy, programs, training, and matters relating to terrorism in order to ensure that the Customs Service maximized its antiterrorism efforts with regards to Customs border security mission, and within the federal law enforcement community, national intelligence community, and homeland security structure.

Josh Filler, Director of the Office of State and Local Government Coordination

As director of the Office of State and Local Government Coordination for the Department of Homeland Security, Josh Filler is responsible for coordinating the programs and policies of the department as they relate to state and local governments, including funding issues and information sharing. Prior to joining the DHS, Josh was director of local affairs for the White House Office of Homeland Security.

Filler graduated from Boston University with a BA in political science and holds a law degree from St. John's University School of Law. Prior to his government service he was an attorney in private practice in New York. He served in the cabinet of New York mayor Rudolph Giuliani as director of legislative affairs for the mayor and chief of staff to the deputy mayor for operations. Following 9/11, he was responsible for emergency operational issues and managing contacts with local, state, and federal officials on behalf of New York City in connection with the attack on the World Trade Center.

Others Involved in the Creation of the U.S. DHS

John Ashcroft, Attorney General

John Ashcroft served as U.S. attorney general of the Department of Justice during President George W. Bush's first administration. One of the critical tools Ashcroft pushed for was the Patriot Act, passed in late October 2001.

Ashcroft graduated with honors from Yale University and received his JD from the University of Chicago. His career of public service began in 1973 as Missouri auditor. He was later elected to two terms as Missouri's attorney general.

Ashcroft served as governor of Missouri from 1985 through 1993, spearheading the state's efforts to reduce the use of illegal drugs, balancing eight consecutive budgets, and serving as chairman of the Education Commission of the States. He was elected to the U.S. Senate in 1994.

George W. Bush, President

George W. Bush is the forty-third president of the United States. He was sworn into office January 20, 2001, after a campaign in which he outlined sweeping proposals to reform America's public schools, transform our national defense, provide tax relief, modernize Social Security and Medicare, and encourage faith-based and community organizations to work with government to help Americans in need. (Most of these proposals did not see the light of day because of Bush's decision, in 2003, to go to war against Iraq.) Bush was reelected president in November 2004 and was sworn in on January 20, 2005.

Bush received a bachelor's degree from Yale University and an MBA from Harvard Business School. He was elected governor of Texas on November 8, 1994, and became the first governor in Texas history to be elected to two consecutive four-year terms when he was reelected in 1998.

Robert C. Byrd, U.S. Senator (D-WV)

West Virginia native Robert Byrd is a career politician, having served in the U.S. Senate continuously since 1959. Prior to his service as a U.S. senator, he was a state representative and a state senator. He holds a bachelor's degree in political science from Marshall University and a JD from George Washington University Law School.

In the U.S. Senate he has held the positions of minority whip, minority leader, majority leader, and president pro tempore. He has twice chaired the Committee on Appropriations.

Richard B. Cheney, Vice President

Vice President Richard ("Dick") B. Cheney earned his bachelor's and master's of arts degrees from the University of Wyoming. His career in public service began in 1969 when he joined the Nixon administration, serving in a number of positions at the Cost of Living Council, the Office of Economic Opportunity, and within the White House.

When Gerald Ford assumed the presidency in August 1974, Cheney served on the transition team and later as deputy assistant to the president. In November 1975 he was named assistant to the president and White House chief of staff, a position he held throughout the remainder of the Ford administration. After he returned to his home state of Wyoming in 1977 he was elected to serve as the state's sole congressman in the U.S. House of Representatives. He was reelected five times. He served as chairman of the Republican Policy Committee from 1981 to 1987 and was elected House minority whip in 1988.

As Secretary of Defense during the administration of George H.B. Bush, Cheney directed two of the largest military campaigns in recent history—Operation Just Cause in Panama and Operation Desert Storm in the Middle East.

Alberto Gonzales, Attorney General

Texas native Alberto ("Al") Gonzales was nominated by President Bush in February 2005 for the position of United States Attorney General and was confirmed by the Senate the following month after controversy emerged because of some documents prepared by Gonzales for the president while he was the president's counsel. After the announcement of Associate Justice Sandra Day O'Connor's retirement, Gonzales's name emerged as a possible replacement for her.

Gonzales served in the U.S. Air Force, attended the Air Force Academy, and Rice University, then earned a law degree from Harvard University and joined the Houston law firm of Vinson & Elkins. He served as general counsel for George W. Bush during Bush's first term as governor of Texas, and later as secretary of state for Texas and as a justice on the Texas Supreme Court. In 2000 he joined Bush's presidential cabinet White House counsel. After Bush won a second term in 2004, Attorney General Ashcroft resigned and Gonzales became the first Hispanic nominated for the position.

Bernard B. Kerik

Bernard Kerik is a former New York City commissioner of corrections and New York City police commissioner. He was nominated on December 3, 2004, by President George W. Bush to serve as secretary of the DHS, replacing Tom Ridge.

Only one week after being nominated for DHS, December 10, 2004, Kerik unexpectedly withdrew his name from consideration for the top post at DHS. The initial reason for his withdrawal was that he had employed a nanny who was an illegal alien and for whom he did not pay any income tax during her term of employment. Asked why he withdrew, Kerik said that "it [the confirmation process in the U.S. Senate] would have been messy, ugly, and an embarrassment to President Bush, so I withdrew my name."

Joseph I. Lieberman, U.S. Senator (D-CT)

Senator Joseph Lieberman has served in the Senate since 1988 and was a Connecticut state senator and attorney general prior to that. He holds a law degree from Yale. He chaired the Committee on Governmental Affairs during the 107th Congress. He was a candidate for vice president with Al Gore Jr. in 2000 and a candidate for the Democratic nomination for president in 2004.

Colin C. Powell, Secretary, Department of State

Colin Powell attended the City College of New York (CCNY), where he earned a bachelor's degree in geology and participated in Army ROTC, receiving a commission as an army second lieutenant upon graduation. He later earned an MBA from George Washington University.

Powell served in the U.S. Army for thirty-five years, eventually rising to the highest military position in the Department of Defense as chairman of the Joint Chiefs of Staff. His tenure on the Joint Chiefs included the victorious 1991 Persian Gulf War. General Powell received many U.S. military awards and decorations, including the Defense Distinguished Service Medal Legion of Merit, Bronze Star Medal, and the Purple Heart.

In 2001 President George W. Bush appointed Powell as the first African-American U.S. secretary of state. Powell served as the president's principal adviser on U.S. foreign policy and negotiated all treaties with foreign governments. He submitted his resignation following Bush's November 2004 reelection.

Tom Ridge, Secretary of OHS, 2002–2003; Secretary of DHS, 2003–2004

On January 24, 2003, Tom Ridge became the first Secretary of the Department of Homeland Security. (In December 2004, he announced his resignation from the DHS.)

Tom Ridge was sworn in as the first director of the Office of Homeland Security in October 2001, following the tragic events of September 11. The charge to the nation's new director of homeland defense was to develop and coordinate a comprehensive national strategy to strengthen the United States against terrorist threats or attacks.

Ridge graduated from Harvard with honors and was drafted into the U.S. Army, where he served as an infantry staff sergeant in Vietnam, earning the Bronze Star for Valor. After returning to his home state of Pennsylvania, he earned his law degree and was in private practice before becoming assistant district attorney. He was elected to Congress in 1982. He was the first congressman to have served as an enlisted man in the Vietnam War, and he was overwhelmingly reelected five times. He was twice elected governor of Pennsylvania, serving from 1995 to 2001.

Donald Rumsfeld, Secretary, DOD

Until being sworn in as secretary of defense, Donald Rumsfeld was in private business. He served as nonexecutive chairman of the board of directors of Gilead Sciences, Inc., and on the boards of directors of ABB (Asea Brown Boveri) Ltd. and Amylin Pharmaceuticals. He was chairman of the Salomon Smith Barney International Advisory Board and served as an advisor to a number of companies.

Rumsfeld attended Princeton University on scholarship (AB, 1954) and served in the U.S. Navy (1954–57) as an aviator. During the Eisenhower administration he served as administrative assistant to a representative from Ohio. After a stint with an investment banking firm, he was elected to the U.S. House of Representatives from Illinois in 1962, at the age of 30, and was re-elected in 1964, 1966, and 1968.

Rumsfeld resigned from Congress in 1969 during his fourth term to serve in the Nixon administration. He was first the director of the Office of Economic Opportunity, assistant to the president, and a member of the president's cabinet (1969–1970); later he served as counselor to the president, director of the Economic Stabilization Program, and a member of the president's cabinet (1971–1972). In 1973 he left Washington to serve as U.S. ambassador to the North Atlantic Treaty Organization (NATO) in Brussels, Belgium.

He returned to Washington to serve in the Ford administration, eventually being named secretary of defense, the youngest in U.S. history. After some twenty years of public service, he left to lecture for a semester at Princeton University's Woodrow Wilson School of International Affairs and at Northwestern University's Kellogg Graduate School of Management prior to entering business. From 1977 to 1985 he served as chief executive officer, president, and then chairman of G. D. Searle & Co., a worldwide pharmaceutical company.

Arlen Specter, U.S. Senator (R-PA)

Arlen Specter was born in Wichita, Kansas, to immigrant parents and grew up in a small town in western Kansas. He served as a stateside air force officer during the Korean War and later settled in Philadelphia, Pennsylvania. He was elected to the U.S. Senate in 1980 and has since become Pennsylvania's first four-term senator. He has chaired the Senate Intelligence Committee and currently chairs the Veterans Affairs Committee, the Appropriations Subcommittee on Labor, Health, and Human Service, and Education (which controls funding on medical research for the National Institutes of Health), and since December 2004 the Judiciary Committee.

6

Documents

This chapter contains five documents relating to the successful effort to create an executive Department of Homeland Security.

Executive Order 13688. Office of Homeland Security and Homeland Security Council, October 2001

Within a month of the September 11, 2001 terrorist attacks on the World Trade Center and the Pentagon, President Bush on October 8, 2001, issued an executive order creating the Office of Homeland Security and a Homeland Security Council. This response reflected the president's view that Homeland Security was a critical, new responsibility in the wake of 9/11. This initial response by the administration reflected their unwillingness to create a new executive department to deal with national security. Less than six months later, President Bush changed his mind and supported such a creation.

Executive Order Establishing the Office of Homeland Security and the Homeland Security Council

By the authority vested in me as President by the Constitution and the laws of the United States of America, it is hereby ordered as follows:

Section 1. Establishment. I hereby establish within the Executive Office of the President an Office of Homeland Security (the "Office") to be headed by the Assistant to the President for Homeland Security.

Section 2. Mission. The mission of the Office shall be to develop and coordinate the implementation of a comprehensive national strategy to secure the United States from terrorist threats or attacks. The Office shall perform the functions necessary to carry out this mission, including the functions specified in section 3 of this order.

Section 3. Functions. The functions of the Office shall be to coordinate the executive branch's efforts to detect, prepare for, prevent, protect against, respond to, and recover from terrorist attacks within the United States.

(a) National Strategy. The Office shall work with executive departments and agencies, State and local governments, and private entities to ensure the adequacy of the national strategy for detecting, preparing for, preventing, protecting against, responding to, and recovering from terrorist threats or attacks within the United States and shall periodically review and coordinate revisions to that strategy as necessary.

(b) Detection. The Office shall identify priorities and coordinate efforts for collection and analysis of information within the United States regarding threats of terrorism against the United States and activities of terrorists or terrorist groups within the United States. The Office also shall identify, in coordination with the Assistant to the President for National Security Affairs, priorities for collection of intelligence outside the United States regarding threats of terrorism within the United States.

(i) In performing these functions, the Office shall work with Federal, State, and local agencies, as appropriate, to:

(A) facilitate collection from State and local governments and private entities of information pertaining to terrorist threats or activities within the United States;

(B) coordinate and prioritize the requirements for foreign intelligence relating to terrorism within the United States of executive departments and agencies responsible for homeland security and provide these requirements and priorities to the Director of Central Intelligence and other agencies responsible collection of foreign intelligence;

(C) coordinate efforts to ensure that all executive departments and agencies that have intelligence collection responsibilities have sufficient technological capabilities and resources to collect intelligence and data relating to terrorist activities or possible terrorist acts within the United States, working with the Assistant to the President for National Security Affairs, as appropriate;

(D) coordinate development of monitoring protocols and equipment for use in detecting the release of biological, chemical, and radiological hazards; and

(E) ensure that, to the extent permitted by law, all appropriate and necessary intelligence and law enforcement information relating to homeland security is disseminated to and exchanged among appropriate executive departments and agencies responsible for homeland security and, where appropriate for reasons of homeland security, promote exchange of such information with and among State and local governments and private entities.

(ii) Executive departments and agencies shall, to the extent permitted by law, make available to the Office all information relating to terrorist threats and activities within the United States.

(c) Preparedness. The Office of Homeland Security shall coordinate national efforts to prepare for and mitigate the consequences of terrorist threats or attacks within the United States. In performing this function, the Office shall work with Federal, State, and local agencies, and private entities, as appropriate, to:

(i) review and assess the adequacy of the portions of all Federal emergency response plans that pertain to terrorist threats or attacks within the United States;

(ii) coordinate domestic exercises and simulations designed to assess and practice systems that would be called upon to respond to a terrorist threat or attack within the United States and coordinate programs and activities for training Federal, State, and local employees who would be called upon to respond to such a threat or attack;

(iii) coordinate national efforts to ensure public health preparedness for a terrorist attack, including reviewing vaccination policies and reviewing the adequacy of and, if necessary, increasing vaccine and pharmaceutical stockpiles and hospital capacity;

(iv) coordinate Federal assistance to State and local authorities and nongovernmental organizations to prepare for and respond to terrorist threats or attacks within the United States;

(v) ensure that national preparedness programs and activities for terrorist threats or attacks are developed and are regularly evaluated under appropriate standards and that resources are allocated to improving and sustaining preparedness based on such evaluations; and

(vi) ensure the readiness and coordinated deployment of Federal response teams to respond to terrorist threats or attacks, working with the Assistant to the President for National Security Affairs, when appropriate.

(d) Prevention. The Office shall coordinate efforts to prevent terrorist attacks within the United States. In performing this function, the Office shall work with Federal, State, and local agencies, and private entities, as appropriate, to:

(i) facilitate the exchange of information among such agencies relating to immigration and visa matters and shipments of cargo; and, working with the Assistant to the President for National Security Affairs, ensure coordination among such agencies to prevent the entry of terrorists and terrorist materials and supplies into the United States and facilitate removal of such terrorists from the United States, when appropriate;

(ii) coordinate efforts to investigate terrorist threats and attacks within the United States; and

(iii) coordinate efforts to improve the security of United States borders, territorial waters, and airspace in order to prevent acts of terrorism within the United States, working with the Assistant to the President for National Security Affairs, when appropriate.

(e) Protection. The Office shall coordinate efforts to protect the United States and its critical infrastructure from the consequences of terrorist attacks. In performing this function, the Office shall work with Federal, State, and local agencies, and private entities, as appropriate, to:

(i) strengthen measures for protecting energy production, transmission, and distribution services and critical facilities; other utilities; telecommunications; facilities that produce, use, store, or dispose of nuclear material; and other critical infrastructure services and critical facilities within the United States from terrorist attack;

(ii) coordinate efforts to protect critical public and privately owned information systems within the United States from terrorist attack;

(iii) develop criteria for reviewing whether appropriate security measures are in place at major public and privately owned facilities within the United States;

(iv) coordinate domestic efforts to ensure that special events determined by appropriate senior officials to have national significance are protected from terrorist attack;

(v) coordinate efforts to protect transportation systems within the United States, including railways, highways, shipping, ports and waterways, and airports and civilian aircraft, from terrorist attack;

(vi) coordinate efforts to protect United States livestock, agriculture, and systems for the provision of water and food for human use and consumption from terrorist attack; and

(vii) coordinate efforts to prevent unauthorized access to, development of, and unlawful importation into the United States of, chemical, biological, radiological, nuclear, explosive, or other related materials that have the potential to be used in terrorist attacks.

(f) Response and Recovery. The Office shall coordinate efforts to respond to and promote recovery from terrorist threats or attacks within the United States. In performing this function, the Office shall work with Federal, State, and local agencies, and private entities, as appropriate, to:

(i) coordinate efforts to ensure rapid restoration of transportation systems, energy production, transmission, and distribution systems; telecommunications; other utilities; and other critical infrastructure facilities after disruption by a terrorist threat or attack;

(ii) coordinate efforts to ensure rapid restoration of public and private critical information systems after disruption by a terrorist threat or attack;

(iii) work with the National Economic Council to coordinate efforts to stabilize United States financial markets after a terrorist threat or attack and manage the immediate economic and financial consequences of the incident;

(iv) coordinate Federal plans and programs to provide medical, financial, and other assistance to victims of terrorist attacks and their families; and

(v) coordinate containment and removal of biological, chemical, radiological, explosive, or other hazardous materials in the event of a terrorist threat or attack involving such hazards and coordinate efforts to mitigate the effects of such an attack.

(g) Incident Management. The Assistant to the President for Homeland Security shall be the individual primarily responsible for coordinating the domestic response efforts of all departments and agencies in the event of an imminent terrorist threat and during and in the immediate aftermath of a terrorist attack within the United States and shall be the principal point of contact for and to the President with respect to coordination of such efforts. The Assistant to the President for Homeland Security shall coordinate with the Assistant to the President for National Security Affairs, as appropriate.

(h) Continuity of Government. The Assistant to the President for Homeland Security, in coordination with the Assistant to the President for National Security Affairs, shall review plans and preparations for ensuring the continuity of the Federal Government in the event of a terrorist attack that threatens the safety and security of the United States Government or its leadership.

(i) Public Affairs. The Office, subject to the direction of the White House Office of Communications, shall coordinate the strategy of the executive branch for communicating with the public in the event of a terrorist threat or attack within the United States. The Office also shall coordinate the development of programs for educating the public about the nature of terrorist threats and appropriate precautions and responses.

(j) Cooperation with State and Local Governments and Private Entities. The Office shall encourage and invite the participation of State and local governments and private entities, as appropriate, in carrying out the Office's functions.

(k) Review of Legal Authorities and Development of Legislative Proposals. The Office shall coordinate a periodic review and assessment of the legal authorities available to executive departments and agencies to permit them to perform the functions described in this order. When the Office determines that such legal authorities are inadequate, the Office shall develop, in consultation with executive departments and agencies, proposals for presidential action and legislative proposals for submission to the Office of Management and Budget to enhance the ability of executive departments and agencies to perform those functions. The Office shall work with State and local governments in assessing the adequacy of their legal authorities to permit them to detect, prepare for, prevent, protect against, and recover from terrorist threats and attacks.

(l) Budget Review. The Assistant to the President for Homeland Security, in consultation with the Director of the Office of Management and Budget (the "Director") and the heads of executive departments and agencies, shall identify programs that contribute to the Administration's strategy for homeland security and, in the development of the President's annual budget submission, shall review and provide advice to the heads of departments and agencies for such programs. The Assistant to the President for Homeland Security shall provide advice to the Director on the level and use of funding in departments and agencies for homeland security-related activities and, prior to the Director's forwarding of the proposed annual budget submission to the President for transmittal to the Congress, shall certify to the Director the funding levels that the Assistant to the President for Homeland Security believes are necessary and appropriate for the homeland security-related activities of the executive branch.

Section 4. Administration.

(a) The Office of Homeland Security shall be directed by the Assistant to the President for Homeland Security.

(b) The Office of Administration within the Executive Office of the President shall provide the Office of Homeland Security with such personnel, funding, and administrative support, to the extent permitted by law and subject to the availability of appropriations, as directed by the Chief of Staff to carry out the provisions of this order.

(c) Heads of executive departments and agencies are authorized, to the extent permitted by law, to detail or assign personnel of such departments and agencies to the Office of Homeland Security upon request of the Assistant to the President for Homeland Security, subject to the approval of the Chief of Staff.

Section 5. Establishment of Homeland Security Council.

(a) I hereby establish a Homeland Security Council (the "Council"), which shall be responsible for advising and assisting the President with respect to all aspects of homeland security. The Council shall serve as the mechanism for ensuring coordination of homeland security-related activities of executive departments and agencies and effective development and implementation of homeland security policies.

(b) The Council shall have as its members the President, the Vice

President, the Secretary of the Treasury, the Secretary of Defense, the Attorney General, the Secretary of Health and Human Services, the Secretary of Transportation, the Director of the Federal Emergency Management Agency, the Director of the Federal Bureau of Investigation, the Director of Central Intelligence, the Assistant to the President for Homeland Security, and such other officers of the executive branch as the President may from time to time designate. The Chief of Staff, the Chief of Staff to the Vice President, the Assistant to the President for National Security Affairs, the Counsel to the President, and the Director of the Office of Management and Budget also are invited to attend any Council meeting. The Secretary of State, the Secretary of Agriculture, the Secretary of the Interior, the Secretary of Energy, the Secretary of Labor, the Secretary of Commerce, the Secretary of Veterans Affairs, the Administrator of the Environmental Protection Agency, the Assistant to the President for Economic Policy, and the Assistant to the President for Domestic Policy shall be invited to attend meetings pertaining to their responsibilities. The heads of other executive departments and agencies and other senior officials shall be invited to attend Council meetings when appropriate.

(c) The Council shall meet at the President's direction. When the President is absent from a meeting of the Council, at the President's direction the Vice President may preside. The Assistant to the President for Homeland Security shall be responsible, at the President's direction, for determining the agenda, ensuring that necessary papers are prepared, and recording Council actions and Presidential decisions.

Section 6. Original Classification Authority. I hereby delegate the authority to classify information originally as Top Secret, in accordance with Executive Order 12958 or any successor Executive Order, to the Assistant to the President for Homeland Security.

Section 7. Continuing Authorities. This order does not alter the existing authorities of United States Government departments and agencies. All executive departments and agencies are directed to assist the Council and the Assistant to the President for Homeland Security in carrying out the purposes of this order.

Section 8. General Provisions.

(a) This order does not create any right or benefit, substantive or procedural, enforceable at law or equity by a party against the United States, its departments, agencies or instrumentalities, its officers or employees, or any other person.

(b) References in this order to State and local governments shall be construed to include tribal governments and United States territories and other possessions.

(c) References to the "United States" shall be construed to include United States territories and possessions.

Section 9. Amendments to Executive Order 12656. Executive Order 12656 of November 18, 1988, as amended, is hereby further amended as follows:

(a) Section 101(a) is amended by adding at the end of the fourth sentence: "except that the Homeland Security Council shall be responsible for administering such policy with respect to terrorist threats and attacks within the United States."

(b) Section 104(a) is amended by adding at the end: "except that the Homeland Security Council is the principal forum for consideration of policy relating to terrorist threats and attacks within the United States."

(c) Section 104(b) is amended by inserting the words "and the Homeland Security Council" after the words "National Security Council."

(d) The first sentence of section 104(c) is amended by inserting the words "and the Homeland Security Council" after the words "National Security Council."

(e) The second sentence of section 104(c) is replaced with the following two sentences: "Pursuant to such procedures for the organization and management of the National Security Council and Homeland Security Council processes as the President may establish, the Director of the Federal Emergency Management Agency also shall assist in the implementation of and management of those processes as the President may establish. The Director of the Federal Emergency Management Agency also shall assist in the implementation of national security emergency preparedness policy by coordinating with the other Federal departments and agencies and with State and local governments, and by providing periodic reports to the National Security Council and the Homeland Security Council on implementation of national security emergency preparedness policy."

(f) Section 201(7) is amended by inserting the words "and the Homeland Security Council" after the words "National Security Council."

(g) Section 206 is amended by inserting the words "and the Homeland Security Council" after the words "National Security Council."

(h) Section 208 is amended by inserting the words "or the Homeland Security Council" after the words "National Security Council."

George W. Bush
The White House
October 8, 2001

Presidential Message to the Congress of the United States on the Need to Create a Department of Homeland Security, June 18, 2002

On June 18, 2002, President Bush sent a lengthy message to the Congress of the United States "On the Need to Create a[n Executive Branch Cabinet] Department of Homeland Security." Realizing that a director of an Office of Homeland Security did not have the power to reorganize the U.S. government's capacity to deal with terrorist attacks, and aware of the fact that there were a number of congressional proposals calling for the creation of a new executive bureaucracy, the White House, in this message, tried to channel legislative demands for such a bureaucratic creation into support for the presidential proposal. This strategy proved to be a very successful one, as a view of the final legislative action (section 3) illustrates.

TO THE CONGRESS OF THE UNITED STATES:

I hereby transmit to the Congress proposed legislation to create a new Cabinet Department of Homeland Security.

Our Nation faces a new and changing threat unlike any we have faced before—the global threat of terrorism. No nation is immune, and all nations must act decisively to protect against this constantly evolving threat.

We must recognize that the threat of terrorism is a permanent condition, and we must take action to protect America against the terrorists that seek to kill the innocent.

Since September 11, 2001, all levels of government and leaders from across the political spectrum have cooperated like never before. We have strengthened our aviation security and tightened our borders. We have stockpiled medicines to defend against bioterrorism and improved our ability to combat weapons of mass destruction. We have dramatically improved information sharing among our intelligence agencies, and we have taken new steps to protect our critical infrastructure.

Our Nation is stronger and better prepared today than it was on September 11. Yet, we can do better. I propose the most extensive reorganization of the Federal Government since the 1940s by creating a new Department of Homeland Security. For the first time we would have a single Department whose primary mission is to secure our homeland. Soon after the Second World War, President Harry Truman recognized that our Nation's fragmented military defenses needed reorganization to help win the Cold War. President Truman proposed uniting our military forces under a single entity, now the Department of Defense, and creating the National Security Council to bring together defense, intelligence, and diplomacy. President Truman's reforms are still helping us to fight terror abroad, and today we need similar dramatic reforms to secure our people at home.

President Truman and Congress reorganized our Government to meet a very visible enemy in the Cold War. Today our nation must once again reorganize our Government to protect against an often-invisible enemy, an enemy that hides in the shadows and an enemy that can strike with many different types of weapons. Our enemies seek to obtain the most dangerous and deadly weapons of mass destruction and use them against the innocent. While we are winning the war on terrorism, Al Qaeda and other terrorist organizations still have thousands of trained killers spread across the globe plotting attacks against America and the other nations of the civilized world.

Immediately after last fall's attack, I used my legal authority to establish the White House Office of Homeland Security and the Homeland Security Council to help ensure that our Federal response and protection efforts were coordinated and effective. I also directed Homeland Security Advisor Tom Ridge to study the Federal Government as a whole to determine if the current structure allows us to meet the threats of today while preparing for the unknown threats of tomorrow. After careful study of the current structure, coupled with the experience gained since September 11 and new information we have learned while fighting a war—the president concluded that our Nation needs a more unified homeland security structure.

I propose to create a new Department of Homeland Security by substantially transforming the current confusing patchwork of government activities into a single department whose primary mission is to secure our homeland. My proposal builds on the strong bipartisan work on the issue of homeland security that has been conducted by Members of Congress. In designing the new Department, my Administration considered a number of homeland security organizational proposals that have emerged from outside studies, commissions, and Members of Congress.

The Need for a Department of Homeland Security

Today no Federal Government agency has homeland security as its primary mission. Responsibilities for homeland security are dispersed among more than 100 different entities of the Federal Government. America needs a unified homeland security structure that will improve protection against today's threats and be flexible enough to help meet the unknown threats of the future.

The mission of the new Department ι
attacks within the United States, to reduce
terrorism, and to minimize the damage anc
may occur. The Department of Homeland S
focus the resources of the Federal Governm(
ments, the private sector, and the American
mission.

The Department of Homeland Security ι
safer because for the first time we would havε
cated to securing the homeland. One departm   ͟ ͟εcure our
borders, transportation sector, ports, and critical infrastructure. One department would analyze homeland security intelligence from multiple
sources, synthesize it with a comprehensive assessment of America's
vulnerabilities, and take action to secure our highest risk facilities and
systems. One department would coordinate communications with
State and local governments, private industry, and the American people about threats and preparedness. One department would coordinate
our efforts to secure the American people against bioterrorism and
other weapons of mass destruction. One department would help train
and equip our first responders. One department would manage Federal emergency response activities.

Our goal is not to expand Government, but to create an agile organization that takes advantage of modern technology and management techniques to meet a new and constantly evolving threat. We can
improve our homeland security by minimizing the duplication of efforts, improving coordination, and combining functions that are currently fragmented and inefficient. The new Department would allow
us to have more security officers in the field working to stop terrorists
and fewer resources in Washington managing duplicative activities
that drain critical homeland security resources.

The Department of Homeland Security would have a clear and ef-
ficient organizational structure with four main divisions: Border and
Transportation Security; Emergency Preparedness and Response;
Chemical, Biological, Radiological and Nuclear Countermeasures; and
Information Analysis and Infrastructure Protection.

Border and Transportation Security

Terrorism is a global threat and we must improve our border security
to help keep out those who mean to do us harm. We must closely monitor who is coming into and out of our country to help prevent foreign
terrorists from entering our country and bringing in their instruments
of terror. At the same time, we must expedite the legal flow of people
and goods on which our economy depends. Securing our borders and

...ing entry to the United States has always been the responsibil-
...the Federal Government. Yet, this responsibility and the security
...our transportation systems is now dispersed among several major
Government organizations. Under my proposed legislation, the Department of Homeland Security would unify authority over major Federal security operations related to our borders, territorial waters, and
transportation systems.

The Department would assume responsibility for the United
States Coast Guard, the United States Customs Service, the Immigration and Naturalization Service (including the Border Patrol), the Animal and Plant Health Inspection Service, and the Transportation Security Administration. The Secretary of Homeland Security would have
the authority to administer and enforce all immigration and nationality
laws, including the visa issuance functions of consular officers. As a result, the Department would have sole responsibility for managing
entry into the United States and protecting our transportation infrastructure. It would ensure that all aspects of border control, including
the issuing of visas, are informed by a central information-sharing
clearinghouse and compatible databases.

Emergency Preparedness and Response

Although our top priority is preventing future attacks, we must also
prepare to minimize the damage and recover from attacks that may
occur.

My legislative proposal requires the Department of Homeland Security to ensure the preparedness of our Nation's emergency response
professionals, provide the Federal Government's response, and aid
America's recovery from terrorist attacks and natural disasters. To fulfill
these missions, the Department of Homeland Security would incorporate the Federal Emergency Management Agency (FEMA) as one of its
key components. The Department would administer the domestic disaster preparedness grant programs for firefighters, police, and emergency
personnel currently managed by FEMA, the Department of Justice, and
the Department of Health and Human Services. In responding to an incident, the Department would manage such critical response assets as
the Nuclear Emergency Search Team (from the Department of Energy)
and the National Pharmaceutical Stockpile (from the Department of
Health and Human Services). Finally, the Department of Homeland Security would integrate the Federal interagency emergency response
plans into a single, comprehensive, Government-wide plan, and would
work to ensure that all response personnel have the equipment and capability to communicate with each other as necessary.

Chemical, Biological, Radiological, and Nuclear Countermeasures

Our enemies today seek to acquire and use the most deadly weapons known to mankind—chemical, biological, radiological, and nuclear weapons.

The new Department of Homeland Security would lead the Federal Government's efforts in preparing for and responding to the full range of terrorist threats involving weapons of mass destruction. The Department would set national policy and establish guidelines for State and local governments. The Department would direct exercises for Federal, State, and local chemical, biological, radiological, and nuclear attack response teams and plans. The Department would consolidate and synchronize the disparate efforts of multiple Federal agencies now scattered across several departments. This would create a single office whose primary mission is the critical task of securing the United States from catastrophic terrorism.

The Department would improve America's ability to develop diagnostics, vaccines, antibodies, antidotes, and other countermeasures against new weapons. It would consolidate and prioritize the disparate homeland security-related research and development programs currently scattered throughout the executive branch, and the Department would assist State and local public safety agencies by evaluating equipment and setting standards.

Information Analysis and Infrastructure Protection

For the first time the Government would have under one roof the capability to identify and assess threats to the homeland, map those threats against our vulnerabilities, issue timely warnings, and take action to help secure the homeland.

The Information Analysis and Infrastructure Protection division of the new Department of Homeland Security would complement the reforms on intelligence-gathering and information-sharing already underway at the FBI and the CIA. The Department would analyze information and intelligence from the FBI, CIA, and many other Federal agencies to better understand the terrorist threat to the American homeland.

The Department would comprehensively assess the vulnerability of America's key assets and critical infrastructures, including food and water systems, agriculture, health systems and emergency services, information and telecommunications, banking and finance, energy, transportation, the chemical and defense industries, postal and shipping entities, and national monuments and icons. The Department would integrate its own and others' threat analyses with its comprehensive vulnerability assessment to identify protective priorities and support protective steps to be taken by the Department, other Federal departments and agencies, State and local agencies, and the private sector. Working closely with State and local officials, other Federal agencies, and the private sector, the Department would help ensure that proper steps are taken to protect high-risk potential targets.

Other Components

In addition to these four core divisions, the submitted legislation would also transfer responsibility for the Secret Service to the Department of Homeland Security. The Secret Service, which would report directly to the Secretary of Homeland Security, would retain its primary mission to protect the President and other Government leaders. The Secret Service would, however, contribute its specialized protective expertise to the fulfillment of the Department's core mission.

Finally, under my legislation, the Department of Homeland Security would consolidate and streamline relations with the Federal Government for America's State and local governments.

The new Department would contain an intergovernmental affairs office to coordinate Federal homeland security programs with State and local officials. It would give State and local officials one primary contact instead of many when it comes to matters related to training, equipment, planning, and other critical needs such as emergency response.

The consolidation of the Government's homeland security efforts as outlined in my proposed legislation can achieve great efficiencies that further enhance our security. Yet, to achieve these efficiencies, the new Secretary of Homeland Security would require considerable flexibility in procurement, integration of information technology systems, and personnel issues. My proposed legislation provides the Secretary of Homeland Security with just such flexibility and managerial authorities. I call upon the Congress to implement these measures in order to ensure that we are maximizing our ability to secure our homeland.

Continued Interagency Coordination at the White House

Even with the creation of the new Department, there will remain a strong need for a White House Office of Homeland Security. Protecting America from terrorism will remain a multi-departmental issue and will continue to require interagency coordination. Presidents will continue to require the confidential advice of a Homeland Security Advisor, and I intend for the White House Office of Homeland Security and the Homeland Security Council to maintain a strong role in coordinating our government-wide efforts to secure the homeland.

The Lessons of History

History teaches us that new challenges require new organizational structures. History also teaches us that critical security challenges require clear lines of responsibility and the unified effort of the U.S. Government.

President Truman said, looking at the lessons of the Second World War: "It is now time to discard obsolete organizational forms, and to provide for the future the soundest, the most effective, and the most economical kind of structure for our armed forces." When skeptics told President Truman that this proposed reorganization was too ambitious to be enacted, he simply replied that it had to be. In the years to follow, the Congress acted upon President Truman's recommendation, eventually laying a sound organizational foundation that enabled the United States to win the Cold War. All Americans today enjoy the inheritance of this landmark organizational reform: a unified Department of Defense that has become the most powerful force for freedom the world has ever seen.

Today America faces a threat that is wholly different from the threat we faced during the Cold War. Our terrorist enemies hide in shadows and attack civilians with whatever means of destruction they can access. But as in the Cold War, meeting this threat requires clear lines of responsibility and the unified efforts of government at all levels—Federal, State, local, and tribal—the private sector, and all Americans. America needs a homeland security establishment that can help prevent catastrophic attacks and mobilize national resources for an enduring conflict while protecting our Nation's values and liberties.

Years from today, our world will still be fighting the threat of terrorism. It is my hope that future generations will be able to look back on the Homeland Security Act of 2002—as we now remember the National Security Act of 1947—as the solid organizational foundation for America's triumph in a long and difficult struggle against a formidable enemy.

History has given our Nation new challenges—and important new assignments. Only the United States Congress can create a new department of Government. We face an urgent need, and I am pleased that Congress has responded to my call to act before the end of the current congressional session with the same bipartisan spirit that allowed us to act expeditiously on legislation after September 11.

These are times that demand bipartisan action and bipartisan solutions to meet the new and changing threats we face as a Nation. I urge the Congress to join me in creating a single, permanent department with an overriding and urgent mission—securing the homeland of America and protecting the American people. Together we can meet this ambitious deadline and help ensure that the American homeland is secure against the terrorist threat.

GEORGE W. BUSH
THE WHITE HOUSE,
June 18, 2002.

Congressional Summary of PL 107–296, The Department of Homeland Security Act of 2002. November 25, 2002.

This document is the official congressional summary of the as-passed Department of Homeland Security Act of 2002. It summarizes the om-nibus bill in a succinct manner, clearly conveying the essential ingredi-ents found in the multi-hundred-page piece of domestic security reorga-nization bill.

H.R.5005
Title: To establish the Department of Homeland Security, and for other purposes.

Sponsor: Rep Armey, Richard K. [TX-26] (by request) (introduced 6/24/2002) Cosponsors (118)

Related Bills: H.RES.502, H.R.4635, H.R.4660, H.R.5506, H.R.5710, S.1534, S.2452, S.2546, S.2554, S.2794 **Latest Major Action:** Became Pub-lic Law No: 107–296 [Text, PDF] **House Reports:** 107–609 Part 1 **Note:** On 11/19/2002, S.Amdt. 4901 substituted text essentially the same as H.R. 5710 in H.R. 5005. The House agreed to the Senate amendment on 11/22/2002. Other earlier bills included H.R. 4660, S. 1534, S. 2452, and S. 2794.

SUMMARY AS OF:
11/19/2002—Passed Senate, amended.
Homeland Security Act of 2002

Title I: Department of Homeland Security—(Sec. 101)

Establishes a Department of Homeland Security (DHS) as an executive department of the United States, headed by a Secretary of Homeland Security (Secretary) appointed by the President, by and with the advice and consent of the Senate, to: (1) prevent terrorist attacks within the United States; (2) reduce the vulnerability of the United States to terrorism; (3) minimize the damage, and assist in the recovery, from terrorist attacks that occur within the United States; (4) carry out all functions of entities transferred to DHS; (5) ensure that the functions of the agencies and subdivisions within DHS that are not related directly to securing the homeland are not diminished or neglected except by a specific Act of Congress; (6) ensure that the overall economic security of the United States is not diminished by efforts, activities, and programs aimed at securing the homeland; and (7) monitor connections between illegal drug trafficking and terrorism, coordinate efforts to sever such connections, and otherwise contribute to efforts to interdict illegal drug trafficking. Vests primary responsibility for investigating and prosecuting acts of terrorism in Federal, State, and local law enforcement agencies with proper jurisdiction except as specifically provided by law with respect to entities transferred to DHS under this Act.

(Sec. 102) Directs the Secretary to appoint a Special Assistant to carry out specified homeland security liaison activities between DHS and the private sector.

(Sec. 103) Creates the following: (1) a Deputy Secretary of Homeland Security; (2) an Under Secretary for Information Analysis and Infrastructure Protection; (3) an Under Secretary for Science and Technology; (4) an Under Secretary for Border and Transportation Security; (5) an Under Secretary for Emergency Preparedness and Response; (6) a Director of the Bureau of Citizenship and Immigration Services; (7) an Under Secretary for Management; (8) not more than 12 Assistant Secretaries; and (9) a General Counsel. Establishes an Inspector General (to be appointed under the Inspector General Act of 1978). Requires the following individuals to assist the Secretary in the performance of the Secretary's functions: (1) the Commandant of the Coast Guard; (2) the Director of the Secret Service; (3) a Chief Information Officer; (4) a Chief Human Capital Officer; (5) a Chief Financial Officer; and (6) an Officer for Civil Rights and Civil Liberties.

Title II: Information Analysis and Infrastructure Protection

Subtitle A: Directorate for Information Analysis and Infrastructure Protection; Access to Information — (Sec. 201)

Establishes in the Department: (1) a Directorate for Information Analysis and Infrastructure Protection, headed by an Under Secretary for Information Analysis and Infrastructure Protection; (2) an Assistant Secretary for Information Analysis; and (3) an Assistant Secretary for Infrastructure Protection.

Requires the Under Secretary to: (1) access, receive, and analyze law enforcement and intelligence information from Federal, State, and local agencies and the private sector to identify the nature, scope, and identity of terrorist threats to the United States, as well as potential U.S. vulnerabilities; (2) carry out comprehensive assessments of vulnerabilities of key U.S. resources and critical infrastructures; (3) integrate relevant information, analyses, and vulnerability assessments to identify protection priorities; (4) ensure timely and efficient Department access to necessary information for discharging responsibilities; (5) develop a comprehensive national plan for securing key U.S. resources and critical infrastructures; (6) recommend necessary measures to protect such resources and infrastructure in coordination with other entities; (7) administer the Homeland Security Advisory System; (8) review, analyze, and make recommendations for improvements in policies and procedures governing the sharing of law enforcement, intelligence, and intelligence-related information and other information related to homeland security within the Federal Government and between the Federal Government and State and local government agencies and authorities; (9) disseminate Department homeland security information to other appropriate Federal, State, and local agencies; (10) consult with the Director of Central Intelligence (DCI) and other appropriate Federal intelligence, law enforcement, or other elements to establish collection priorities and strategies for information relating the terrorism threats; (11) consult with State and local governments and private entities to ensure appropriate exchanges of information relating to such threats; (12) ensure the protection from unauthorized disclosure of homeland security and intelligence information; (13) request additional information from appropriate entities relating to threats of terrorism in the United States; (14) establish and utilize a secure communications and information technology infrastructure for receiving and analyzing data; (15) ensure the compatibility and privacy protection of shared information databases and analytical tools; (16) coordinate training and other support to facilitate the identification and sharing of information; (17) coordinate activities with elements of the intelligence community, Federal, State, and local law enforcement agencies, and the private sector; and (18) provide intelligence and information analysis and support to other elements of the Department. Provides for: (1) staffing, including the use of private sector analysts; and (2) cooperative agreements for the detail of appropriate personnel.

Transfers to the Secretary the functions, personnel, assets, and liabilities of the following entities: (1) the National Infrastructure Protection Center of the Federal Bureau of Investigation (other than the Computer Investigations and Operations Section); (2) the National Communications System of the Department of Defense; (3) the Critical Infrastructure Assurance Offices of the Department of Commerce; (4) the National Infrastructure Simulation and Analysis Center of the Department of Energy and its energy security and assurance program;

and (5) the Federal Computer Incident Response Center of the General Services Administration.

Amends the National Security Act of 1947 to include as elements of the intelligence community the Department elements concerned with analyses of foreign intelligence information.

(Sec. 202) Gives the Secretary access to all reports, assessments, analyses, and unevaluated intelligence relating to threats of terrorism against the United States, and to all information concerning infrastructure or other vulnerabilities to terrorism, whether or not such information has been analyzed. Requires all Federal agencies to promptly provide to the Secretary: (1) all reports, assessments, and analytical information relating to such threats and to other areas of responsibility assigned to the Secretary; (2) all information concerning the vulnerability of U.S. infrastructure or other U.S. vulnerabilities to terrorism, whether or not it has been analyzed; (3) all other information relating to significant and credible threats of terrorism, whether or not it has been analyzed; and (4) such other information or material as the President may direct. Requires the Secretary to be provided with certain terrorism-related information from law enforcement agencies that is currently required to be provided to the DCI.

Subtitle B: Critical Infrastructure Information—

Critical Infrastructure Information Act of 2002—(Sec. 213) Allows a critical infrastructure protection program to be so designated by either the President or the Secretary.

(Sec. 214) Exempts from the Freedom of Information Act and other Federal and State disclosure requirements any critical infrastructure information that is voluntarily submitted to a covered Federal agency for use in the security of critical infrastructure and protected systems, analysis, warning, interdependency study, recovery, reconstitution, or other informational purpose when accompanied by an express statement that such information is being submitted voluntarily in expectation of such nondisclosure protection. Requires the Secretary to establish specified procedures for the receipt, care, and storage by Federal agencies of critical infrastructure information voluntarily submitted. Provides criminal penalties for the unauthorized disclosure of such information.

Authorizes the Federal Government to issue advisories, alerts, and warnings to relevant companies, targeted sectors, other governmental entities, or the general public regarding potential threats to critical infrastructure.

Subtitle C: Information Security

(Sec. 221) Requires the Secretary to establish procedures on the use of shared information that: (1) limit its re-dissemination to ensure it is not used for an unauthorized purpose; (2) ensure its security and confidentiality; (3) protect the constitutional and statutory rights of individuals who are subjects of such information; and (4) provide data integrity through the timely removal and destruction of obsolete or erroneous names and information.

(Sec. 222) Directs the Secretary to appoint a senior Department official to assume primary responsibility for information privacy policy.

(Sec. 223) Directs the Under Secretary to provide: (1) to State and local government entities and, upon request, to private entities that own or operate critical information systems, analysis and warnings related to threats to and vulnerabilities of such systems, as well as crisis management support in response to threats to or attacks upon such systems; and (2) technical assistance, upon request, to private sector and other government entities with respect to emergency recovery plans to respond to major failures of such systems.

(Sec. 224) Authorizes the Under Secretary to establish a national technology guard (known as NET Guard) to assist local communities to respond to and recover from attacks on information systems and communications networks.

(Sec. 225) Cyber Security Enhancement Act of 2002—Directs the U.S. Sentencing Commission to review and amend Federal sentencing guidelines and otherwise address crimes involving fraud in connection with computers and access to protected information, protected computers, or restricted data in interstate or foreign commerce or involving a computer used by or for the Federal Government. Requires a Commission report to Congress on actions taken and recommendations regarding statutory penalties for violations. Exempts from criminal penalties any disclosure made by an electronic communication service to a Federal, State, or local governmental entity if made in the good faith belief that an emergency involving danger of death or serious physical injury to any person requires disclosure without delay. Requires any government entity receiving such a disclosure to report it to the Attorney General.

Amends the Federal criminal code to: (1) prohibit the dissemination by electronic means of any such protected information; (2) increase criminal penalties for violations which cause death or serious bodily injury; (3) authorize the use by appropriate officials of emergency pen register and trap and trace devices in the case of either an immediate threat to a national security interest or an ongoing attack on a protected computer that constitutes a crime punishable by a prison term of greater than one year; (4) repeal provisions which provide a shorter term of imprisonment for certain offenses involving protection from the unauthorized interception and disclosure of wire, oral, or electronic communications; and (5) increase penalties for repeat offenses in connection with unlawful access to stored communications.

Subtitle D: Office of Science and Technology — (Sec. 231)

Establishes within the Department of Justice (DOJ) an Office of Science and Technology whose mission is to: (1) serve as the national focal point for work on law enforcement technology (investigative and forensic technologies, corrections technologies, and technologies that support the judicial process); and (2) carry out programs that improve the safety and effectiveness of such technology and improve technology access by Federal, State, and local law enforcement agencies. Sets forth Office duties, including: (1) establishing and maintaining technology advisory groups and performance standards; (2) carrying out research, development, testing, evaluation, and cost-benefit analyses for improving the safety, effectiveness, and efficiency of technologies used by Federal, State, and local law enforcement agencies; and (3) operating the regional National Law Enforcement and Corrections Technology Centers (established under this Subtitle) and establishing additional centers. Requires the Office Director to report annually on Office activities.

(Sec. 234) Authorizes the Attorney General to transfer to the Office any other DOJ program or activity determined to be consistent with its mission. Requires a report from the Attorney General to the congressional judiciary committees on the implementation of this Subtitle.

(Sec. 235) Requires the Office Director to operate and support National Law Enforcement and Corrections Technology Centers and, to the extent necessary, establish new centers through a merit-based, competitive process. Requires such Centers to: (1) support research and development of law enforcement technology; (2) support the transfer and implementation of such technology; (3) assist in the development and dissemination of guidelines and technological standards; and (4) provide technology assistance, information, and support for law enforcement, corrections, and criminal justice purposes. Requires the Director to: (1) convene an annual meeting of such Centers; and (2) report to Congress assessing the effectiveness of the Centers and identifying the number of Centers necessary to meet the technology needs of Federal, State, and local law enforcement in the United States.

(Sec. 237) Amends the Omnibus Crime Control and Safe Streets Act of 1968 to require the National Institute of Justice to: (1) research and develop tools and technologies relating to prevention, detection, investigation, and prosecution of crime; and (2) support research, development, testing, training, and evaluation of tools and technology for Federal, State, and local law enforcement agencies.

Title III: Science and Technology in Support of Homeland Security — (Sec. 301)

Establishes in DHS a Directorate of Science and Technology, headed by an Under Secretary for Science and Technology, to be responsible for: (1)

advising the Secretary regarding research and development (R&D) efforts and priorities in support of DHS missions; (2) developing a national policy and strategic plan for, identifying priorities, goals, objectives and policies for, and coordinating the Federal Government's civilian efforts to identify and develop countermeasures to chemical, biological, radiological, nuclear, and other emerging terrorist threats; (3) supporting the Under Secretary for Information Analysis and Infrastructure Protection by assessing and testing homeland security vulnerabilities and possible threats; (4) conducting basic and applied R&D activities relevant to DHS elements, provided that such responsibility does not extend to human health-related R&D activities; (5) establishing priorities for directing, funding, and conducting national R&D and procurement of technology systems for preventing the importation of chemical, biological, radiological, nuclear, and related weapons and material and for detecting, preventing, protecting against, and responding to terrorist attacks; (6) establishing a system for transferring homeland security developments or technologies to Federal, State, and local government and private sector entities; (7) entering into agreements with the Department of Energy (DOE) regarding the use of the national laboratories or sites and support of the science and technology base at those facilities; (8) collaborating with the Secretary of Agriculture and the Attorney General in the regulation of certain biological agents and toxins as provided in the Agricultural Bioterrorism Protection Act of 2002; (9) collaborating with the Secretary of Health and Human Services and the Attorney General in determining new biological agents and toxins that shall be listed as select agents in the Code of Federal Regulations; (10) supporting U.S. leadership in science and technology; (11) establishing and administering the primary R&D activities of DHS; (12) coordinating and integrating all DHS R&D activities; (13) coordinating with other appropriate executive agencies in developing and carrying out the science and technology agenda of DHS to reduce duplication and identify unmet needs; and (14) developing and overseeing the administration of guidelines for merit review of R&D projects throughout DHS and for the dissemination of DHS research.

(Sec. 303) Transfers to the Secretary: (1) specified DOE functions, including functions related to chemical and biological national security programs, nuclear smuggling programs and activities within the proliferation detection program, the nuclear assessment program, designated life sciences activities of the biological and environmental research program related to microbial pathogens, the Environmental Measurements Laboratory, and the advanced scientific computing research program at Lawrence Livermore National Laboratory; and (2) the National Bio-Weapons Defense Analysis Center of DOD.

(Sec. 304) Requires the HHS Secretary, with respect to civilian human health-related R&D activities relating to HHS countermeasures for chemical, biological, radiological, and nuclear and other emerging terrorist threats, to: (1) set priorities, goals, objectives, and policies and develop a coordinated strategy for such activities in collaboration with the Secretary to ensure consistency with the national policy and strategic plan; and (2) collaborate with the Secretary in developing specific benchmarks and outcome measurements for evaluating progress toward achieving such priorities and goals.

Amends the Public Health Service Act to: (1) authorize the HHS Secretary to declare that an actual or potential bioterrorist incident or other public health emergency makes advisable the administration of a covered countermeasure against smallpox to a category or categories of individuals; (2) require the HHS Secretary to specify the substances to be considered countermeasures and the beginning and ending dates of the period of the declaration; and (3) deem a covered person to be an employee of the Public Health Service with respect to liability arising out of administration of such a countermeasure.

Extends liability to the United States (with an exception) with respect to claims arising out of an administration of a covered countermeasure to an individual only if: (1) the countermeasure was administered by a qualified person for the purpose of preventing or treating smallpox during the effective period; (2) the individual was within a covered category; or (3) the qualified person administering the countermeasure had reasonable grounds to believe that such individual was within such category. Provides for a rebuttable presumption of an administration within the scope of a declaration in the case where an individual who is not vaccinated contracts vaccinia. Makes the remedy against the United States provided under such Act exclusive of any other civil action or proceeding against a covered person for any claim or suit arising out of the administration of a covered countermeasure.

(Sec. 305) Authorizes the Secretary, acting through the Under Secretary, to establish or contract with one or more federally funded R&D centers to provide independent analysis of homeland security issues or to carry out other responsibilities under this Act.

(Sec. 306) Directs the President to notify the appropriate congressional committees of any proposed transfer of DOE life sciences activities.

(Sec. 307) Establishes the Homeland Security Advanced Research Projects Agency to be headed by a Director who shall be appointed by the Secretary and who shall report to the Under Secretary. Requires the Director to administer the Acceleration Fund for Research and Development of Homeland Security Technologies (established by this Act) to award competitive, merit-reviewed grants, cooperative agreements, or contracts to public or private entities to: (1) support basic and applied homeland security research to promote revolutionary changes in technologies that would promote homeland security; (2) advance the development, testing and evaluation, and deployment of critical homeland security technologies; and (3) accelerate the prototyping and deployment of technologies that would address homeland security vulnerabilities. Allows the Director to solicit proposals to address specific vulnerabilities. Requires the Director to periodically hold homeland security technology demonstrations to improve contact among technology developers, vendors, and acquisition personnel.

Authorizes appropriations to the Fund. Earmarks ten percent of such funds for each fiscal year through FY 2005 for the Under Secretary, through joint agreement with the Commandant of the Coast Guard, to carry out R&D of improved ports, waterways, and coastal security surveillance and perimeter protection capabilities to minimize the possibility that Coast Guard cutters, aircraft, helicopters, and personnel will be diverted from non-homeland security missions to the ports, waterways, and coastal security mission.

(Sec. 308) Requires the Secretary, acting through the Under Secretary, to: (1) operate extramural R&D programs to ensure that colleges, universities, private research institutes, and companies (and consortia thereof) from as many areas of the United States as practicable participate; and (2) establish a university-based center or centers for homeland security which shall establish a coordinated, university-based system to enhance the Nation's homeland security. Authorizes the Secretary, through the Under Secretary, to: (1) draw upon the expertise of any Government laboratory; and (2) establish a headquarters laboratory for DHS and additional laboratory units.

(Sec. 309) Allows the Secretary, in carrying out DHS missions, to utilize DOE national laboratories and sites through: (1) a joint sponsorship arrangement; (2) a direct contact between DHS and the applicable DOE laboratory or site; (3) any "work for others" basis made available by that laboratory or site; or (4) any other method provided by law. Allows DHS to be a joint sponsor: (1) with DOE of one or more DOE national laboratories; and (2) of a DOE site in the performance of work as if such site were a federally funded R&D center and the work were performed under a multiple agency sponsorship arrangement with DHS. Directs the Secretary and the Secretary of DOE to ensure that direct contracts between DHS and the operator of a DOE national laboratory or site for programs or activities transferred from DOE to DHS are separate from the direct contracts of DOE with such operator.

Establishes within the Directorate of Science and Technology an Office for National Laboratories which shall be responsible for the coordination and utilization of DOE national laboratories and sites in a manner to create a networked laboratory system to support DHS missions.

(Sec. 310) Directs the Secretary of Agriculture to transfer to the Secretary the Plum Island Animal Disease Center of the Department of Agriculture and provides for continued Department of Agriculture access to such Center.

(Sec. 311) Establishes within DF
and Technology Advisory Committee
respect to the activities of the Under S

(Sec. 312) Directs the Secretary to
Institute, a federally funded R&D cente
duties for the Institute: (1) determinatio
Nation's critical infrastructures; (2) asses
of alternative approaches to enhancing s
the effectiveness of measures deployed to
tutions, facilities, and infrastructure that r

(Sec. 313) Requires the Secretary to est
gram to encourage technological innovation ......ung the mission of
DHS, to include establishment of: (1) a centralized Federal clearinghouse
to further the dissemination of information on technologies; and (2) a
technical assistance team to assist in screening submitted proposals.

Title IV: Directorate of Border and Transportation Security—Subtitle A: Under Secretary for Border and Transportation Security—(Sec. 401)

Establishes in DHS a Directorate of Border and Transportation Security
to be headed by an Under Secretary for Border and Transportation Security. Makes the Secretary, acting through the Under Secretary for Border and Transportation Security, responsible for: (1) preventing the
entry of terrorists and the instruments of terrorism into the United
States; (2) securing the borders, territorial waters, ports, terminals, waterways, and air, land, and sea transportation systems of the United
States; (3) carrying out the immigration enforcement functions vested
by statute in, or performed by, the Commissioner of Immigration and
Naturalization immediately before their transfer to the Under Secretary; (4) establishing and administering rules governing the granting of
visas or other forms of permission to enter the United States to individuals who are not citizens or aliens lawfully admitted for permanent
residence in the United States; (5) establishing national immigration
enforcement policies and priorities; (6) administering the customs laws
of the United States (with certain exceptions); (7) conducting the inspection and related administrative functions of the Department of
Agriculture transferred to the Secretary; and (8) ensuring the speedy,
orderly, and efficient flow of lawful traffic and commerce in carrying
out the foregoing responsibilities.

(Sec. 403) Transfers to the Secretary the functions, personnel, assets, and liabilities of: (1) the U.S. Customs Service; (2) the Transportation Security Administration; (3) the Federal Protective Service of the

...ces Administration (GSA); (4) the Federal Law Enforce-
...ing Center of the Department of the Treasury; and (5) the
...for Domestic Preparedness of the Office of Justice Programs of
...Department of Justice (DOJ).

Subtitle B: United States Customs Service — (Sec. 411)

Establishes in DHS the U.S. Customs Service (transferred from the Department of the Treasury, but with certain customs revenue functions remaining with the Secretary of the Treasury). Authorizes the Secretary of the Treasury to appoint up to 20 new personnel to work with DHS personnel in performing customs revenue functions.

(Sec. 414) Requires the President to include a separate budget request for the U.S. Customs Service in the annual budget transmitted to Congress.

(Sec. 416) Directs the Comptroller General to report to Congress on all trade functions performed by the executive branch, specifying each agency that performs each such function.

(Sec. 417) Directs the Secretary to ensure that adequate staffing is provided to assure that levels of current customs revenue services will continue to be provided. Requires the Secretary to notify specified congressional committees prior to taking any action which would: (1) result in any significant reduction in customs revenue services (including hours of operation provided at any office within DHS or any port of entry); (2) eliminate or relocate any office of DHS which provides customs revenue services; or (3) eliminate any port of entry.

(Sec. 419) Amends the Consolidated Omnibus Budget Reconciliation Act of 1985 to create in the Treasury a separate Customs Commercial and Homeland Security Automation Account to contain merchandise processing (customs user) fees. Authorizes appropriations for FY 2003 through 2005 for establishment of the Automated Commercial Environment computer system for the processing of merchandise that is entered or released and for other purposes related to the functions of DHS.

Subtitle C: Miscellaneous Provisions — (Sec. 421)

Transfers to the Secretary the functions of the Secretary of Agriculture relating to agricultural import and entry inspection activities under specified animal and plant protection laws.

Requires the Secretary of Agriculture and the Secretary to enter into an agreement to effectuate such transfer and to transfer periodically funds collected pursuant to fee authorities under the Food, Agriculture, Conservation, and Trade Act of 1990 to the Secretary for activities carried out by the Secretary for which such fees were collected.

Directs the Secretary of Agriculture to transfer to the Secretary not more than 3,200 full-time equivalent positions of the Department of Agriculture.

(Sec. 423) Directs the Secretary to establish a liaison office within DHS for the purpose of consulting with the Administrator of the Federal Aviation Administration before taking any action that might affect aviation safety, air carrier operations, aircraft airworthiness, or the use of airspace.

(Sec. 424) Requires the Transportation Security Administration to be maintained as a distinct entity within DHS under the Under Secretary for Border Transportation and Security for two years after enactment of this Act.

(Sec. 425) Amends Federal aviation law to require the Under Secretary of Transportation for Security to take certain action, if, in his discretion or at the request of an airport, he determines that the Transportation Security Administration is not able to deploy explosive detection systems at all airports required to have them by December 31, 2002. Requires the Under Secretary, in such circumstances, to: (1) submit to specified congressional committees a detailed plan for the deployment of explosive detection systems at such airport by December 31, 2003; and (2) take all necessary action to ensure that alternative means of screening all checked baggage is implemented.

(Sec. 426) Replaces the Secretary of Transportation with the Secretary of Homeland Security as chair of the Transportation Security Oversight Board. Requires the Secretary of Transportation to consult with the Secretary before approving airport development project grants relating to security equipment or the installation of bulk explosive detection systems.

(Sec. 427) Directs the Secretary, in coordination with the Secretary of Agriculture, the Secretary of Health and Human Services, and the head of each other department or agency determined to be appropriate by the Secretary, to ensure that appropriate information concerning inspections of articles that are imported or entered into the United States, and are inspected or regulated by one or more affected agencies, is timely and efficiently exchanged between the affected agencies. Requires the Secretary to report to Congress on the progress made in implementing this section.

(Sec. 428) Grants the Secretary exclusive authority to issue regulations with respect to, administer, and enforce the Immigration and Nationality Act (INA) and all other immigration and nationality laws relating to the functions of U.S. diplomatic and consular officers in connection with the granting or refusal of visas, and authority to refuse visas in accordance with law and to develop programs of homeland security training for consular officers, which authorities shall be exercised through the Secretary of State. Denies the Secretary authority, however, to alter or reverse the decision of a consular officer to refuse a visa to an alien.

Grants the Secretary authority also to confer or impose upon any U.S. officer or employee, with the consent of the head of the executive agency under whose jurisdiction such officer or employee is serving, any of these specified functions.

Authorizes the Secretary of State to direct a consular officer to refuse a visa to an alien if the Secretary of State deems such refusal necessary or advisable in the foreign policy or security interests of the United States.

Authorizes the Secretary to assign employees of DHS to any diplomatic and consular posts abroad to review individual visa applications and provide expert advice and training to consular officers regarding specific security threats relating to such applications and to conduct investigations with respect to matters under the Secretary's jurisdiction.

Directs the Secretary to study and report to Congress on the role of foreign nationals in the granting or refusal of visas and other documents authorizing entry of aliens into the United States.

Requires the Director of the Office of Science and Technology Policy to report to Congress on how the provisions of this section will affect procedures for the issuance of student visas.

Terminates after enactment of this Act all third party screening visa issuance programs in Saudi Arabia. Requires on-site personnel of DHS to review all visa applications prior to adjudication.

(Sec. 429) Requires visa denial information to be entered into the electronic data system as provided for in the Enhanced Border Security and Visa Entry Reform Act of 2002. Prohibits an alien denied a visa from being issued a subsequent visa unless the reviewing consular officer makes specified findings concerning waiver of ineligibility.

(Sec. 430) Establishes within the Directorate of Border and Transportation Security the Office for Domestic Preparedness to: (1) coordinate Federal preparedness for acts of terrorism, working with all State, local, tribal, county, parish, and private sector emergency response providers; (2) coordinate or consolidate systems of communications relating to homeland security at all levels of government; (3) direct and supervise Federal terrorism preparedness grant programs for all emergency response providers; and (4) perform specified other related duties.

Subtitle D: Immigration Enforcement Functions — (Sec. 441)

Transfers from the Commissioner of Immigration and Naturalization to the Under Secretary for Border and Transportation Security all functions performed under the following programs, and all personnel, assets, and liabilities pertaining to such programs, immediately before such transfer occurs: (1) the Border Patrol program; (2) the detention and removal program; (3) the intelligence program; (4) the investigations program; and (5) the inspections program.

(Sec. 442) Establishes in the Department of Homeland Security (DHS) the Bureau of Border Security, headed by the Assistant Secretary of the Bureau of Border Security who shall: (1) report directly to the Under Secretary; (2) establish and oversee the policies for performing functions transferred to the Under Secretary and delegated to the Assistant Secretary by the Under Secretary; and (3) advise the Under Secretary with respect to any policy or operation of the Bureau that may affect the Bureau of Citizenship and Immigration Services.

Directs the Assistant Secretary to: (1) administer the program to collect information relating to nonimmigrant foreign students and other exchange program participants; and (2) implement a managerial rotation program.

Establishes the position of Chief of Policy and Strategy for the Bureau of Border Security, who shall: (1) make immigration enforcement policy recommendations; and (2) coordinate immigration policy issues with the Chief of Policy and Strategy for the Bureau of Citizenship and Immigration Services.

(Sec. 443) Makes the Under Secretary responsible for: (1) investigating noncriminal allegations of Bureau employee misconduct, corruption, and fraud that are not subject to investigation by the Inspector General for DHS; (2) inspecting and assessing Bureau operations; and (3) analyzing Bureau management.

(Sec. 444) Authorizes the Under Secretary to impose disciplinary action pursuant to policies and procedures applicable to FBI employees.

(Sec. 445) Requires the Secretary of Homeland Security to report on how the Bureau will enforce relevant INA provisions.

(Sec. 446) Expresses the sense of Congress that completing the 14-mile border fence project near San Diego, California, mandated by the Illegal Immigration Reform and Immigrant Responsibility Act of 1996 should be a priority for the Secretary.

Subtitle E: Citizenship and Immigration Services — (Sec. 451)

Establishes in DHS a Bureau of Citizenship and Immigration Services, headed by the Director of the Bureau of Citizenship and Immigration Services, who shall: (1) establish the policies for performing and administering transferred functions; (2) establish national immigration services policies and priorities; and (3) implement a managerial rotation program.

Authorizes the Director to implement pilot initiatives to eliminate the backlog of immigration benefit applications.

Transfers all Immigration and Naturalization Service (INS) adjudications and related personnel and funding to the Director.

Establishes for the Bureau positions of: (1) Chief of Policy and Strategy; (2) legal adviser; (3) budget officer; and (4) Chief of the Office of Citizenship to promote citizenship instruction and training for aliens interested in becoming naturalized U.S. citizens.

(Sec. 452) Establishes within the DHS a Citizenship and Immigration Services Ombudsman, with local offices, to: (1) assist individuals and employers in resolving problems with the Bureau; (2) identify problem areas; and (3) propose administrative and legislative changes.

(Sec. 453) Makes the Director responsible for (1) investigating noncriminal allegations of Bureau employee misconduct, corruption, and fraud that are not subject to investigation by the Inspector General of DHS; (2) inspecting and assessing Bureau operations; and (3) analyzing Bureau management.

(Sec. 454) Authorizes the Director to impose disciplinary action pursuant to policies and procedures applicable to FBI employees.

(Sec. 456) Sets forth transfer of authority and transfer and allocation of appropriations and personnel provisions.

(Sec. 457) Amends the INA to repeal the provision permitting fees for adjudication and naturalization services to be set at a level that will ensure recovery of the costs of similar services provided without charge to asylum applicants.

(Sec. 458) Amends the Immigration Services and Infrastructure Improvements Act of 2000 to change the deadline for the Attorney General to eliminate the backlog in the processing of immigration benefit applications to one year after enactment of this Act.

(Sec. 459) Directs the Secretary to report on how the Bureau of Citizenship and Immigration Services will efficiently complete transferred INS adjudications.

(Sec. 460) Directs the Attorney General to report on changes in law needed to ensure an appropriate response to emergent or unforseen immigration needs.

(Sec. 461) Directs the Secretary to: (1) establish an Internet-based system that will permit online information access to a person, employer, immigrant, or nonimmigrant about the processing status of any filings for any benefit under the INA; (2) conduct a feasibility study for online filing and improved processing; and (3) establish a Technology Advisory Committee.

(Sec. 462) Transfers to the Director of the Office of Refugee Resettlement of the Department of Health and Human Services (HHS) INS functions with respect to the care of unaccompanied alien children (as defined by this Act).

Sets forth the responsibilities of the Office for such children, including: (1) coordinating and implementing the care and placement of unaccompanied alien children who are in Federal custody, including appointment of independent legal counsel to represent the interests of each child; (2) identifying and overseeing individuals, entities, and facilities to house such children; (3) family reunification; (4) compiling, updating, and publishing at least annually a State-by-State list of professionals or other entities qualified to provide guardian and attorney representation services; (5) maintaining related biographical and statistical information; and (6) conducting investigations and inspections of residential facilities.

Directs the Office to: (1) consult with juvenile justice professionals to ensure such children's safety; and (2) not release such children upon their own recognizance.

Subtitle F: General Immigration Provisions — (Sec. 471)

Abolishes INS upon completion of all transfers from it as provided for by this Act.

(Sec. 472) Authorizes the Attorney General and the Secretary to make voluntary separation incentive payments, after completion of a strategic restructuring plan, to employees of: (1) INS; (2) the Bureau of Border Security of DHS; and (3) the Bureau of Citizenship and Immigration Services of DHS.

(Sec. 473) Directs the Attorney General and the Secretary to conduct a demonstration project to determine whether policy or procedure revisions for employee discipline would result in improved personnel management.

(Sec. 474) Expresses the sense of Congress that: (1) the missions of the Bureau of Border Security and the Bureau of Citizenship and Immigration Services are equally important and should be adequately funded; and (2) the functions transferred should not operate at levels below those in effect prior to the enactment of this Act.

(Sec. 475) Establishes within the Office of Deputy Secretary a Director of Shared Services who shall be responsible for: (1) information resources management; and (2) records, forms, and file management.

(Sec. 476) Provides for budgetary and funding separation with respect to the Bureau of Citizenship and Immigration Services and the Bureau of Border Security.

(Sec. 477) Sets forth reporting and implementation plan provisions.

(Sec. 478) Directs the Secretary to annually report regarding: (1) the aggregate number of all immigration applications and petitions received, and processed; (2) regional statistics on the aggregate number of denied applications and petitions; (3) application and petition backlogs and a backlog elimination plan; (4) application and petition processing periods; (5) number, types, and disposition of grievances and plans to improve immigration services; and (6) appropriate use of immigration-related fees.

Expresses the sense of Congress that: (1) the quality and efficiency of immigration services should be improved after the transfers made by Act; and (2) the Secretary should undertake efforts to guarantee that such concerns are addressed after such effective date.

Title V: Emergency Preparedness and Response—(Sec. 501)

Establishes in DHS a Directorate of Emergency Preparedness and Response, headed by an Under Secretary.

(Sec. 502) Requires the responsibilities of the Secretary, acting through the Under Secretary, to include: (1) helping to ensure the effectiveness of emergency response providers to terrorist attacks, major disasters, and other emergencies; (2) with respect to the Nuclear Incident Response Team, establishing and certifying compliance with standards, conducting joint and other exercises and training, and providing funds to the Department of Energy and the Environmental Protection Agency for homeland security planning, training, and equipment; (3) providing the Federal Government's response to terrorist attacks and major disasters; (4) aiding recovery from terrorist attacks and major disasters; (5) building a comprehensive national incident management system with Federal, State, and local governments to respond to such attacks and disasters; (6) consolidating existing Federal Government emergency response plans into a single, coordinated national response plan; and (7) developing comprehensive programs for developing interoperative communications technology and helping to ensure that emergency response providers acquire such technology.

(Sec. 503) Transfers to the Secretary the functions, personnel, assets, and liabilities of: (1) the Federal Emergency Management Agency (FEMA); (2) the Integrated Hazard Information System of the National Oceanic and Atmospheric Administration, which shall be renamed FIRESAT; (3) the National Domestic Preparedness Office of the FBI; (4) the Domestic Emergency Support Teams of DOJ; (5) the Office of Emergency Preparedness, the National Disaster Medical System, and the Metropolitan Medical Response System of HHS; and (6) the Strategic National Stockpile of HHS.

(Sec. 504) Requires the Nuclear Incident Response Team, at the direction of the Secretary (in connection with an actual or threatened terrorist attack, major disaster, or other emergency in the United States), to operate as an organizational unit of DHS under the Secretary's authority and control.

(Sec. 505) Provides that, with respect to all public health-related activities to improve State, local, and hospital preparedness and response to chemical, biological, radiological, and nuclear and other emerging terrorist threats carried out by HHS (including the Public Health Service), the Secretary of HHS shall set priorities and preparedness goals and further develop a coordinated strategy for such activities in collaboration with the Secretary.

(Sec. 506) Defines the Nuclear Incident Response Team to include: (1) those entities of the Department of Energy that perform nuclear or radiological emergency support functions, radiation exposure functions at the medical assistance facility known as the Radiation Emergency Assistance Center/Training Site (REAC/TS), radiological assistance functions, and related functions; and (2) Environmental Protection Agency entities that perform such support functions and related functions.

(Sec. 507) Includes in the homeland security role of FEMA: (1) all functions and authorities prescribed by the Robert T. Stafford Disaster Relief and Emergency Assistance Act; and (2) a comprehensive, risk-based emergency management program of mitigation, of planning for building the emergency management profession, of response, of recovery, and of increased efficiencies. Maintains FEMA as the lead agency for the Federal Response Plan established under Executive Orders 12148 and 12656. Requires the FEMA Director to revise the Plan to reflect the establishment of and incorporate DHS.

(Sec. 508) Directs the Secretary, to the maximum extent practicable, to use national private sector networks and infrastructure for emergency response to major disasters.

(Sec. 509) Expresses the sense of Congress that the Secretary should: (1) use off-the-shelf commercially developed technologies to allow DHS to collect, manage, share, analyze, and disseminate information securely over multiple channels of communication; and (2) rely on commercial sources to supply goods and services needed by DHS.

Title VI: Treatment of Charitable Trusts for Members of the Armed Forces of the United States and Other Governmental Organizations—(Sec. 601)

Sets forth requirements a charitable corporation, fund, foundation, or trust must meet to designate itself as a Johnny Micheal Spann Patriot Trust (a charitable trust for the spouses, dependents, and relatives of military and Federal personnel who lose their lives in the battle against terrorism that is named after the first American to die in such service following the September 11th terrorist attacks). Requires at least 85 percent of each Trust corpus to be distributed to such survivors and prohibits more than 15 percent from being used for administrative purposes. Prohibits: (1) any Trust activities from violating any prohibition against attempting to influence legislation; and (2) any such Trust from participating in any political campaign on behalf of a candidate for public office. Requires: (1) audits of each Trust that annually receives contributions of more than $1 million; and (2) Trust distributions to be made at least once a year. Provides for the notification of Trust beneficiaries.

Title VII: Management—(Sec. 701)

Makes the Secretary, acting through the Under Secretary for Management, responsible for the management and administration of DHS. Details certain responsibilities of the Under Secretary with respect to immigration statistics. Transfers to the Under Secretary functions previously performed by the Statistics Branch of the Office of Policy and Planning of the Immigration and Naturalization Service (INS) with respect to: (1) the Border Patrol program; (2) the detention and removal program; (3) the intelligence program; (4) the investigations program; (5) the inspections program; and (6) INS adjudications.

(Sec. 702) Requires a chief financial officer, a chief information officer, and a chief human capital officer to report to the Secretary. Requires the chief human capital officer to ensure that all DHS employees are informed of their rights and remedies under merit system protection and principle provisions.

(Sec. 705) Requires the Secretary to appoint an Officer for Civil Rights and Civil Liberties who shall: (1) review and assess information alleging abuses of civil rights, civil liberties, and racial and ethnic profiling by employees and officials of DHS; and (2) make public information on the responsibilities and functions of, and how to contact, the Office.

(Sec. 706) Requires the Secretary to develop and submit to Congress a plan for consolidating and co-locating: (1) any regional offices or field offices of agencies that are transferred to DHS under this Act, if their officers are located in the same municipality; and (2) portions of regional and field offices of other Federal agencies, to the extent such offices perform functions that are transferred to the Secretary under this Act.

Title VIII: Coordination With Non-Federal Entities; Inspector General; United States Secret Service; Coast Guard; General Provisions—Subtitle A: Coordination with Non-Federal Entities—(Sec. 801)

Establishes within the Office of the Secretary the Office for State and Local Government Coordination to oversee and coordinate Department homeland security programs for and relationships with State and local governments.

Subtitle B: Inspector General—(Sec. 811)

Places the DHS Inspector General under the authority, direction, and control of the Secretary with respect to audits or investigations, or the issuance of subpoenas, that require access to sensitive information concerning intelligence, counterintelligence, or counterterrorism matters; criminal investigations or proceedings; undercover operations; the identify of confidential sources; and certain matters of disclosure.

Amends the Inspector General Act of 1978 to: (1) give such Inspector General oversight responsibility for internal investigations performed by the Office of Internal Affairs of the United States Customs Service and the Office of Inspections of the United States Secret Service; and (2) authorize each Inspector General, any Assistant Inspector General for Investigations, and any special agent supervised by such an Assistant Inspector General to carry a firearm, make arrests without warrants, and seek and execute warrants. Allows the latter only upon certain determinations by the Attorney General (exempts the Inspector General offices of various executive agencies from such requirement). Provides for the rescinding of such law enforcement powers. Requires the Inspector General offices exempted from the determinations requirement to collectively enter into a memorandum of understanding to establish an external review process for ensuring that adequate internal safeguards and management procedures continue to exist to ensure the proper utilization of such law enforcement powers within their departments.

Subtitle C: United States Secret Service — (Sec. 821)

Transfers to the Secretary the functions of the United States Secret Service, which shall be maintained as a distinct entity within DHS.

Subtitle D: Acquisitions — (Sec. 831)

Authorizes the Secretary to carry out a five-year pilot program under which the Secretary may exercise specified authorities in carrying out: (1) basic, applied, and advanced research and development projects for response to existing or emerging terrorist threats; and (2) defense prototype projects. Requires a report from the Comptroller General to specified congressional committees on the use of such authorities.

(Sec. 832) Permits the Secretary to procure temporary or intermittent: (1) services of experts or consultants; and (2) personal services without regard to certain pay limitations when necessary due to an urgent homeland security need.

(Sec. 833) Authorizes the Secretary to use specified micro purchase, simplified acquisition, and commercial item acquisition procedures with respect to any procurement made during the period beginning on the effective date of this Act and ending on September 30, 2007, if the Secretary determines that the mission of DHS would be seriously impaired without the use of such authorities. Requires a report from the Comptroller General.

(Sec. 834) Requires the Federal Acquisition Regulation to be revised to include regulations with regard to unsolicited proposals.

(Sec. 835) Prohibits the Secretary from entering into a contract with a foreign incorporated entity which is treated as an inverted domestic corporation. Sets forth requirements for such treatment. Authorizes the Secretary to waive such prohibition in the interest of homeland security, to prevent the loss of any jobs in the United States, or to prevent the Government from incurring any additional costs.

Subtitle E: Human Resources Management — (Sec. 841)

Expresses the sense of Congress calling for the participation of DHS employees in the creation of the DHS human resources management system.

Amends Federal civil service law to authorize the Secretary, in regulations prescribed jointly with the Director of the Office of Personnel Management (OPM), to establish and adjust a human resources management system for organizational units of DHS. Requires the system to ensure that employees may organize, bargain collectively, and participate through labor organizations of their own choosing in decisions which affect them, subject to an exclusion from coverage or limitation on negotiability established by law. Imposes certain requirements upon the Secretary and the OPM Director to ensure the participation of employee representatives in the planning, development, and implementation of any human resources management system or system adjustments.

Declares the sense of Congress that DHS employees are entitled to fair treatment in any appeals that they bring in decisions relating to their employment.

Terminates all authority to issue regulations under this section five years after enactment of this Act.

(Sec. 842) Prohibits any agency or agency subdivision transferred to DHS from being excluded from coverage under labor-management relations requirements as a result of any order issued after June 18, 2002, unless: (1) the mission and responsibilities of the agency or subdivision materially change; and (2) a majority of the employees within the agency or subdivision have as their primary duty intelligence, counterintelligence, or investigative work directly related to terrorism investigation. Declares that collective bargaining units shall continue to be recognized unless such conditions develop. Prohibits exclusion of positions or employees for a bargaining unit unless the primary job duty materially changes or consists of intelligence, counterintelligence, or investigative work directly related to terrorism investigation. Waives these prohibitions and recognitions in circumstances where the President determines that their application would have a substantial adverse impact on the Department's ability to protect homeland security.

Subtitle F: Federal Emergency Procurement Flexibility — (Sec. 852)

Provides that the simplified acquisition threshold to be applied for any executive agency procurement of property or services that is to be used to facilitate the defense against or recovery from terrorism or nuclear, biological, chemical, or radiological attack and that is carried out in support of a humanitarian or peacekeeping operation or a contingency operation shall be: (1) $200,000 for a contract to be awarded and performed, or a purchase to be made, inside the United States; or (2) $300,000 for a contract to be awarded and performed, or a purchase to be made, outside the United States.

(Sec. 854) Authorizes the head of each agency to designate certain employees to make such procurements below a micro-purchase threshold of $7,500 (currently $2,500) under the Office of Federal Procurement Policy Act.

(Sec. 855) Permits executive agencies to apply to any such procurement specified provisions of law relating to the procurement of commercial items, without regard to whether the property and services are commercial items. Makes the $5 million limitation on the use of simplified acquisition procedures inapplicable to purchases of property or services to which such provisions apply.

(Sec. 856) Requires executive agencies to use specified streamlined acquisition authorities and procedures for such procurements. Waives certain small business threshold requirements with respect to such procurements.

(Sec. 857) Requires the Comptroller General to review and report to specified congressional committees on the extent to which procurements of property and services have been made in accordance with requirements of this Subtitle.

(Sec. 858) Requires each executive agency to conduct market research to identify the capabilities of small businesses and new entrants into Federal contracting that are available to meet agency requirements in furtherance of defense against or recovery from terrorism or nuclear, biological, chemical, or radiological attack.

Subtitle G: Support Anti-terrorism by Fostering Effective Technologies Act of 2002

Support Anti-terrorism by Fostering Effective Technologies Act of 2002 or SAFETY Act—(Sec. 862) Authorizes the Secretary to designate anti-terrorism technologies that qualify for protection under a risk management system in accordance with criteria that shall include: (1) prior Government use or demonstrated substantial utility and effectiveness; (2) availability for immediate deployment in public and private settings; (3) substantial likelihood that such technology will not be deployed unless protections under such system are extended; and (4) the magnitude of risk exposure to the public if such technology is not deployed. Makes the Secretary responsible for administration of such protections.

(Sec. 863) Provides a Federal cause of action for sellers suffering a loss from qualified antiterrorism technologies so deployed. Prohibits punitive damages from being awarded against a seller.

(Sec. 864) Requires sellers of qualified antiterrorism technologies to obtain liability insurance in amounts certified as satisfactory by the Secretary.

Subtitle H: Miscellaneous Provisions — (Sec. 871)

Authorizes the Secretary to establish, appoint members of, and use the services of advisory committees as necessary.

(Sec. 872) Grants the Secretary limited authority to reorganize DHS by allocating or reallocating functions within it and by establishing, consolidating, altering, or discontinuing organizational units.

(Sec. 873) Requires the Secretary to comply with Federal requirements concerning the deposit of proceeds from property sold or transferred by the Secretary. Requires the President to submit to Congress a detailed Department budget request for FY 2004 and thereafter.

(Sec. 874) Requires each such budget request to be accompanied by a Future Years Homeland Security Program structured in the same manner as the annual Future Years Defense Program.

(Sec. 876) Provides that nothing in this Act shall confer upon the Secretary any authority to engage in war fighting, the military defense of the United States, or other military activities or limit the existing authority of the Department of Defense or the armed forces to do so.

(Sec. 878) Directs the Secretary to appoint a senior DHS official to assume primary responsibility for coordinating policy and operations within DHS and between DHS and other Federal departments and agencies with respect to interdicting the entry of illegal drugs into the United States and tracking and severing connections between illegal drug trafficking and terrorism.

(Sec. 879) Establishes within the Office of the Secretary an Office of International Affairs, headed by a Director, to: (1) promote information and education exchange on homeland security best practices and technologies with friendly nations; (2) identify areas for homeland security information and training exchange where the United States has a demonstrated weakness and another friendly nation has a demonstrated expertise; (3) plan and undertake international conferences, exchange programs, and training activities; and (4) manage international activities within DHS in coordination with other Federal officials with responsibility for counter-terrorism matters.

(Sec. 880) Prohibits any Government activity to implement the proposed component program of the Citizen Corps known as Operation TIPS (Terrorism Information and Prevention System).

(Sec. 881) Directs the Secretary to review the pay and benefit plans of each agency whose functions are transferred to DHS under this Act and to submit a plan for ensuring the elimination of disparities in pay and benefits throughout DHS, especially among law enforcement personnel, that are inconsistent with merit system principles.

(Sec. 882) Establishes within the Office of the Secretary the Office of National Capital Region Coordination, headed by a Director, to oversee and coordinate Federal homeland security programs for and relationships with State, local, and regional authorities within the National Capital Region. Requires an annual report from the Office to Congress on: (1) resources needed to fully implement homeland security efforts in the Region; (2) progress made by the Region in implementing such efforts; and (3) recommendations for additional needed resources to fully implement such efforts.

(Sec. 883) Requires DHS to comply with specified laws protecting equal employment opportunity and providing whistle blower protections.

(Sec. 885) Authorizes the Secretary to establish a permanent Joint Interagency Homeland Security Task Force, composed of representatives from military and civilian agencies, for the purpose of anticipating terrorist threats and taking actions to prevent harm to the United States.

(Sec. 886) Reaffirms the continued importance of Federal criminal code proscriptions on the use of the armed forces as posse comitatus and expresses the sense of Congress that nothing in this Act shall be construed to alter the applicability of such proscriptions to any use of the armed forces to execute the laws.

(Sec. 887) Requires the annual Federal response plan developed by DHS to be consistent with public health emergency provisions of the Public Health Service Act. Requires full disclosure of public health emergencies, or potential emergencies, among HHS, DHS, the Department of Justice, and the Federal Bureau of Investigation.

(Sec. 888) Transfers to DHS the authorities, functions, personnel, and assets of the Coast Guard, which shall be maintained as a distinct entity within DHS. Prohibits the Secretary from substantially or significantly reducing current Coast Guard missions or capabilities, with a waiver of such prohibition upon a declaration and certification to Congress that a clear, compelling and immediate need exists. Requires the DHS Inspector General to annually review and report to Congress on performance by the Coast Guard of its mission requirements. Requires the Commandant of the Coast Guard, upon its transfer, to report directly to the Secretary. Prohibits any of the above conditions and restrictions from applying to the Coast Guard when it is operating as a service in the Navy. Directs the Secretary to report to specified congressional committees on the feasibility of accelerating the rate of procurement in the Coast Guard's Integrated Deepwater System from 20 to ten years.

(Sec. 889) Requires the inclusion in the President's annual budget documents of a detailed homeland security funding analysis for the previous, current, and next fiscal years.

(Sec. 890) Amends the Air Transportation Safety and System Stabilization Act, with respect to the September 11th Victim Compensation Fund of 2001, to limit "agents" of an air carrier engaged in the business of providing air transportation security to persons that have contracted directly with the Federal Aviation Administration on or after February 17, 2002, to provide such security and that had not been or are not debarred within six months of that date.

Subtitle I: Information Sharing

Homeland Security Information Sharing Act—(Sec. 891) Expresses the sense of Congress that Federal, State, and local entities should share homeland security information to the maximum extent practicable, with special emphasis on hard-to-reach urban and rural communities.

(Sec. 892) Directs the President to prescribe and implement procedures for Federal agency: (1) sharing of appropriate homeland security information, including with DHS and appropriate State and local personnel; and (2) handling of classified information and sensitive but unclassified information. Authorizes appropriations.

(Sec. 893) Requires an implementation report from the President to the congressional intelligence and judiciary committees.

(Sec. 895) Amends the Federal Rules of Criminal Procedure to treat as contempt of court any knowing violation of guidelines jointly issued by the Attorney General and DCI with respect to disclosure of grand jury matters otherwise prohibited. Allows disclosure to appropriate Federal, State, local, or foreign government officials of grand jury matters involving a threat of grave hostile acts of a foreign power, domestic or international sabotage or terrorism, or clandestine intelligence gathering activities by an intelligence service or network of a foreign power (threat), within the United States or elsewhere. Permits disclosure to appropriate foreign government officials of grand jury matters that may disclose a violation of the law of such government. Requires State, local, and foreign officials to use disclosed information only in conformity with guidelines jointly issued by the Attorney General and the DCI.

(Sec. 896) Amends the Federal criminal code to authorize Federal investigative and law enforcement officers conducting communications interception activities, who have obtained knowledge of the contents of any intercepted communication or derivative evidence, to disclose such contents or evidence to: (1) a foreign investigative or law enforcement officer if the disclosure is appropriate to the performance of the official duties of the officer making or receiving the disclosure; and (2) any appropriate Federal, State, local, or foreign government official if the contents or evidence reveals such a threat, for the purpose of preventing or responding to such threat. Provides guidelines for the use and disclosure of the information.

(Sec. 897) Amends the Uniting and Strengthening America by Providing Appropriate Tools Required to Intercept and Obstruct Terrorism Act (USA PATRIOT ACT) of 2001 to make lawful the disclosure to appropriate Federal, State, local, or foreign government officials of information obtained as part of a criminal investigation that reveals such a threat.

(Sec. 898) Amends the Foreign Intelligence Surveillance Act of 1978 to allow Federal officers who conduct electronic surveillance and physical searches in order to acquire foreign intelligence information to consult with State and local law enforcement personnel to coordinate efforts to investigate or protect against such a threat.

Title IX: National Homeland Security Council—(Sec. 901)

Establishes within the Executive Office of the President the Homeland Security Council to advise the President on homeland security matters.

(Sec. 903) Includes as members of the Council: (1) the President; (2) the Vice President; (3) the Secretary; (4) the Attorney General; and (5) the Secretary of Defense.

(Sec. 904) Requires the Council to: (1) assess the objectives, commitments, and risks of the United States in the interest of homeland security and make recommendations to the President; and (2) oversee and review Federal homeland security policies and make policy recommendations to the President.

(Sec. 906) Authorizes the President to convene joint meetings of the Homeland Security Council and the National Security Council.

Title X: Information Security

Federal Information Security Management Act of 2002—(Sec. 1001) Revises Government information security requirements. Requires the head of each agency operating or exercising control of a national security system to ensure that the agency: (1) provides information security protections commensurate with the risk and magnitude of the harm resulting from the unauthorized access, use, disclosure, disruption, modification, or destruction of the information; and (2) implements information security policies and practices as required by standards and guidelines for national security systems. Authorizes appropriations for FY 2003 through 2007.

(Sec. 1002) Transfers from the Secretary of Commerce to the Director of the Office of Management and Budget (OMB) the authority to promulgate information security standards pertaining to Federal information systems.

(Sec. 1003) Amends the National Institute of Standards and Technology Act to revise and expand the mandate of the National Institute of Standards and Technology to develop standards, guidelines, and associated methods and techniques for information systems. Renames the Computer System Security and Privacy Advisory Board as the Information Security and Privacy Board and requires it to advise the Director of OMB (instead of the Secretary of Commerce) on information security and privacy issues pertaining to Federal Government information systems.

Title XI: Department of Justice Divisions

Subtitle A: Executive Office for Immigration Review—(Sec. 1101)

Declares that there is in the Department of Justice (DOJ) the Executive Office for Immigration Review (EOIR), which shall be subject to the direction and regulation of the Attorney General under the INA.

(Sec. 1102) Amends the INA to grant the Attorney General such authorities and functions relating to the immigration and naturalization of aliens as were exercised by EOIR, or by the Attorney General with respect to EOIR, on the day before the effective date of the Immigration Reform, Accountability and Security Enhancement Act of 2002.

Subtitle B: Transfer of the Bureau of Alcohol, Tobacco and Firearms to the Department of Justice—(Sec. 1111)

Establishes within DOJ, under the Attorney General's authority, the Bureau of Alcohol, Tobacco, Firearms, and Explosives (the Bureau). Transfers to DOJ the authorities, functions, personnel, and assets of the Bureau of Alcohol, Tobacco and Firearms (BATF), which shall be maintained as a distinct entity within DOJ, including the related functions of the Secretary of the Treasury.

Provides that the Bureau shall be headed by a Director and shall be responsible for: (1) investigating criminal and regulatory violations of the Federal firearms, explosives, arson, alcohol, and tobacco smuggling laws; (2) such transferred functions; and (3) any other function related to the investigation of violent crime or domestic terrorism that is delegated to the Bureau by the Attorney General.

Retains within the Department of the Treasury certain authorities, functions, personnel, and assets of BATF relating to the administration and enforcement of the Internal Revenue Code.

Establishes within the Department of the Treasury the Tax and Trade Bureau, which shall retain and administer the authorities, functions, personnel, and assets of BATF that are not transferred to DOJ.

(Sec. 1113) Amends the Federal criminal code to authorize special agents of the Bureau, as well as any other investigator or officer charged by the Attorney General with enforcing criminal, seizure, or forfeiture laws, to carry firearms, serve warrants and subpoenas, and make arrests without warrant for offenses committed in their presence or for felonies on reasonable grounds. Authorizes any special agent to make seizures of property subject to forfeiture to the United States. Sets forth provisions regarding seizure, disposition, and claims pertaining to property.

(Sec. 1114) Establishes within the Bureau an Explosives Training and Research Facility at Fort AP Hill in Fredericksburg, Virginia, to train Federal, State, and local law enforcement officers to: (1) investigate bombings and explosions; (2) properly handle, utilize, and dispose of explosive materials and devices; (3) train canines on explosive detection; and (4) conduct research on explosives. Authorizes appropriations.

(Sec. 1115) Transfers the Personnel Management Demonstration Project to the Attorney General for continued use by the Bureau and to the Secretary of the Treasury for continued use by the Tax and Trade Bureau.

Subtitle C: Explosives

Safe Explosives Act—(Sec. 1122) Rewrites Federal criminal code provisions regarding the purchase of explosives to create a new "limited permit" category. Prohibits a holder of a limited permit: (1) from transporting, shipping, causing to be transported, or receiving in interstate or foreign commerce explosive materials; (2) from receiving explosive materials from a licensee or permittee whose premises are located outside the holder's State of residence; or (3) on more than six separate occasions during the period of the permit, from receiving explosive materials from one or more licensees or permittees whose premises are located within the holder's State of residence.

Requires license, user permit, and limited permit applicants to include the names of and identifying information (including fingerprints and a photograph of each responsible person) regarding all employees who will be authorized by the applicant to possess explosive materials. Caps the fee for limited permits at $50 for each permit. Makes each limited permit valid for not longer than one year.

Modifies criteria for approving licenses and permits. Requires the Secretary of the Treasury to issue to the applicant the appropriate license or permit if, among other conditions: (1) the applicant is not a person who is otherwise prohibited from possessing explosive materials (excluded person); (2) the Secretary verifies by inspection or other appropriate means that the applicant has a place of storage for explosive materials that meets the Secretary's standards of public safety and security against theft (inapplicable to an applicant for renewal of a limited permit if the Secretary has verified such matters by inspection within the preceding three years); (3) none of the applicant's employees who will be authorized to possess explosive materials is an excluded person; and (4) in the case of a limited permit, the applicant has certified that the applicant will not receive explosive materials on more than six separate occasions during the 12-month period for which the limited permit is valid. Authorizes the Secretary to inspect the storage places of an applicant for or holder of a limited permit only as provided under the code. Requires the Secretary of the Treasury to approve or deny an application for licenses and permits within 90 days.

Requires the Secretary: (1) upon receiving from an employer the name and other identifying information with respect to a person or an employee who will be authorized to possess explosive materials, to determine whether such person or employee is an excluded person; (2) upon determining that such person or employee is not an excluded person, to notify the employer and to issue to the person or employee a letter of clearance confirming the determination; and (3) upon determining that such person or employee is an excluded person, to notify the employer and issue to such person or employee a document that confirms the determination, explains the grounds, provides information on how the disability may be relieved, and explains how the determination may be appealed.

(Sec. 1123) Includes among aliens who may lawfully receive or possess explosive materials any alien who is in lawful non-immigrant status, is a refugee admitted under the INA, or is in asylum status under the INA and who is: (1) a foreign law enforcement officer of a friendly government; (2) a person having the power to direct the management and policies of a corporation; (3) a member of a North Atlantic Treaty Organization or other friendly foreign military force; or (4) lawfully present in the United States in cooperation with the DCI and the shipment, transportation, receipt, or possession of the explosive materials is in furtherance of such cooperation.

(Sec. 1124) Requires: (1) licensed manufacturers, licensed importers, and those who manufacture or import explosive materials or ammonium nitrate to furnish samples and relevant information when required by the Secretary; and (2) the Secretary to authorize reimbursement of the fair market value of samples furnished, as well as reasonable shipment costs.

(Sec. 1125) Sets penalties for the destruction of property of institutions receiving Federal financial assistance.

(Sec. 1127) Requires a holder of a license or permit to report any theft of explosive materials to the Secretary not later than 24 hours after discovery. Sets penalties for failure to report.

(Sec. 1128) Authorizes appropriations.

Title XII: Airline War Risk Insurance Legislation—(Sec. 1201)

Amends Federal aviation law to extend the period during which the Secretary of Transportation may certify an air carrier as a victim of terrorism (and thus subject to the $100 million limit on aggregate third-party claims) for acts of terrorism from September 22, 2001, through December 31, 2003.

(Sec. 1202) Directs the Secretary of Transportation to extend through August 31, 2003, and authorizes the Secretary to extend through December 31, 2003, the termination date of any insurance policy that the Department of Transportation (DOT) issues to an American aircraft or foreign-flag aircraft against loss or damage arising out of any risk from operation, and that is in effect on enactment of this Act, on no less favorable terms to such air carrier than existed on June 19, 2002. Directs the Secretary, however, to amend such policy to add coverage for losses or injuries to aircraft hulls, passengers, and crew at the limits carried by air carriers for such losses and injuries as of such enactment, and at an additional premium comparable to the premium charged for third-party casualty under the policy.

Limits the total premium paid by an air carrier for such a policy to twice the premium it was paying for its third party policy as of June 19, 2002. Declares that coverage in such a policy shall begin with the first dollar of any covered loss incurred.

(Sec. 1204) Directs the Secretary of Transportation to report to specified congressional committees concerning: (1) the availability and cost of commercial war risk insurance for air carriers and other aviation entities for passengers and third parties; (2) the economic effect upon such carriers and entities of available commercial war risk insurance; and (3) the manner in which DOT could provide an alternative means of providing aviation war risk reinsurance covering passengers, crew, and third parties through use of a risk-retention group or by other means.

Title XIII: Federal Workforce Improvement

Subtitle A: Chief Human Capital Officers

Chief Human Capital Officers Act of 2002—(Sec. 1302) Requires the heads of Federal departments and agencies currently required to have Chief Financial Officer to appoint or designate a Chief Human Capital Officer to: (1) advise and assist agency officials in selecting, developing, training, and managing a high-quality, productive workforce in accordance with merit system principles; and (2) implement the rules and regulations of the President and the Office of OPM and civil service laws.

Requires such Officer's functions to include: (1) setting the agency's workforce development strategy; (2) assessing workforce characteristics and future needs; (3) aligning the agency's human resources policies and programs with organization mission, strategic goals, and performance outcomes; (4) developing and advocating a culture of continuous learning to attract and retain employees with superior abilities; (5) identifying best practices and benchmarking studies; and (6) applying methods for measuring intellectual capital and identifying links of that capital to organizational performance and growth.

(Sec. 1303) Establishes a Chief Human Capital Officers Council (consisting of the Director of OPM, the Deputy Director for Management of the Office of Management and Budget, and the Chief Human Capital Officers of executive departments and other members designated by the Director of OPM) to advise and coordinate the activities of the agencies of its members on such matters as modernization of human resources systems, improved quality of human resources information, and legislation affecting human resources operations and organizations.

(Sec. 1304) Directs OPM to design a set of systems, including metrics, for assessing the management of human capital by Federal agencies.

Subtitle B: Reforms Relating to Federal Human Capital Management — (Sec. 1311)

Requires each agency's: (1) performance plan to describe how its performance goals and objectives are to be achieved; and (2) program performance report to include a review of the goals and evaluation of the plan relative to the agency's strategic human capital management.

(Sec. 1312) Authorizes the President to prescribe rules which grant authority for agencies to appoint candidates directly to certain positions for which there exists a severe candidate shortage or a critical hiring need.

Allows OPM to establish quality category rating systems for evaluating applicants for competitive service positions under two or more quality categories based on merit rather than numerical ratings. Requires agencies that establish a quality category rating system to report to Congress on that system, including information on the number of employees hired, the impact that system has had on the hiring of veterans and minorities, and the way in which managers were trained in the administration of it.

(Sec. 1313) Sets forth provisions governing Federal employee voluntary separation incentive payments. Requires each agency, before obligating any resources for such payments, to submit to OPM for modification and approval a plan outlining the intended use of such payments and a proposed organizational chart for the agency once such payments have been completed. Requires such plan to include the positions and functions affected, the categories of employees to be offered such payments, the timing and amounts of payments, and how the agency will subsequently operate. Limits voluntary separation incentive payments to the lesser of: (1) the amount of severance pay to which an employee would be entitled; or (2) an amount determined by the agency head, not to exceed $25,000. Sets forth provisions regarding the repayment and waiver of repayment of such incentive payments upon subsequent employment with the Government. Authorizes the Director of the Administrative Office of the United States Courts to establish a substantially similar program for the judicial branch. Continues existing voluntary separation incentives authority until expiration.

Amends Federal employee early retirement provisions to apply to employees who are: (1) voluntarily separated by an agency undergoing substantial delayering, reorganization, reductions in force, functions transfer, or workforce restructuring; or (2) identified as being in positions that are becoming surplus or excess to the agency's future ability to carry out its mission effectively; and (3) within the scope of the offer of voluntary early retirement on the basis of specific periods or such employee's organizational unit, occupational series, geographical location, and/or skills, knowledge, and other factors related to a position. Expresses the sense of Congress that the implementation of this section is intended to reshape, and not downsize, the Federal workforce.

(Sec. 1314) Includes students who provide voluntary services for the Government as "employees" for purposes of provisions authorizing agency programs to encourage employees to commute by means other than single-occupancy motor vehicles.

Subtitle C: Reforms Relating to the Senior Executive Service—(Sec. 1321)

Repeals recertification requirements for senior executives.

(Sec. 1322) Changes the limitation on total annual compensation (basic pay and cash payments) from the annual rate of basic pay payable for level I of the Executive Schedule to the total annual compensation payable to the Vice President for certain senior level executive and judicial employees who hold a position in or under an agency that has been certified as having a performance appraisal system which makes meaningful distinctions based on relative performance.

Subtitle D: Academic Training—(Sec. 1331)

Revises agency academic degree training criteria to allow agencies to select and assign employees to academic degree training and to pay and reimburse such training costs if such training: (1) contributes significantly to meeting an agency training need, resolving an agency staffing problem, or accomplishing goals in the agency's strategic plan; (2) is part of a planned, systemic, and coordinated agency employee development program linked to accomplishing such goals; and (3) is accredited and is provided by a college or university that is accredited by a nationally recognized body.

(Sec. 1332) Amends the David L. Boren National Security Education Act of 1991 to modify service agreement requirements for recipients of scholarships and fellowships under the National Security Education Program to provide for recipients to work in other Federal offices or agencies when no national security position is available.

Title XIV: Arming Pilots Against Terrorism

Arming Pilots Against Terrorism Act—(Sec. 1402) Amends Federal law to direct the Under Secretary of Transportation for Security (in the Transportation Security Administration) to establish a two-year pilot program to: (1) deputize volunteer pilots of air carriers as Federal law enforcement officers to defend the flight decks of aircraft against acts of criminal violence or air piracy (Federal flight deck officers); and (2) provide training, supervision, and equipment for such officers.

Requires the Under Secretary to begin the process of training and deputizing qualified pilots to be Federal flight deck officers under the program. Allows the Under Secretary to request another Federal agency to deputize such officers.

Directs the Under Secretary to authorize flight deck officers to carry firearms and to use force, including lethal force, according to standards and circumstances the Under Secretary prescribes. Shields air carriers from liability for damages in Federal or State court arising out of a Federal flight deck officer's use of or failure to use a firearm. Shields flight deck officers from liability for acts or omissions in defending the flight deck of an aircraft against acts of criminal violence or air piracy, except in cases of gross negligence or willful misconduct.

Declares that if an accidental discharge of a firearm results in the injury or death of a passenger or crew member on the aircraft, the Under Secretary: (1) shall revoke the deputization of the responsible Federal flight deck officer if such discharge was attributable to the officer's negligence; and (2) may temporarily suspend the pilot program if the Under Secretary determines that a shortcoming in standards, training, or procedures was responsible for the accidental discharge.

Prohibits an air carrier from prohibiting a pilot from becoming a Federal flight deck officer, or threatening any retaliatory action against the pilot for doing so.

Declares the sense of Congress that the Federal air marshal program is critical to aviation security, and that nothing in this Act shall be construed as preventing the Under Secretary from implementing and training Federal air marshals.

(Sec. 1403) Directs the Under Secretary, in updating the guidance for training flight and cabin crews, to issue a rule to: (1) require both classroom and effective hands-on situational training in specified elements of self-defense; (2) require training in the proper conduct of a cabin search, including the duty time required to conduct it; (3) establish the required number of hours of training and the qualifications for training instructors; (4) establish the intervals, number of hours, and elements of recurrent training; (5) ensure that air carriers provide the initial training within 24 months of the enactment of this Act. Directs the Under Secretary to designate an official in the Transportation Security Administration to be responsible for overseeing the implementation of the training program; and (6) ensure that no person is required to participate in any hands-on training activity that such person believes will have an adverse impact on his or her health or safety.

Amends the Aviation and Transportation Security Act to authorize the Under Secretary to take certain enhanced security measures, including to require that air carriers provide flight attendants with a discreet, hands-free, wireless method of communicating with the pilot of an aircraft.

Directs the Under Secretary to study and report to Congress on the benefits and risks of providing flight attendants with nonlethal weapons to aide in combating air piracy and criminal violence on commercial airlines.

(Sec. 1404) Directs the Secretary of Transportation to study and report within six months to Congress on: (1) the number of armed Federal law enforcement officers (other than Federal air marshals) who travel on commercial airliners annually, and the frequency of their travel; (2) the cost and resources necessary to provide such officers with supplemental aircraft antiterrorism training comparable to the training that Federal air marshals receive; (3) the cost of establishing a program at a Federal law enforcement training center for the purpose of providing new Federal law enforcement recruits with standardized training comparable to Federal air marshal training; (4) the feasibility of implementing a certification program designed to ensure that Federal law enforcement officers have completed aircraft antiterrorism training, and track their travel over a six-month period; and (5) the feasibility of staggering the flights of such officers to ensure the maximum amount of flights have a certified trained Federal officer on board.

(Sec. 1405) Amends Federal aviation law to require the Under Secretary to respond within 90 days of receiving a request from an air carrier for authorization to allow pilots of the air carrier to carry less-than-lethal weapons.

Title XV: Transition—Subtitle A: Reorganization Plan—(Sec. 1502)

Requires the President, within 60 days after enactment of this Act, to transmit to the appropriate congressional committees a reorganization plan regarding: (1) the transfer of agencies, personnel, assets, and obligations to DHS pursuant to this Act; and (2) any consolidation, reorganization, or streamlining of agencies transferred to DHS pursuant to this Act.

(Sec. 1503) Expresses the sense of Congress that each House of Congress should review its committee structure in light of the reorganization of responsibilities within the executive branch by the establishment of DHS.

Subtitle B: Transitional Provisions—(Sec. 1511)

Outlines transitional provisions with regard to assistance from officials having authority before the effective date of this Act; details of personnel and services to assist in the transition; acting officials during the transition period; the transfer of personnel, assets, obligations and functions; and the status of completed administrative actions, pending proceedings and civil actions, and Inspector General oversight. Prohibits DHS use of any funds derived from the Highway Trust Fund, the Airport and Airway Trust Fund, the Inland Waterway Trust Fund, or the Harbor Maintenance Trust Fund, with a specified exception for certain security-related funds provided to the Federal Aviation Administration.

(Sec. 1514) Provides that nothing in this Act shall be construed to authorize the development of a national identification system or card.

(Sec. 1516) Authorizes and directs the Director of OMB to make additional necessary incidental dispositions of personnel, assets, and liabilities in connection with the functions transferred by this Act.

Title XVI: Corrections to Existing Law Relating to Airline Transportation Security—(Sec. 1601)

Amends Federal aviation law to require the Administrator of the Federal Aviation Administration (FAA), along with the Under Secretary of Transportation for Security, to each conduct research (including behavioral research) and development activities to develop, modify, test, and evaluate a system, procedure, facility, or device to protect passengers and property against acts of criminal violence, aircraft piracy, and terrorism and to ensure security.

Directs the Secretary of Transportation (currently, the Under Secretary) to prescribe regulations prohibiting disclosure of information obtained or developed in ensuring security under this section if the Secretary of Transportation decides disclosing such information would:

(1) be an unwarranted invasion of personal privacy; (2) reveal a trade secret or privileged or confidential commercial or financial information; or (3) be detrimental to the safety of passengers in transportation. Sets forth similar provisions requiring the Under Secretary to prescribe regulations prohibiting the disclosure of information obtained or developed in carrying out security under authority of the Aviation and Transportation Security Act (PL107–71).

(Sec. 1602) Increases the maximum civil penalty to $25,000 for a person who violates certain aviation security requirements while operating an aircraft for the transportation of passengers or property for compensation (except an individual serving as an airman).

(Sec. 1603) Revises certain hiring security screener standards to allow a national (currently, only a citizen) of the United States to become a security screener.

Title XVII: Conforming and Technical Amendments—(Sec. 1701)

Sets forth technical and conforming amendments.

(Sec. 1706) Transfers from the Administrator of General Services to the Secretary of Homeland Security law enforcement authority for the protection of Federal property.

(Sec. 1708) Establishes in DOD a National Bio-Weapons Defense Analysis Center to develop countermeasures to potential attacks by terrorists using weapons of mass destruction.

(Sec. 1714) Amends the Public Health Service Act to define "vaccine" to mean any preparation or suspension, including one containing an attenuated or inactive microorganism or toxin, developed or administered to produce or enhance the body's immune response to a disease and to include all components and ingredients listed in the vaccine's product license application and product label.

Testimony, The Nomination of The Honorable Tom Ridge to Be Secretary of the Department of Homeland Security before the U.S. Senate Committee on Government Affairs, January 17, 2003

Immediately after signing the new legislation in late 2003, President Bush nominated Tom Ridge to be the first secretary of the Department

*of Homeland Security. Ridge, a former Republican governor of Penn-
sylvania, was at the time the director of the Office of Homeland Security in the White House. On January 17, 2003, he presented written testimony and answered questions posed by the members of the U.S.
Senate Committee on Government Affairs. The committee quickly and
unanimously recommended to the full Senate that Ridge be confirmed
as the secretary of the Department of Homeland Security. This document is the formal statement by the nominee to the Senate.*

I would like to first thank you, Senator Collins and Senator
Lieberman, and all the members of the Committee for moving expeditiously to conduct today's hearing. As I have said many times before
my nomination was announced, and as I have said many times since,
to me there is no more serious job in all the land than stopping future
terrorist incidents from occurring on American soil. I can imagine no
mission more imperative than protecting the American people; and
should another terrorist attack occur, I can think of nothing more crucial than working to ensure that every single echelon of society is as
prepared as possible to respond. I wish to commend the Congress
again for pressing forward and taking bold and historic steps to establish this new Department of Homeland Security. Together, the Congress and the Executive Branch realized the current structure of our
government limited our ability to protect America. Now, for the first
time, we will have a Federal Department whose primary mission is the
protection of the American people. America is undoubtedly safer and
better prepared today than on September 10th, 2001. We have taken
key steps to protect America—from pushing our maritime borders farther from shore and professionalizing airport screening to developing
vaccination plans and tightening our borders. Public servants at all
levels of government, private sector employees, and citizens all across
the United States have changed the way in which they live and work
in a unified effort to improve our security since the September 11th attacks. For the first time in our Nation's history, the President has created a *National Strategy for Homeland Security,* a strategy which provides the framework to mobilize and organize the nation—the federal
government, state and local governments, the private sector, and the
American people—in the complex mission to protect our homeland.
We have begun the very first steps of critical work in the initiative by
identifying and assessing our vulnerabilities to see where we are exposed to an unpredictable enemy. That said, we are only at the beginning of what will be a long struggle to protect our Nation from terrorism. While much has been accomplished, there is much more work to
do. We are a country that is built from ingenuity and hard work and
we will not rest on our laurels. We must stay focused. We must stay
vigilant. We have no higher purpose than to ensure the security of our

people to protect and preserve our democratic way of life. Terrorism directly threatens the foundations of our Nation, our people, our freedom, and our economic prosperity. We face a hate-filled, remorseless enemy that takes many forms, has many places to hide, and is often invisible.

The role of the Secretary of Homeland Security will be, first and foremost, the protection of the American people. Since being sworn in by the President as the first Homeland Security Advisor on October 8th, 2001, I have been focused solely on this mission.

Shortly after the President made his speech to the nation announcing his intention to propose the creation of the Department of Homeland Security, he also appointed me as Director of the Transition Planning Office. It was in that capacity that I testified in front of Congressional committees in both the House and Senate about the vision we were undertaking that began the critical partnership of working with Congress to ensure the success of this venture.

In the time since, I have helped to guide the men and women in the Transition Planning Office, who are detailed from all of the agencies affected by the legislation. They have been working undeterred and with a strong sense of urgency. In the nearly 60 days since the President signed the Homeland Security Act of 2002 into law, our Transition staff has laid the framework for an organizational structure that will best accomplish our goals and create a professional workforce focused first and foremost on the mission of protecting our homeland. The Secretary of Homeland Security, however, is only one person who, without the support of those who have dedicated and risked their lives to protecting America, will not succeed. Should I be confirmed as the Secretary of Homeland Security, I will go to work every single morning with the mission of protecting the American people from the threat of terrorist attack, knowing that the most valuable asset the new Department will have is not funding, or technology, or equipment, but the men and women who work there.

These are the true patriots in every sense of the term. They are vital to the mission.

The more than 170,000 future employees of the Department of Homeland Security will be doing the same job in the new Department that they are doing today: protecting our country from terrorist attack. That focus exists now, and it will exist long after the Department is created. We will also not forget the breadth of the task at hand. This is the largest and most significant transformation of the U.S. government in over a half-century. We will not be naive to the challenge of merging 22 separate work cultures, operating procedures and management procedures into one cohesive organization. At the same time, we cannot lose sight of the individual missions of each of the agencies. But we must create a mindset in which everyone is thinking about how each of their missions fit into the larger mission of protecting our homeland. From day one, we will not allow for invisible barriers to lead to the breakdown of information. To be successful, we will need to foster teamwork and a strong sense of pride about working together to accomplish the mission. However, unifying in one Department on the federal level will not in itself be able to stop all attempts to do harm to America. We must realize fully the value of cultivating partnerships and cooperating with our partners in other federal agencies, state and local governments, the private sector and with the American people.

As a former Governor, I am keenly aware of the shared responsibility that exists between the federal, state, and local governments for homeland security. In fact, over the past year I have often said that "when our hometowns are secure, our homeland will be secure." That is not merely rhetoric, but a fundamental principle of the nation's homeland security effort. I'm pleased to report that all 50 states and the territories have appointed homeland security advisors and that they participate regularly in meetings at the White House and in bimonthly conference calls with the Office of Homeland Security. We have, for the first time, created a single entry point to address many of the homeland security concerns of our Governors and Mayors.

We know, however, that much more needs to be done. We must recognize that communities and state and local governments face new and unprecedented threats. As such, the new Department should stand ready to work with them to obtain the tools, resources, and information they need to do their jobs. We also must develop new channels of communication with private sector organizations, and provide clear, concise, scientifically sound and easily accessible information so that Americans citizens can be prepared in the event their community is affected by a terrorist act. If I should become the new Secretary, you have my pledge that I will focus on increased collaboration and coordination so that public and private resources are better aligned to secure the homeland and support each one of our critical missions.

Supporting the *National Strategy for Homeland Security*

I also wish to state my promise that I will do everything in my power to use the office of the secretary to keep the Department focused on all six of its critical missions outlined in the *National Strategy for Homeland Security*. They include:

- Intelligence and Warning,
- Border and Transportation Security,
- Domestic Counterterrorism,
- Protecting Critical Infrastructure and Key Assets,

- Defending Against Catastrophic Threats, and
- Emergency Preparedness and Response.

While each of these missions is unique, each is essential to our primary mission of protecting the security of the United States. Some, such as Emergency Preparedness and Response, have long played key roles in helping society overcome hardship and emergencies; while others are byproducts of the harsh reality that terrorism can strike on our soil. As I said earlier, the future employees of the Department of Homeland Security will be doing the same job in the new Department that they are doing today. The difference is that the new structure of the Department will refocus, consolidate and reorganize the functions of each of the 22 agencies involved in protecting the homeland.

The Department will be structured into four Directorates, each responsible for implementing the applicable components of the six critical missions. They are:

- Border and Transportation Security,
- Information Analysis and Critical Infrastructure Protection,
- Emergency Response and Preparedness, and
- Science and Technology

The United States Coast Guard and Secret Service will retain their independence and will play key roles in supporting all of the critical missions.

I would like to give you a sense of how I believe this unified homeland security structure will mobilize and focus the resources of the federal government, state and local governments, the private sector, and the American people to accomplish its mission; beginning first with one of the most sizable challenges, border and transportation security.

Border and Transportation Security

America has historically relied on two vast oceans and two friendly neighbors for border security. And our country has long cherished its identity as a nation of immigrants. Nearly 500 million people enter our country each year at our numerous border checkpoints, seaports and airports. The sheer volume of those wishing to visit our great country or move here permanently in search of the American dream, coupled with the burden of processing vast amounts of information from disparate federal agencies, has severely taxed our border security and immigration systems. Even before September 11th, it had become apparent that the system could no longer determine who exactly was in our country, for what reason, and whether they left when they said they were going to leave.

Since then, we have made substantial improvements to tighten security in areas like visa issuances and border patrol; but more importantly, we have laid the foundation for a comprehensive plan with tangible benchmarks to measure success through the *National Strategy for Homeland Security.* The new Department will be organized to implement this plan efficiently and meet its two inherent strategic goals: to improve border security while at the same time, facilitate the unimpeded flow of legitimate commerce and people across our borders. We will implement the President's plan to separate the Immigration and Naturalization Service into two functions: services and enforcement. This plan will allow the new Department to greatly improve the administration of benefits and services for applicants, while at the same time ensuring full enforcement of the laws that regulate the flow of aliens to the United States. I realize that this is no simple task. But if we are to remain the land of freedom and opportunity, we must retain complete control over who enters our country and maintain the integrity of our immigration system so that we always know who is in our country and for what purpose.

The integrity of our borders goes hand-in-hand with the security of our transportation systems. Today, Americans are more mobile than ever. We enjoy the freedom to go where we want, when we want, using the best transportation system in the world. This efficient system is also one of the engines that drives our economy. Shutting down that engine is not a viable option. But the destructive potential of modern terrorism requires that we fundamentally rethink how we should protect this system. Virtually every community in America is connected to the global transportation network by seaports, airports, highways, railroads, and waterways. One area in which we have shown significant progress is security at our nation's airports. The Transportation Security Administration, under the leadership of the Department of Transportation, has hired, trained and deployed a new federal screening workforce that is professional and focused on providing the highest levels of security without hindering our aviation system. We need to build on that success, but at the same time realize we have farther still to go. The new Department must work with its federal and private sector partners to assess and take the necessary steps to secure our means of transportation, including our railways, roadways, bridges, waterways and especially our seaports. We must take immediate action to make sure our seaports are open to process the flow of goods and commercial traffic, but are closed to terrorists. A vast majority of container cargo remains unscreened. Port security remains the responsibility of a myriad of local port authorities, federal agencies and the Coast Guard. However, we are making changes. We must enhance risk management and implement practices that allow for higher efficiency screening of goods. Our fundamental goal is to make certain that heightened security does not obstruct legitimate trade. Progress, however, is already underway. Programs like the Container Security Initiative are helping nations spot and screen the highest-risk containers. Operation Safe Commerce focuses on business driven initiatives to enhance security for the movement of cargo throughout the entire supply chain. Most recently, Congress passed the Maritime Transportation Security Act, which gives authority to the Coast Guard and Customs Service to develop standards and procedures for conducting port vulnerability assessments.

United States Coast Guard

The men and women of the United States Coast Guard, who live under the guiding principle *SemperParatus* or Always Ready, have been performing the mission of Homeland Security in a complex and dangerous maritime environment for more than 200 years. The Coast Guard's fundamental responsibilities—preparedness, protection, response and recovery—cut across all facets of the Department's mission.

Every day since the September 11th terrorist attacks, the Coast Guard pushes our maritime borders farther from shore. All ships bound for the U.S., regardless of registry, face a multi-layered, interagency security screening process in addition to traditional safety, environmental and operational standards enforcement, plus random boardings. Vessels now must provide 96-hour advance notice of arrival to the Coast Guard National Vessel Movement Center, including detailed crew and passenger information, cargo details, and voyage history. The Coast Guard has also created highly trained and specially equipped Maritime Safety and Security Teams to add an extra layer of security and additional quick-response capabilities in key U.S. ports. But let me make one thing clear. The new Department will not lose focus of the Coast Guard's other critical missions. From search and rescue, anti-drug and illegal migrant patrols to fisheries enforcement and aids to navigation, I will work personally to ensure that the Department continues to support the entirety of the Coast Guard mission. No branch of the Armed Forces has as much history in protecting the homeland, and should I be confirmed as Secretary, I can think of no honor that would make me more proud than calling myself a Service Secretary of the Coast Guard.

United States Secret Service

The Secret Service represents another unique critical mission that aligns with the core competencies of the new Department and will remain independent. Through its two distinct missions, protection and criminal investigation, the Secret Service is responsible for the protection of the President, the Vice President and their families; heads of state; the security for designated National Special Security Events; and the investigation and enforcement of laws relating to counterfeiting, fraud and financial crimes.

The Secret Service is, and has been for decades, in the business of assessing vulnerabilities and designing ways to reduce them in advance of an attack. This expertise will greatly benefit the Department as we strive to create an overall culture of anticipation, vulnerability assessment, and threat reduction. Building on these institutional ideals will be of the utmost importance as it pertains to nearly all of the missions in the Department, but none more so than protecting our critical infrastructure.

Information Analysis and Critical Infrastructure Protection

On September 11th, we were dealt a grave, horrific blow, and today we face the real possibility of additional attacks of similar or even greater magnitude. Our enemy will choose their targets deliberately based upon weaknesses in our defenses and preparations. Thus, a fundamental priority in our mission must be to analyze the threat, while concurrently and continuously assessing our vulnerabilities. The Department is structured in such a way as to efficiently conduct this task. The Information Analysis and Critical Infrastructure Directorate will bring together for the first time under one roof the capability to identify and assess threats to the homeland, map those threats against our vulnerabilities, issue warnings, and provide the basis from which to organize protective measures to secure the homeland. For this Directorate to play an effective role in the mission of securing our homeland, I believe a top priority will be to work with the CIA, the FBI and other intelligence-gathering agencies to define the procedures from which to obtain the appropriate intelligence. This means that the Department will be a full participant, at all levels, in the mechanisms for setting foreign intelligence requirements, including the prioritization for terrorism, weapons of mass destruction, and other relevant foreign intelligence collection activities. We also must continue to work with the FBI as they reorganize to most effectively collect domestic intelligence. More than just countering each identified threat, the Department will design and implement a longterm comprehensive and nationwide plan for protecting America's critical infrastructure and key assets. A key mission of the Information Analysis and Critical Infrastructure Protection division will be to catalogue and reduce the Nation's domestic vulnerability.

America's critical infrastructure encompasses a large number of sectors ranging from energy and chemical to banking and agriculture. Each has unique vulnerabilities, and each requires different kinds of protection. This, coupled with the fact that nearly 85 percent of critical infrastructure is owned by the private sector—and that 12 separate federal agencies have oversight authority—creates an enormous challenge. Realizing the breadth of this task, the Office of Homeland Security began working with the federal lead departments and agencies for each of the 14 critical infrastructure sectors designated in the President's *National Strategy for Homeland Security.* This cooperation has included the identification of infrastructures and assets of national-level criticality within each sector; facilitating the sharing of risk and vulnerability assessment methodologies and best practices; and enabling cooperation between federal departments and agencies, state and local governments, and the private sector.

This process, however, is only the beginning. The Department of Homeland Security will provide greater uniformity to these efforts and further strengthen the relationships with the private sector and state and local governments so that we can integrate the threat and vulnerability analysis in a way that will help produce effective countermeasures. As this information is collected and mapped to critical infrastructure vulnerabilities, our top priority must be to get this information to those federal, state and local officials to whose mission the information is relevant. These individuals represent the first line of defense against and response to a terrorist attack, and we must make it a priority to keep them properly informed and aware.

Emergency Preparedness and Response

Our nation's three million firefighters, police officers, and EMTs are the first on the scene in a crisis and the last to leave. Their heroic efforts saved lives and speeded the recovery from the attacks of September 11th, and they will be called upon to do so in the event of future attacks against our hometowns. They're living proof that homeland security is a national, not a federal effort.

We must give these brave men and women all the assistance and support possible. Under the Emergency Preparedness and Response Directorate in the new Department, we will strengthen our relationship with first responders and partner with the states, cities and counties that manage and fund them. We will work with Congress to provide them with the resources they need, beginning with the President's First Responder Initiative, which offered a thousand-percent increase in funding to equip, train and drill first responders to meet a conventional attack or one involving a weapon of mass destruction. We will build on the strong foundation already in place by the Federal Emergency Management Agency, which for decades has provided command and control support and funding support in disasters, whether caused by man or Mother Nature.

The new Department of Homeland Security will consolidate at least five different plans that currently govern federal response to disasters into one genuinely all-discipline, all-hazard plan—between "crisis management" and "consequence management." Moreover, it will consolidate grant programs for first responders and citizen volunteers that are now scattered across numerous federal agencies.

This will prevent waste and duplication, and ultimately save lives, including the lives of first responders. In a crisis, the Department will for the first time provide a direct line of authority from the President through the Secretary of Homeland Security to a single on-site federal response coordinator. All levels of government will have complete incident awareness and open communication. The Department will also direct our federal crisis response assets, such as the National Pharmaceutical Stockpile and nuclear incident response teams—assets that work best when they work together. In doing all this, we believe we can build the capabilities for a proactive emergency management culture—one that is well-planned, well-organized and well-equipped to not just manage the risk, but reduce the risk of death and damage to property. It is vitally important to remember that no matter what steps we take to preempt terrorists, we cannot guarantee that another attack will not occur. However, we must be prepared to respond. We must also take brave new steps, think creatively and invest in homeland security technologies that aim to stay one step ahead of the technologically proficient terrorists.

Science and Technology

As stated in the President's *National Strategy for Homeland Security,* our Nation enjoys a distinct advantage in science and technology. We must exploit that advantage. And just as technology has helped us to defeat enemies from afar, so too will it help us to protect our homeland. Creating a Directorate in the new Department specifically devoted to Science and Technology for the homeland represents an exciting milestone. For the first time, the federal government will harness American ingenuity to develop new synergies and form robust partnerships with the private sector to research, develop and deploy homeland security technologies that will make America safer.

The science and technology organizational structure, while still being defined, is envisioned to be a streamlined, integrated team that will access the technical resources and assets of the private sector, academia, and federal government. It will be based on customer-focused portfolios for countering chemical, biological, radiological and nuclear attacks and for conducting and enhancing the normal operations of the Department. Research, development, test and evaluation programs will address the greatest threats and highest priorities based on assessments of threats, customer requirements and technological capabilities.

The technologies developed through this research and development should not only make us safer, but also make our daily lives better. These technologies fit well within our physical and economic structure and our national habits. And the Science and Technology Directorate will have a structure that ensures those who are the end users of all technologies provide their expertise throughout the entire lifecycle of research, development and acquisition of systems.

Before any new homeland security technologies are deployed, we will ensure that we are upholding the laws of the land. Any new data mining techniques or programs to enhance information sharing and collecting must and will respect the civil rights and civil liberties guaranteed to the American people under the Constitution. Furthermore, as we go about developing new technologies and programs to strengthen our homeland, treating citizens differently on the basis of religion or ethnicity will not be tolerated.

Before I close, I wish to again underscore an earlier point. No matter how this organization is structured it will not achieve its mission without the dedication of its employees. And the key to ensuring the Department's mission and focus throughout the transition will be the continuing support of those conducting the day-to-day work. This will be an all-inclusive effort. We will eagerly solicit and consider advice from employees, unions, professional associations and other stakeholders. We will create a human resource model that will be collaborative, responsive to both its employees and the mission of the agency. First, we will work to create some measure of stability for employees even as we undergo the transition. For the first year, employees can expect to receive at least the same pay and benefits, and probably in the same location. Some people will certainly be able to take advantage of new career opportunities. Second, we will work hard to create a modern, flexible, fair, merit-based personnel system. Third, we will communicate to ensure that personnel know what to expect and when to expect it. Fourth, we will work hard to ensure that employees continue to receive the same civil service protections that they currently enjoy. Most importantly, we aim for the Department's employees to be better able to do their jobs with more support and more effective use of resources. Finally, I will insist on measurable progress from all of the agencies and bureaus that will make up the Department of Homeland Security. Americans must and will know when improvements have been made. In a town hall I hosted with future employees of the Department in December, I made all of these promises to them, as well as the pledge to keep them informed and aware of historic changes before them. Should I be confirmed, I make that same pledge to you. In closing, during our darkest hour on September 11th, American spirit and pride rose above all else to unify our Nation. In the time since, we have fought a new kind of war—one that has a new enemy, new techniques, new strategies, new soldiers and is fought on a new battlefield—our own homeland.

Our response has been strong, measured and resolute. But nothing has been more profound as the creation of one Department whose primary mission is the protection of the American people.

The Department of Homeland Security will better enable every level of federal, state and local government; every private sector employee; and, ultimately, every citizen in our Nation to prevent terrorist attacks, reduce America's vulnerability and respond and recover when attacks do occur. The road will be long, and the mission difficult. We will not have truly succeeded until the day when terrorists know the futility of attacking Americans and Americans know we have the ability to protect them. The bottom line is, we will secure the homeland—whether by the efforts of thousands of people working together, or by a single scientist working alone in a laboratory—whether from behind a desk in Washington, or at the far corners of the continent. We will accomplish our mission.

Advancing the Management of Homeland Security: Protecting the Homeland; Lessons from Prior Governmental Reorganizations. National Academy of Public Administration. April 2003.

Everyone, from President Bush and DHS Secretary Tom Ridge to members of Congress, from the bureaucratic leaders managing the twenty-two federal agencies that were to become the Department of Homeland Security to all those in the public administration academic community, knew that bringing together the 180,000 people working in these many separate and distinct federal agencies would be a nightmarish problem for the DHS secretary and his political appointees, one that might take decades before there was a successful reorganization. This document, an executive summary of a lengthy report of the highly respected non-governmental, nonpartisan organization the National Academy of Public Administration, issued in April 2003, presented a comprehensive set of recommendations for the successful reorganization of those agencies responsible for domestic security. These recommendations were the

*product of an examination of earlier federal and state bureaucratic reor-
ganizations and the mistakes made in these earlier efforts.*

A NATIONAL ACADEMY OF PUBLIC ADMINISTRATION
FORUM ON HOMELAND SECURITY
SUMMARY REPORT
NATIONAL ACADEMY OF PUBLIC ADMINISTRATION
WASHINGTON, DC
APRIL 29, 2003

FOREWORD

*The National Academy of Public Administration is an independent non-profit,
non-partisan corporation chartered by Congress. Founded in 1967, it provides
trusted advice to leaders on issues of governance and public management. The
Academy works closely with all three branches of government at the federal,
state, and local levels; with philanthropic and non-governmental organizations;
and with foreign and international institutions that request advice or assistance.*

Howard M. Messner
President
Jonathan D. Breul
Chair, Homeland Security
Steering Committee

Organizing the Department of Homeland Security is an immense challenge that requires visionary leadership, exemplary management, and
effective intergovernmental coordination. To successfully defend the
homeland from terrorist threats, departmental leadership must draw
on the knowledge of men and women who have directed large-scale
government **reorganizations** in the past. Over their decades in public
service, Academy Fellows have amassed unique expertise and per-
spectives that can be proactively applied to the structure, organization, and management of the Department of Homeland Security. The
Academy's 550 Fellows are elected from the nation's top policy makers, public administrators, and scholars of public policy and public
administration. They include public managers and scholars, business
executives and labor leaders, current and former cabinet officers,
members of Congress, governors, mayors, state legislators, and diplo-
mats. On April 29, 2003, Academy Fellow Frank C. Carlucci, former
Secretary of Defense and National Security Advisor, moderated the
Academy forum *Protecting the Homeland: Lessons from Prior Government
Reorganizations.* At this event, a panel of Fellows engaged in lively discussion on such topics as personnel systems, budgeting, forging departmental identity and decentralized management. The 11 panelists

have more than 400 years of collective experience—many of those years as distinguished leaders and senior executives. They have worked at more than 30 federal departments and agencies and have served on commissions, councils, and delegations. Drawing on their public sector leadership and extensive backgrounds in past government reorganizations, the panelists illuminated and clarified the management issues associated with the creation of the Department of Homeland Security.

As Netscape founder Jim Barksdale once stated, "The main thing is to keep the main thing the main thing." We believe that clarifying major management issues will allow the department's leadership to focus on its "main thing": fulfilling its crucial mission of protecting the homeland. The Academy often forms a Panel of Fellows to issue a research report on a specific topic. This publication, however, is intended to serve as a summary of the April 29 forum's proceedings. By capturing the broad knowledge and cogent anecdotes that Fellows offered at the forum, this report provides insights and practical management advice to top-level department and administration officials, as well as public and private sector stakeholders.

HOMELAND SECURITY: MANAGEMENT CHALLENGES AND OPTIONS

Good morning, Mr. Secretary, Congratulations on your appointment. Here's your charge:

- Mold 22 disparate agencies into one department.
- Protect more than 12,350 miles of coastland, 5,700 miles of borders, all essential power, transportation and other infrastructure networks, and the lives and safety of 281.4 million Americans.
- Do it now.

Keep in mind that your success depends heavily on state, local and private organizations you do not control. And while your office may have security at the door, it has glass walls through which the President, Congress, the media and stakeholders are watching—closely.

Good luck . . . and keep in touch.

This might well have been the greeting card on the desk of the nation's first Secretary of Homeland Security: Officially launched January 24, 2003 with 180,000 employees and a budget of nearly $40 billion, the Department of Homeland Security (DHS) is, at its inception, the third largest cabinet agency in the U.S. government. No U.S. government reorganization of this magnitude has been accomplished since the creation of the Department of Defense following World War II. The challenges of establishing and organizing such a large undertaking cover the entire spectrum of public management issues and, as the forum Chair noted in his opening remarks, "the transformation of the new department into a high-performance organization is not going to be self-executing."

Recognizing the difficulties the new Secretary would encounter, Congress provided for an Under Secretary for Management.[1] That appointee was given the broadest set of responsibilities ever specified by law for such an internal management official.

The Under Secretary is subsuming, for example, jurisdiction over critical systems that in other departments are managed by separate high-level managers, such as the Chief Information Officer or Chief Financial Officer. The provision for a unified managerial post gives the Secretary a chance to focus more attention on the fundamental mission of preventing and mitigating the effects of terrorist attacks. With billions of dollars to be spent wisely or wasted, and with nothing less than the national security at stake, the panelists at the Academy's forum offered some significant **lessons** from their combined 400-plus years of high-level, hands-on government and organizational development experience. These **lessons** fell into two obvious categories: 1. organizational barriers that led to incomplete or ineffective reorganizations in the past, 2. strategies, principles, and tactics that proved successful in past **reorganizations.**

While the forum panelists agreed that the challenges facing the new department are formidable, all viewed its creation as an exciting event. As one panelist framed it, one possible outcome could be the creation of "a strong and effective cabinet department that can, quite possibly, become a 21st Century model of management excellence."

DHS is tasked with making sure that America is stronger, safer, and more secure. "The federal government has no more important mission," said one panelist. But if the Secretary, the Under Secretary for Management and other top DHS officials are to be successful, they must not be overwhelmed with crises and detail. In order for that to happen, panelists agreed that much thought will have to be devoted to managerial process, structure, and style. The general consensus was that much can be learned from other **reorganizations**, such as those that created the Departments of Health, Education and Welfare (HEW, the predecessor to Health and Human Services), Housing and Urban Development (HUD), Transportation (DOT), and the Environmental Protection Agency (EPA). While those organizations were dissimilar to DHS in magnitude and diversity of missions, the panelists were confident that many **lessons** and insights gleaned from past **reorganizations** are, in fact, relevant to DHS.

The panelists identified six major challenges:

1. diversity of incoming agencies, missions, and management cultures
2. coordination with the White House, Congress, and other departments and agencies
3. dependence on shared authority with local, state, and regional entities
4. establishment of an improved personnel system
5. the tendency to build departmental budgets by aggregation rather than by mission priorities
6. high public expectations

Agency diversity. DHS is absorbing a significantly higher number of organizations with disparate missions than has been the case with previous large **reorganizations**. In the Transportation Department reorganization, for example, the incoming elements all dealt with moving goods and people. At DHS, some elements, like the Coast Guard, have non-security functions, such as search and rescue off the coasts and inland waters. The Customs Service, which also will be joining the department, has important regulatory powers that deal with conformance to trade laws. This diversity also extends to the management cultures and contrasting records of effective performance. As measured by Government Performance Project ratings, the Coast Guard ranks near the top with A ratings, while Customs and the Immigration and Naturalization Service are described as "on the sick list" with Cs. There also are relatively new elements, such as the Transportation Security Administration, which has had insufficient time (prior to being absorbed by DHS) to be able to establish a management culture. Panelists suggested that, based on previous experience, a first priority would be to get everyone involved in the planning process so that there would be no surprises and there would be a sense of ownership. In the past, this often was successful because a strong internal communications system was put into place early in the effort. Several stressed the use of a number of task forces, with members drawn from different levels of DHS' various components, to generate innovative thinking and to help break down organizational walls. Also suggested was that policy and operations were two distinct but interdependent areas, with policy set in the secretarial office and operations with the administrators. In former **reorganizations**, important **lessons** learned were that people should understand their roles, and that the focus should remain on the mission, especially at the highest levels. By doing just that, one avoided including agencies or tasks that did not fit into the mission.

Coordination with the White House, Congress, and other departments and agencies. The panelists recognized that coordination within the federal arena should be of primary importance to the Secretary. While DHS will initiate some of its own policies and programs, many others will be initiated on the outside, with operational responsibility, including implementation and funding, left to the department. For instance, a decision made by the Attorney General in April 2003 regarding indefinite detention of refugees and asylum seekers becomes an operational function of the department. This will have a direct effect on detention resources, both physical capacity as well as dollars. Such a decision may limit DHS' ability to manage limited resources in a manner that most effectively protects public safety and immigration enforcement. Without constant, comprehensive communications channels in place, the department will continually be surprised with added operational responsibilities. Every time the White House, Congress, an agency, or international body makes a decision that impacts the security of the United States, DHS must be in a position to know what will happen before it happens so that it can have a voice in the discussion prior to the decision going into effect.

Another good example of an everyday issue that will span departmental boundaries may be the manner in which security measures are exercised on goods crossing the nation's borders, or arriving via sea or air. This is clearly of interest not only to the Departments of Agriculture, Commerce, Transportation, and State, but also to businesses and consumers at large. A further challenge to coordination will be DHS' relationship to the White House Office of Homeland Security, National Homeland Security Council, and the National Security Council. These relationships will take time to build. And because the exercise of law enforcement and security historically has clashed head-on with highly protected individual freedoms and rights, the department can expect these conflicts to surface even more noticeably as its operations are weaved into the tapestry of the nation's business. This raises issues of jurisdiction and impacts on agency budgets. The Secretary should expect to spend a lot of time building support with Congress, the White House, and other federal constituents.

A particularly difficult coordination challenge is crafting the roles and procedures under which the various levels of government must function as a closely knit team in the immediate responses to terrorist attacks. Achieving operational coordination to avoid, mitigate, and respond to attacks is a daunting challenge, yet this task is the essence of the department's mission.

Dependence on shared authority with local, state, and regional entities. The panelists recognized that accomplishing DHS' mission requires the cooperation of state and local governments and private entities, and that the choices concerning the structure of field and regional operations demand close attention. One question already being raised is whether to funnel most homeland security assistance funds through the states to local jurisdictions or pass them directly to the latter.

As one panelist put it, "unless we can somehow enhance coordination between the federal government and the state and local government, we've done something with much sound and fury, signifying nothing."

Again, clear channels of communications will be of primary importance. Regional offices, should they be established, as well as field operations and local leadership must be well informed. The panelists agreed that any regional structure must be thought out very carefully. Regions need to have added value, and not merely constitute another layer of government operations, to be effective. The regional experience of the 1970s should be looked at, though a whole new approach may be needed today.

The federal personnel system. The panelists noted that personnel reform was under design for DHS and under consideration for the Department of Defense. Some viewed reform as essential to accomplishing DHS' mission, and they called for more flexibility in hiring, reassigning, paying, and classifying personnel, while retaining the merit principles and the capacity to enforce them. Others cautioned that such reforms as "pay for performance" can become subjective and erode the principles established in creating the civil service, if the system becomes politicized. It is important to retain the capacity to quickly detect and correct abuses of the increased flexibilities needed.

Budget processes and priorities. The usual budgeting process, in which agency elements submit requests and the department Secretary or budget function subtracts from or adds to them, was viewed as unfavorable to the process of achieving integration. The alternative is to use the budget process to prioritize resources by function rather than organization. It was suggested that DHS have the program drive the process. Strong emphasis was given to having adequate resources, and to implementing top-down structuring of resource allocations to facilitate change. Regardless of how the department puts its budget together, it can expect the congressional committees with jurisdiction to have their own priorities.

High public expectations. Despite warnings from the President, CIA, FBI, and others that there is no sure defense against future terrorist attacks, public expectations of DHS are high. Furthermore, the department is relying on the general public for preparedness in the event of further attacks and for their assistance in detecting potential threats.

While the panelists suggested some specific actions that the Secretary might undertake, they emphasized overarching goals that, based on prior experience, would help ensure the success of the new department:

- establishing departmental identity
- forging good relationships with employees and stakeholders
- determining what should be integrated vs. what should be co-ordinated
- determining what should be decentralized, to what extent it should be decentralized, what field capacity is needed to accept decentralized work, and what headquarters capacity is required to provide adequate oversight

Departmental identity. DHS is absorbing personnel ranging from Coast Guard midshipmen and border patrol officers to intelligence analysts and explosives experts, all operating under differing pay scales, personnel systems, and management cultures. Panelists emphasized several approaches for "bringing them on board" and establishing a public presence. These included early and ongoing consultation, collaboration, and communication with employees at all levels and taking visible actions and conveying consistent messages from the department to the public.

To illustrate the importance of consistent public communication, three examples from the early days of past **reorganizations** were cited. Establishing trust in the department's decisions and ability to make progress in countering terrorism was seen as essential. In addition, the panelists stressed the need to involve important stakeholders such as Congress, private industry, academia, and nonprofits in the departmental planning and decision process. To the extent possible, it is of great value to provide enough participation to develop some sense of ownership among the stakeholders, thus increasing their motivation for success. Panelists also thought it important to have early symbols of presence and process. Citing both the DOT and EPA reorganizations, panelists mentioned speeches, public appearances, symbols, and initiatives that jump-started a positive public awareness of those entities.

Secretary Elliot Richardson sent senior administrators out to speak, particularly those who didn't agree with some of the policies. Another example of early leadership in addressing public concerns and establishing departmental identity came from EPA. Two weeks after the start of operations, Administrator William Ruckelshaus announced that the agency was suing a major city, thus establishing that EPA would use its enforcement mechanism to achieve the agency's environmental goals. In another case, HUD suspended payments to half of the first group of Model Cities one afternoon because initial audits showed flaws in the cities' capacity to protect the grant funds.

Methods of Forging Departmental Identity within the New Organization

Plan and implement task forces with broad representation at various levels, including the field.

- Create a sense of ownership.
- Show people from different agencies how to work together.
- Provide a good way to evaluate potential of task force members, including young employees. Keep key congressional committees informed and build ongoing department-wide relationships with them.
- Avoid surprises and counter the alignment of different committees with different pieces of the organization. Keep employees informed via meetings at each level, bulletin boards, e-mail and other means; encourage discussion and listen to different points of view.
- Mitigate employee fears about changes in status and assignment (facts are better than rumors). Have senior officials make policy speeches, particularly on controversial issues; maintain contact with groups that disagree.
- Maintain the public presence.
- Strive to bring stakeholders behind the unified mission. Take strong early action.
- Establish that the department is up and running. Run a logo contest.
- Involve lower-level employees.
- Create a sense of belonging to the organization.

Consultation with stakeholders. Among the important groups identified were DHS employees, the White House, congressional committees and staffs, elements of the Executive Office of the President (such as the Office of Management and Budget), state and local governments, the private sector, academia, and nonprofits. Several panelists emphasized the importance of true consultation rather than simply informing stakeholders.

Some felt that the Office of Homeland Security and the National Homeland Security Council might interfere with the operation of the department. That type of interference has been the case with the Environmental Policy Council and many others. A contrasting view was that these White House agencies could be useful in coordinating the department's role with other departments and agencies.

Integration vs. coordination. Opinions varied sharply about the best strategy for consolidating 22 agencies. Some advocated tearing down old structures and "stovepipes" to realign department organization by functions. Others argued for leaving in place those elements that were functioning well, but integrating some of the processes that involve different units. Participants advocated the use of information systems as a tool for helping to achieve departmental integration, though there was lack of agreement on how much information systems alone could achieve.

Two examples of agency mergers were presented to shed light on the process of integration. In the (early years) of the formation of the National Imagery Mapping Agency (from the Defense Mapping Agency and parts of the CIA and State Department and other agencies in the mid-90s), the discussion focused almost entirely on who was going to get the money, who was going to get the people, and who was going to be in this box or that box. They never talked about the new mission. And I worry that could happen with the Department of Homeland Security.

A more recent example is the formation of the Defense Threat Reduction Agency (1998) from a number of existing agencies. It has a lot of analogies to DHS, although on a much smaller scale. I would argue that there were five characteristics that made it succeed. It picked people who were leaders rather than managers. It didn't keep any of the original organizations—it forced them together to form new structural organizations. It increased the funding because some new missions were added. There was a very clear mission and a strategy and alignment that everybody understood. And it spent a lot of time trying to communicate that.

The synergy that one gets when bringing in private sector people, people from the universities, people from the non-profits—the clash of ideas that one often achieves from that kind of group is extremely helpful, especially in formulating policies. If one finds a function that's working, do not let anybody try to put a template over it to remake it DHS.

The differing approaches—"breaking eggs" vs. coordinating existing boxes—were both seen as valid in some cases. Even at a lower level of integration, contrasting advice was offered. Based on experience with large industry mergers and earlier government consolidations, two panelists urged DHS *not* to seek uniformity among information systems, but rather to overlay them with off-the-shelf "middleware" that makes information accessible and useful to top management. In the case of personnel systems, however, considerable unification was seen as essential to align job classifications with the new functions, facilitate mobility, and counter pay disparities.

Centralization vs. Decentralization

Several panelists agreed that a crucial issue in DHS' organization was how to manage activities in the field and how to coordinate them with state and local governments and with private industry. The result was a discussion of centralized vs. decentralized authority in carrying out the department's mission. Several facets of this issue follow:

- What degree of management control should there be from the top and in the office of the Under Secretary for Management?
- What should be the relationship of headquarters offices to regional and field offices and to existing local organizations?
- What should be the relationship between policy and operations staff?
- Where should key staff persons be housed?

The organization of DHS includes four functional divisions headed by Under Secretaries. Given the depth and reach of those functions, some argued that it is impossible to manage the department from the top down. Others suggested that there are some basic management and leadership roles that must come from the top, but that operational management should be left to the lower levels. The consensus was that it will be impossible for the Secretary to make all the decisions, and that delegation of authority to lower levels is imperative. Panelists also mentioned that it would be important for the Secretary to have an information system that brought key conflicts and policy issues to his attention in a timely manner.

Resolving conflicts between the policy-making and operational functions was one such conflict that panelists stressed as an appropriate role for the Secretary. As for the role of the Under Secretary for Management, several panelists advised that the Secretary should rely on the Under Secretary to see that the human resources, budget, audit, support services, and accounting functions are properly carried out in a coordinated system. Another stressed the importance of the Under Secretary being responsible for the integration of program and administrative management.

Several panelists emphasized the need to delegate authority to the field.

"If you have any notion of 'controlling' this department, please remove that word from your vocabulary," one panelist said in describing his first advice to the Secretary. "You cannot even make all of the decisions. You must rely upon your principal subordinates."

Science and Technology, Information Analysis and Infrastructure Protection, Border and Transportation Security, and Emergency Preparedness and Response.

"The regional structure is one that people really need to think through very carefully," said one, stimulating an extensive discussion.

Among the points that emerged were the following:

- The field structure is particularly relevant to successful coordination of DHS functions at the local level.
- As much of the operational authority as possible should be delegated to the field where the services are actually delivered, requiring the development of field capacity to exercise this authority.
- Good communication is required among the Secretary, headquarters, and the field.
- No uniform model for the field structure is mandatory. The structure might vary, for example, according to geographical location and the nature of the security threat in the area.
- Regardless of the degree of authority vested in field managers, they should have access to headquarters to share information with the Secretary's office.
- Since not everyone in such a large department can be brought under one roof, it is important to think about who sits where—such as whether heads of operational functions should be located with the employees they supervise or be placed close to the Secretary's office. The panelists brought up an example of successful interagency coordination in the field from a prior organizational effort: regional councils, which had liaison with the Office of Management and Budget. They were seen as a forum for reaching out to state and local officials and the private sector, monitoring the regional apparatus and interagency functioning, and bringing problems to the attention of managers who had the capacity to take action. In 1969, President Nixon divided the country into 10 standard regions for departments most heavily involved with grants to state and local governments. A city was designated for each region and a regional council was set up in those cities. The councils were composed of the senior field person from each participating department and independent agency. The councils had no authority, relying instead on the authority each member had from his or her agency. The OMB Assistant Director for Executive Management designated seven of his management staff to spend roughly half their time in the field, assuring that the councils served as coordinating and expediting organs, rather than another layer of government. Effective during their first few years, the councils declined as most top career people in the field were replaced by less informed political appointees, and as the management staff in OMB phased out and OMB could no longer provide coordinating and expediting leadership in the field.

You can't have a uniform regional structure for each function. It depends on the mission. . . .Regional directors have to have common functions to coordinate. Otherwise you're just layering over problems with another level of management.

The forum was not intended to lead to formal recommendations, but it did yield valuable guidance for the DHS organization.

- Do not try to make all the management decisions at the top.
- Delegate maximum operational authority to the field.
- Invite in and listen to important stakeholders, especially if they oppose what you are doing.
- Use task forces to help make the various elements work together and to foster ownership.
- Involve various levels of the staffs from different agencies in the reorganization plans.
- Use the budget process for building consensus on program priorities.
- Do not let the urgent overcome the important in day-to-day administration.
- Have a good information system to bring important issues to the attention of the Secretary and other department leaders.
- Establish streamlined processes for delivering services (e.g., ease of grant applications, small business relief assistance, or response to attack).
- Carefully design the organization of the field structure, and reevaluate it from time to time.
- Establish continuous employee communications. Be sure employees first hear about changes from the Secretary's office, not Congress or the media.
- Establish some early wins to show the department is up and running.
- Choose administrators by competency in the particular assigned mission, not by political influence or seniority in existing pay scales.
- Don't force uniformity in departmental information systems. Use technology and middleware to achieve integration.
- Use advisers with experience in more than one organization when formulating reorganization plans.

In sum, the forum produced a number of specific suggestions for undertaking the complex problems presented by the reorganization of homeland security functions. It also identified the critical management issues facing the new department and the options for addressing them. While the panelists offered different strategies for addressing these issues, all are reality-tested strategies from the past that could be used to make the DHS organization process more effective and possibly create a "model for public administration in the 21st Century."

Notes

1. The specific statutory responsibilities assigned to the Under Secretary for Management include budget, appropriations, expenditures, and accounting and finance; procurement; human resources and personnel; information technology and communications; facilities and other material resources; security for personnel, information technology, communications, and physical facilities of the department; performance measures; grants and other assistance management programs; the reorganization process; internal audits, and any others assigned by the Secretary.

7

Directory of Organizations

Governmental

American Federation of Government Employees (AFGE)
80 F Street NW
Washington, DC 20001
Tel: (202) 737-8700
E-mail: comments@afge.org

The American Federation of Government Employees (AFGE) is the largest federal employee union, representing 600,000 federal and D.C. government workers nationwide and overseas. The AFGE has been nationally affiliated with the AFL-CIO since it was founded in 1932. In addition to negotiating working conditions at the bargaining table, AFGE coordinates a full-scale legislative and political action program to monitor issues that impact the government work force. The union is headquartered in Washington, D.C., and divided into twelve geographical districts consisting of some 1,100 locals. Over one-half of the AFGE's members are consolidated into agency-wide bargaining units. Agencies with the highest concentration of union membership include the Department of Defense, the Department of Veterans Affairs, the Social Security Administration, the Department of Justice, and the newly created Department of Homeland Security.

Department of Defense
http://www.defenselink.mil/

Initially called the War Department (1789), the Department of Defense was created in 1949 in an effort to place the multi-task defense organizations under a single leader, the secretary of defense. The major military components are the Department of the Army (1798), the Department of the Navy (1798), and the Department of the Air Force (1949). The U.S. Army, the U.S. Marines, and the U.S. Navy were established in 1775 by the Continental Congress. The U.S. Coast Guard was created in 1798, and the U.S. Air Force in 1947. In July 2005, there were 5.3 million persons in the Department of Defense:

> 1.4 million active duty personnel
> 654,000 civilian employees
> 1.2 million guard and reserve forces
> 2.0 million retirees and families receiving benefits.

Seen as a "company," the Defense Department employs 2.04 million persons and its annual budget (2005) is $371 billion. It is America's largest company. Wal-Mart, with 1.383 million employees, is the second largest company in America.

Department of Homeland Security
Web site: http://www.whitehouse.gov/homeland/
Tel: 1-800-BE-READY
Web site: www.Ready.gov

The Department of Homeland Security originated as the Office of Homeland Security. The following description comes from the State of Georgia Office of Homeland Security web site:

> The mission of the Office of Homeland Security was to develop and coordinate the implementation of a comprehensive national strategy to secure the United States from terrorist threats or attacks. Until the DHS was established in November 2002, the OHS coordinated the executive branch's efforts to detect, prepare for, prevent, protect against, respond to, and recover from terrorist attacks within the United States. The Office was to work with federal, state, and local agencies to:
>
> • facilitate collection from state and local governments and private entities of information pertaining to terrorist threats or activities within the United States;

- coordinate and prioritize the requirements for foreign intelligence relating to terrorism within the United States of executive departments and agencies responsible for homeland security, and provide these requirements and priorities to the Director of Central Intelligence and other agencies responsible for collection of foreign intelligence;
- coordinate efforts to ensure that all executive departments and agencies that have intelligence collection responsibilities have sufficient technological capabilities and resources to collect intelligence and data relating to terrorist activities or possible terrorist acts within the United States, working with the Assistant to the President for National Security Affairs, as appropriate;
- coordinate development of monitoring protocols and equipment for use in detecting the release of biological, chemical, and radiological hazards; and
- ensure that, to the extent permitted by law, all appropriate and necessary intelligence and law enforcement information relating to homeland security is disseminated to and exchanged among appropriate executive departments and agencies responsible for homeland security and, where appropriate for reasons of homeland security, promote exchange of such information with and among state and local governments and private entities.

With the passage of the Homeland Security Act of 2002, the OHS was abolished. The Council on Homeland Security, however, has become part of the DHS.

The Department of Homeland Security's *Ready* Campaign seeks to help American families be better prepared for even unlikely emergency scenarios. It was established "because intelligence reports indicate that terrorists are seeking to obtain biological, chemical, and radiological weapons, and the threat of an attack on civilians in America is real."

Department of Justice, Office of the Attorney General
U.S. Department of Justice
950 Pennsylvania Avenue NW
Washington, DC 20530-0001

Tel: (202) 353-1555
E-mail: AskDOJ@usdoj.gov.

The position of U.S. attorney general was created by the Judiciary Act of 1789. In June 1870 Congress enacted a law entitled "An Act to Establish the Department of Justice." This act established the attorney general as head of the Department of Justice and gave the attorney general direction and control of U.S. attorneys general and all other counsel employed on behalf of the United States. The act also vested in the U.S. attorney general supervisory power over the accounts of U.S. attorneys, U.S. marshals, clerks, and other officers of the federal courts.

The mission of the Office of the Attorney General is to supervise and direct the administration and operation of the Department of Justice, including the Federal Bureau of Investigation; Drug Enforcement Administration; Bureau of Alcohol, Tobacco, Firearms, and Explosives; Bureau of Prisons; Office of Justice Programs; and the Offices of U.S. Attorneys and U.S. Marshals, which are all within the Department of Justice.

The major functions of the attorney general are to:

- Represent the United States in legal matters
- Supervise and direct the administration and operation of the offices, boards, divisions, and bureaus that comprise the Department
- Furnish advice and opinions, formal and informal, on legal matters to the president and the cabinet and to the heads of the executive departments and agencies of the government, as provided by law
- Make recommendations to the president concerning appointments to federal judicial positions and to positions within the department, including U.S. attorneys and U.S. marshals
- Represent or supervise the representation of the United States government in the Supreme Court of the United States and all other courts, foreign and domestic, in which the United States is a party or has an interest as may be deemed appropriate
- Perform or supervise the performance of other duties required by statute or executive order

Environmental Protection Agency (EPA)
Ariel Rios Building
1200 Pennsylvania Avenue NW
Washington, DC 20460
Tel: (202) 272-0167
Web site: http://www.epa.gov/

The Environmental Protection Agency (EPA) was established in 1970 in response to the growing public demand for cleaner water, air, and land. Prior to the establishment of the EPA, "the federal government was not structured to make a coordinated attack on the pollutants that harm human health and degrade the environment. The EPA was assigned the daunting task of repairing the damage already done to the natural environment and to establish new criteria to guide Americans in making a cleaner environment a reality." The EPA employs 18,000 people nationwide, with headquarters in Washington, D.C., ten regional offices, and more than a dozen labs. More than half of the EPA staff are engineers, scientists, and policy analysts. In addition, a large number of employees are legal, public affairs, financial, information management, and computer specialists. The EPA is led by the administrator, who is appointed by the president.

First Gov
Federal Citizen Information Center
Office of Citizen Services and Communications, U.S. General
    Services Administration
1800 F Street NW
Washington, DC 20405
Tel: 1-800-FED INFO (1-800-333-4636)
Web site: FirstGov.gov

FirstGov.gov is the official U.S. gateway to all government information. Its work, all done over the Internet, transcends the traditional boundaries of government. On FirstGov.gov, one can search millions of web pages from federal and state governments, the District of Columbia, and U.S. territories. Most of these pages are not available on commercial web sites. FirstGov works with agencies to encourage portals organized around customer groups and topics instead of agency names. Examples of cross-agency portals include students, people with disabilities, and exporters. FirstGov.gov enables users to find and do business with government online, on the phone, by mail, or in person. Customer gateways—for example, citizens, businesses and nonprofits, federal employees, and government-to-government—can be selected to find exactly what is needed.

National Science Advisory Biosecurity Board (NSABB)
Office of Biotechnology Activities
National Institutes of Health
6705 Rockledge Drive, Suite 750
Bethesda, MD 20892-7985
Tel: (301) 496-9838
Fax: (301) 496-9839
E-mail: oba@od.nih.gov
Web site: http://www.biosecurityboard.gov/

The NSABB provides advice to federal departments and agencies on ways to minimize the possibility that knowledge and technologies emanating from vitally important biological research will be misused to threaten public health or national security. The NSABB is chartered to have up to twenty-five voting members with a broad range of expertise in molecular biology, microbiology, infectious diseases, biosafety, public health, veterinary medicine, plant health, national security, biodefense, law enforcement, scientific publishing, and related fields. The NSABB also includes nonvoting ex officio members from fifteen federal agencies and departments.

9/11 Commission on Terrorist Attacks upon the United States

The National Commission on Terrorist Attacks Upon the United States (known as the 9/11 Commission), was an independent, bipartisan commission created by congressional legislation and the signature of President George W. Bush in late 2002. It was chartered to prepare a full and complete account of the circumstances surrounding the September 11, 2001, terrorist attacks, including preparedness for and the immediate response to the attacks. The commission was also mandated to provide recommendations designed to guard against future attacks. On July 22, 2004, the commission released its public report, available for download from http://www.911commission.gov/about/index.htm.

On August 21, 2004, the commission released two staff monographs, available at http://www.911commission.gov/about/index.htm. The commission disbanded on August 21, 2004.

Office of Homeland Security

See Department of Homeland Security

Occupational Safety and Health Administration (OSHA)
200 Constitution Avenue NW
Washington, DC 20210
Web site: www.osha.gov

OSHA's mission is "to assure the safety and health of America's workers by setting and enforcing standards; providing training, outreach, and education; establishing partnerships; and encouraging continual improvement in workplace safety and health." OSHA employs approximately 2,100 federal and state inspectors, plus complaint discrimination investigators, engineers, physicians, educators, standards writers, and other technical and support personnel spread over more than 200 offices throughout the country. Nearly every working man and woman in the nation comes under OSHA's jurisdiction (with some exceptions such as miners, transportation workers, many public employees, and the self-employed).

Nongovernmental

American Chemical Society
1155 16th Street NW
Washington, DC 20036
Tel: 1-800-227-5558 (United States only); (202) 872-4600
(outside the United States)
Fax: (202) 872-4615
E-mail: help@acs.org

The American Chemical Society is a self-governed individual membership organization that consists of more than 159,000 members at all degree levels and in all fields of chemistry. The organization provides a broad range of opportunities for peer interaction and career development, regardless of professional or scientific interests.

American Chemistry Council (ACC)
1300 Wilson Boulevard
Arlington, VA
Tel: (703) 741-5000

The American Chemistry Council (ACC) provides both government and the general public with information about the comprehensive, risk-based security measures ACC member companies have taken—and continue to take—to further ensure that the chemical industry and all Americans are increasingly secure against threats of terrorism.

American Civil Liberties Union (ACLU)
125 Broad Street, 18th Floor
New York, NY 10004
Web site: www.aclu.org/

Founded in 1920, the nonprofit, nonpartisan ACLU works daily in courts, legislatures, and communities to defend and preserve the individual rights and liberties guaranteed to every person in the United States by the Constitution and laws of the United States. The primary mission of the ACLU is to conserve America's original civic values—the Constitution and the Bill of Rights.

The ACLU works to extend rights to segments of our population that have traditionally been denied their rights, including Native Americans and other people of color; lesbians, gay men, bisexuals, and transgendered people; women; mental-health patients; prisoners; people with disabilities; and the poor.

The organization handles nearly 6,000 court cases annually from offices in almost every state.

American Institute for Chemical Engineers
3 Park Avenue
New York, NY 10016-5991
Tel: 1-800-242-4363; international calls, (212) 591-8100
Fax: (212) 591-8888
Web site: http://www.aiche.org/help/keycontacts.htm

The American Institute of Chemical Engineers is a professional association of more than 50,000 members that provides leadership in advancing the chemical engineering profession. The institute fosters and disseminates chemical engineering knowledge and applies the expertise of its members to address societal needs throughout the world.

American Nuclear Society (ANS)
555 N. Kensington Avenue

La Grange Park, IL 60526
Tel: (708) 352-6611
Fax: (708) 352-0499
Web site: http://www.ans.org/contact/

The American Nuclear Society is a not-for-profit scientific and educational organization composed of approximately 10,500 engineers, scientists, administrators, and educators. Its members work to develop and safely apply nuclear science and technology for public benefit through knowledge exchange, professional development, and enhanced public understanding.

American Red Cross
2025 E Street NW
Washington, DC 20006
Tel: (202) 303-4498
Web site: http://www.redcross.org

Since its founding in 1881 by Clara Barton, the American Red Cross has been the nation's premier emergency response organization. As part of a worldwide movement that offers neutral humanitarian care to the victims of war, the American Red Cross has distinguished itself by also aiding victims of devastating natural disasters worldwide. Governed by volunteers and supported by community donations, the American Red Cross is a nationwide network of nearly 1,000 chapters and Blood Services regions dedicated to saving lives and helping people prevent, prepare for and respond to emergencies. More than a million Red Cross volunteers and 30,000 employees annually mobilize relief to families affected by more than 67,000 disasters, train almost 12 million people in lifesaving skills and exchange more than a million emergency messages for U.S. military service personnel and their families. The Red Cross is also the largest supplier of blood and blood products to more than 3,000 hospitals across the nation.

Center for Chemical Process Safety
American Institute of Chemical Engineers
3 Park Avenue
New York, NY 10016-5991
Tel: (212) 591-7319
Fax: (212) 591-8895
E-mail: ccps@aiche.org

The Center for Chemical Process Safety brings together manufacturers, insurers, government, academia, and expert consultants to improve chemical manufacturing process safety. The center and its sponsors are committed to protecting employees, communities, and the environment by developing engineering and management practices to prevent or mitigate catastrophic releases of chemicals, hydrocarbons, and other hazardous materials.

Chlorine Institute, Inc.
1300 Wilson Boulevard
Rosslyn, VA 22209
Tel: (703) 741-5760
Fax: (703) 741-6068
Web site: http://www.cl2.com/contact_info/index.html

The Chlorine Institute is a trade association of companies and other entities that are involved or interested in the safe production, distribution, and use of chlorine, sodium, and potassium hydroxides, and sodium hypochlorite, and the distribution and use of hydrogen chloride. The institute has 240 members located in the United States, Canada, Mexico, Central and South America, and overseas countries. Institute members account for 98 percent of the U.S. production of chlorine and related alkali chemicals—nearly 30 million tons of material annually.

The institute works with government agencies, its members, and other stakeholders to encourage the use of credible science and proven technology in the development of voluntary actions and regulations to enhance safety and security in operations involving the aforementioned chemicals.

Eli Lilly Pharmaceutical
Lilly Corporate Center
Indianapolis, IN 46285
Tel: (317) 276-2000
Web site: http://www.lilly.com/contact.html

Eli Lilly Pharmaceutical employs more than 46,000 people worldwide and markets its medicines in 138 countries. Lilly has major research and development facilities in nine countries and conducts clinical trials in more than sixty countries. The corporation develops its growing portfolio of pharmaceutical products by applying the latest research from its laboratories, collaborating with eminent scientific organizations, and using cutting-edge technological tools.

Federation of American Scientists

1717 K Street NW, Suite 209
Washington, DC 20036
Web site: http://www.fas.org/main/home.jsp

The Federation of American Scientists "focuses the resources of the scientific and technical community on some of the nation's most critical challenges." Its programs and publications advance the mission of informed public debate.

Federation of American Societies for Experimental
   Biology (FASEB)

9650 Rockville Pike
Bethesda, MD 20814
Tel: (301) 634-7000
Web site: http://www.faseb.org/

FASEB's mission is "to enhance the ability of biomedical and life scientists to improve, through their research, the health, well-being, and productivity of all people." FASEB is a coalition of independent member societies that serve the interests of biomedical and life scientists, particularly those related to public policy issues, through scientific conferences and publications.

Homeland One

Tel: (866) 424-5663
E-mail: HomelandOne@pwpl.com
Web site: http://www.homelandone.com/About_Us.asp

Homeland One is designed "to link emergency response communities together, giving immediate access to government leadership at virtually every level." The network helps the government to communicate directly to first responders—providing briefings and updates, investigation leads, emergency deployment plans, personnel and equipment mobilization, evacuation notices, and other timely information. It also develops and offers training programs designed for the specific requirements of the first-responder communities.

Mary Kay O'Connor Center for Chemical Process
   Safety, Texas A&M University

Texas A&M University System
3574 TAMU

College Station, TX 77843-3574
Tel: (979) 845-3489
Fax (979) 458-1493
Web site: http://process-safety.tamu.edu/

The Mary Kay O'Connor Center conducts research and develops undergraduate, graduate, and continuing education programs. Its service to industry and government includes accident investigation and analysis services, particularly for chemical accidents suggesting new phenomena or complex technologies. The center also helps private and public enterprises evaluate and minimize the risk of chemical catastrophes.

National Association of Chemical Distributors (NACD)
1560 Wilson Boulevard, Suite 1250
Arlington, VA 22209
Tel: (703) 527-NACD (6223)
Fax: (703) 527-7747
E-mail: nacdpublicaffairs@nacd.com

The National Association of Chemical Distributors (NACD) is an international association of chemical distributor companies that purchase and take title of chemical products from manufacturers. Member companies process, formulate, blend, repackage, warehouse, transport, and market these chemical products exclusively for an industrial customer base.

National League of Cities (NLC)
1301 Pennsylvania Avenue NW, Suite 550
Washington, DC 20004
Phone: (202) 626-3000
Fax: (202) 626-3043
Web site: http://www.nlc.org/nlc_org/site/inside_nlc/
  staff_contacts/

The National League of Cities (NLC) is the oldest and largest national organization representing municipal governments throughout the United States. Its mission is "to strengthen and promote cities as centers of opportunity, leadership, and governance." Working in partnership with state municipal leagues, the NLC serves as a national resource to and an advocate for the more than 18,000 cities, villages, and towns it represents.

Regional Alliances for Infrastructure and Network Security (RAINS)

PO Box 6955
Portland, OR 97228-6955
Web site: http://www.rainsnet.org/contact/index.asp

RAINS is a nonprofit private/public partnership formed to "accelerate development and deployment of innovative technology for homeland security." The companies that make up the RAINS alliance work to strengthen the U.S. information infrastructure and build awareness about the urgency of increasing domestic security.

Synthetic Organic Chemical Manufacturers Association (SOCMA)

1850 M Street NW, Suite 700
Washington, DC 20036-5810
Tel: (202) 721-4100
Fax: (202) 296-8120
Web site: http://www.socma.com/about/index.htm

The Synthetic Organic Chemical Manufacturers Association (SOCMA) is a trade association serving the specialty-batch and custom chemical industry. Its 300 member companies have more than 2,000 manufacturing sites and 100,000 employees. SOCMA members encompass every segment of the industry—from small specialty producers to large multinational corporations—and manufacture 50,000 products annually valued at $60 billion.

Batch chemical manufacturers play a key role in the U.S. chemical industry by producing intermediates, specialty chemicals, and ingredients that are used to develop a wide range of commercial and consumer products. Thus, SOCMA's member companies manufacture products that are key building blocks and ingredients for a range of other production operations. In batch manufacturing, the raw materials, processes, operating conditions, configuration of equipment and end products change on a regular basis. Batch producers must respond quickly to new requests by customers, fill small market niches, and participate in the development of new products. U.S. batch producers are at the cutting edge of new technology and provide products often made nowhere else in the world.

WMD First Responders
Web site: http://www.wmdfirstresponders.com/Index.htm

The WMD First Responders Web site was created "to help improve the response capabilities of members assigned to organizations and agencies that could respond to attacks or events involving the use of a weapon of mass destruction (WMD) (e.g., chemical, biological, radiological, nuclear, and explosive material)." First responders are members of emergency communications centers (ECCs); emergency medical services (EMS), fire, and rescue; HAZMAT teams; law enforcement agencies; bomb squads; SWAT; hospitals; public health; risk management; security; emergency and disaster management; transportation and public works; gas, water, and electric companies; the American Red Cross, and so on. Through information sharing, networking, planning, exercises, and research, first responders are better prepared to respond to and manage terrorist events involving WMD.

8

Print and Nonprint Resources

Print Resources

Books, Monographs, and Reports

Ball, Howard. 2004. *The U.S.A. Patriot Act: A Reference Handbook.* Santa Barbara, CA: ABC-CLIO.

A general overview of the Patriot Act, including observations by supporters and opponents of the legislation.

Badley, Thomas J. 2004. *Homeland Security, 2004–2005.* Guilford, CT: McGraw-Hill/Dushkin.

A good contemporary anthology of important essays on the status of homeland security.

Brzezinski, Matthew. 2004. *Fortress America: On the Frontlines of Homeland Security.* New York: Bantam.

An excellent critical assessment of the state of homeland security in 2005.

Bush, George W. 2002. *The Department of Homeland Security.* Washington, DC: The White House.

The official White House document that defends the decision of President Bush to recommend the creation of the U.S. Department of Homeland Security.

Byrd, Robert C. 2004. *Losing America: Confronting a Reckless and Arrogant Presidency.* New York: W.W. Norton.

One of the most critical books about the Bush presidency, this one focusing on the many errors of judgment and policy initiated by the president.

Chang, Nancy. 2002. *Silencing Political Dissent.* New York: Seven Stories.

An unsparing and critical assessment of steps the federal executive and the Congress have taken to counter threats from terrorists and other subversive groups that allegedly threaten U.S. domestic security.

Clancy, Tom. 2003. *Teeth of the Tiger.* New York: G. P. Putnams' Sons.

This Clancy novel eerily sketches terrorist activities in America's heartland.

Clarke, Richard A. 2004. *Against All Enemies: Inside America's War on Terror.* New York: Free Press.

An examination of the U.S. intelligence community's efforts to track and identify terrorists and a criticism of the Bush administration's foreign and national security policy leadership in the months before and after the 9/11 tragedy.

Cole, David. 2003. *Enemy Aliens: Double Standards and Constitutional Freedoms in the War on Terrorism.* New York: New Press.

A sharp critique of the government's treatment of enemy aliens in the contemporary United States.

Conley, Richard S. 2002. **"The War on Terrorism and Homeland Security."**

A paper presented at the conference Assessing the Presidency of President George W. Bush at Midpoint, November 22, Gulfport, MS: University of Southern Mississippi.

Department of Homeland Security, Inspector General's Report. 2004. *DHS Challenges in Consolidating Terrorist Watch List Information.* Washington, DC: Department of Homeland Security.

This is an in-house report from October 4, 2004, one of a number that have found many faults in the organizational structure of the DHS.

DiStasi, Lawrence. 2001. *Una Storia Segreta: The Secret History of the Italian American Evacuation and Internment during World War II.* Berkeley: Heyday.

An examination of a heretofore invisible problem involving governmental efforts in a time of war to maintain domestic security against foreign aliens living in the United States. This book focuses on the plight of tens of thousands of aliens of Italian heritage, as well as a number of Italian Americans, who were registered by the government and placed under tight curfews, with many thousands sent to "internment centers" across the country during World War II.

Flynn, Steven. 2004. *America the Vulnerable: How Our Government Is Failing to Protect Us from Terrorism.* New York: Harper-Collins.

Another book that exposes the many vulnerable situations that, if not fixed, will continue to lead millions of illegal aliens to cross U.S. borders for employment—and terrorist planning and action.

Gottfried, Ted. 2003. *Homeland Security Versus Constitutional Rights.* Brookfield, CT: Twenty First Century.

Hoyt, Edwin P. 1969. *The Palmer Raids, 1919–1920: An Attempt to Suppress Dissent.* Boston: Seabury Press.

An older book that examines the excesses of governmental actions against alleged threats to U.S. homeland security, this time concerning aliens who were socialists, communists, and anarchists during the first five decades of the twentieth century.

Korb, Lawrence J. 2003. *A New National Security Strategy in an Age of Terrorists, Tyrannies, and Weapons of Mass Destruction.* New York: Council on Foreign Relations.

This book, including an appendix containing the actual new national security strategy—preemptive war—issued by the Bush administration in 2002, is a must-read for those examining homeland security after 9/11.

Lieberman, Jethro K. 1992. *The Evolving Constitution.* New York: Random House.

Light, Paul C. 2002. **"Assessing the Department of Homeland Security."** *Testimony Before the U.S. Senate Committee on the Judiciary, Subcommittee on Technology, Terrorism, and Government Information.* 107th Congress. Washington, DC: Brookings Institution.

Paul Light is an outstanding public administrator who has studied and written about governmental reorganization efforts. He has also been a practitioner engaged in the effort to reduce the chaos associated with massive governmental reorganizations. This book is a must read for those concerned about the problems facing the DHS.

Lindsay, James, and Ivo Daalder. 2003. **"Whose Job Is It? Organizing the Federal Government for Homeland Security."** In James Lindsay, ed., *American Politics After September 11.* Cincinnati: Atomic Dog.

Maharidge, Dale. 2004. *Homeland.* New York: Seven Stories.

An evocative essay about the human dynamics of homeland security in the years surrounding 9/11.

Malkin, Michelle. 2002. *Invasion: How America Still Welcomes Terrorists, Criminals, and Other Foreign Menaces to Our Shores.* Washington, DC: Regnery.

A conservative scholar's criticism of the government's efforts to provide homeland security both before and after 9/11. A no-holds-barred condemnation of these efforts.

Malkin, Michelle. 2004. *In Defense of Internment: The Case for "Racial Profiling" in World War II and the War on Terror.* Washington, DC: Regnery.

A strong defense of governmental efforts to provide a strong domestic security program during World War II and the present war on terrorism.

9/11 Commission. 2004. *Final Report of the National Commission on Terrorist Attacks upon the United States.* New York: Norton.

The 9/11 Commission's final report is an excellent analysis by a panel of prominent political leaders of the events surrounding the tragedy of September 11, 2001. It was nominated for the National Book Award for 2004. The two staff reports of the 9/11 Commission have also been published; they also provide important information for the student of homeland security.

Office of Homeland Security, the White House. *Homeland Security: U.S. National Security Strategy.* Philadelphia: Pavillion.

An important national security policy change by the Bush Administration announced in 2002 that led directly to the invasion of Iraq.

Ranum, Marcus J. 2004. *The Myth of Homeland Security.* New York: Wiley.

A critical examination of the government's efforts to defend against domestic and foreign terrorists.

Schneier, Bruce. 2003. *Beyond Fear: Thinking Sensibly about Security in an Uncertain World.* New York: Copernicus.

The book carefully and thoughtfully examines the value of cost-benefit analyses of programs, projects, and policy decisions that affect homeland security.

Stone, Geoffrey R. 2004. *Perilous Times: Free Speech in Wartime from the Sedition Act of 1798 to the War on Terrorism.* New York: W.W. Norton.

A well-written, illuminating book on the historical tension between individual liberty and national security in the United States.

Strasser, Steven, ed. 2004. *The 9/11 Investigations: Staff Reports of the 9/11 Commission.* New York: Public Affairs.

Another excellent governmental report about the 9/11 Commission and congressional committee reports on what led to the 9/11 attacks.

Zelikow, Philip, ed. 2004. *9/11 and Terrorist Travel: A Staff Report of the National Commission on Terrorist Attacks upon the United States.* Franklin, TN: Hillsboro.

A truly frightening account of how the 9/11 attackers were able to enter the United States between 1999 and 2001 with great ease even though they made many errors when filling out visa information and the like.

Newspapers, News Weeklies, and Journal Articles

Anderson, Curt. 2004. **"Terror Prosecutors Record Uneven."** *Burlington Free Press,* September 7, 3A.

Barlett, Donald L., and James B. Steele. 2004. **"Who Left the Door Open?"** *Time,* September 20, 51–66.

Becker, Elizabeth. 2002. **"'Prickly Roots' of Homeland Security."** *New York Times,* August 31, 1A.

Becker, Elizabeth. 2002. **"Big Visions for Security Post Shrink Amid Political Drama."** *New York Times,* May 2, A1.

Cha, Ariana Eunjung. 2004. **"From a Virtual Shadow, Messages of Terror."** *Washington Post,* October 2, A1.

Clarke, Richard A. 2005. **"Ten Years Later."** *Atlantic Monthly,* January–February, 61–77.

Cmar, Thomas. 2002. **"Office of Homeland Security."** *Harvard Journal on Legislation* 39 (Summer).

Cohen, Richard E., Siobhan Gorman, and Sydney J. Freedberg Jr. 2003. **"The Ultimate Turf War."** *National Journal* (January 4): 16–23.

A provocative essay that examines the multitude of congressional committees that still oversee the actions of the DHS employees and leadership.

de Rugy, Veronique. 2004. **"What Does Homeland Security Spending Buy?"** *American Enterprise Institute for Public Policy Research* (November 3): 11–27.

Dewar, Helen. 2002. **"Homeland Bill Gets Boost: 3 Key Senators Agree to White House Plan for Department."** *Washington Post,* November 13, A1.

Dimond, Diane. 2004. **"Defending Our Skies against the Elderly."** *Newsweek,* August 30, 11.

Dinsmore, M. R. 2004. **"Make Our Ports Safer."** *Washington Post,* September 27–October 3, national weekly edition, 26.

Donnally, Sally B. 2004. **"Should the No-Fly List Be Grounded?"** *Time,* October 18, 18.

Dunham, Steve. 2002. **"Transportation Security Administration Faces Huge Challenges."** *Journal of Homeland Security* (February): 65–75.

Fallows, James. 2004. **"Bush's Lost Year."** *Atlantic Monthly,* October, 68–84.

Fallows, James. 2005. **"Success without Victory."** *Atlantic Monthly,* January–February, 80–90.

Flynn, Steven. 2002. **"America the Vulnerable."** *Foreign Affairs,* January/February, 60–74.

Hind, Rick, and David Halperin. 2004. **"Lots of Chemicals, Little Reaction."** *New York Times,* September 22.

Hirsch, Daniel. 2003. **"The NRC: What, Me Worry?"** *Bulletin of the Atomic Scientists* (January/February): 39–44.

Hsu, Spencer S., and Sari Horwitz. 2004. **"Impervious Shield Elusive Against Drive-By Terrorists."** *Washington Post,* August 8, A1.

James, Frank. 2004. **"Homeland Security Department Gets Mixed Grades after First Year."** *Macon* (GA) *Telegram,* February 29, A1.

Kristov, Nicholas D. 2004. **"An American Hiroshima."** *New York Times,* August 11, A26.

Lappin, Elena. 2004. **"Letter from a Deportee: Your Country Is Safe from Me."** *New York Times Book Review,* July 4, 11.

Light, Paul. 2004. **"Homeland Security Department Marks a Fractious First Year."** *Seattle Times,* March 1, A1.

Lipton, Eric. 2004. **"Spy Chiefs Say Cooperation Should Begin at Bottom."** *New York Times,* October 14, A1.

Martin, Kate. 2004. **"Irresponsible Intelligence Reform."** *Washington Post,* October 4–10, national weekly edition, 26.

McLaughlin, Abraham. 2002. **"Emerging Plans for Homeland Security Department Focus on Border and Transportation Issues."** *Christian Science Monitor,* June 24, A1.

McLaughlin, Abraham. 2002. **"New U.S. Security Mantra: Keep Bad Guys Out."** *Christian Science Monitor,* June 24, A1.

Miller, Bill. 2002. **"Lieberman Warns of Homeland Bill Hurdles: Senator Aims to Guard Worker Protections."** *Washington Post,* August 30, A6.

Miller, Bill. 2002. **"Standoff on Homeland Security: Bill Stalled as Senators Can't Agree on Workers' Rights."** *Washington Post,* September 26, A12.

Mintz, John, and Joby Warrick. 2004. **"U.S. Unprepared Despite Progress, Experts Say."** *Washington Post,* November 8, A1.

Murphy, Dean E. 2004. **"Security Grants Still Streaming to Rural States."** *New York Times,* October 12, A1.

Noonan, Peggy. 2002. **"Homeland Ain't no American Word."** *Wall Street Journal,* June 14.

Nye, Joseph S., Jr. 2004. **"Watch Out."** *Washington Post,* September 27–October 3, national weekly edition, 32.

Posner, Richard A. 2004. **"The 9/11 Report: A Dissent."** *New York Times Book Review,* August 29, 1, 9–11.

Ramirez, Anthony. 2004. **"Off New Jersey, Coast Guard Seizes Container Ship, and a Million Lemons."** *New York Times,* August 7, A16.

Swarns, Rachel L. 2004. **"Government to Take over Watch-List Screening."** *New York Times,* August 17, A1.

Swarns, Rachel L. 2004. **"Senator? Terrorist? A Watch List Stops Kennedy at Airport."** *New York Times,* August 20, A1.

Swarns, Rachel L. 2004. **"Study Finds Most Border Officers Feel Security Ought to Be Better."** *New York Times,* August 24, A1.

Swarns, Rachel L. 2004. **"U.S. to Give Border Patrol Agents the Power to Deport Illegal Aliens."** *New York Times,* August 11, A1.

Victor, Kirk. 2002. "The Experiment Begins." *National Journal,* June 15, 1775–1787.

Wald, Matthew L. 2004. **"Accusations on Detention of Ex-Singer."** *New York Times,* September 23, A1.

Wald, Matthew L., and John Schwartz. 2004. **"Screening Plans Went beyond Terrorism."** *New York Times,* September 19, A25.

Nonprint Resources

Governmental

Antiterror. https://disasterhelp.gov/portal/jhtml/community.jhtml? community=Acts+of+Terror&index=0&id=19

First Gov for Consumers. http://www.consumer.gov/

First Gov: The Official Web Portal of the U.S. Federal Government. http://www.firstgov.gov/

Chemical Stockpile Emergency Preparedness Program Residential Shelter-in-Place. http://emc.ornl.gov/CSEPPweb/SIP/SIP.htm

CitizenCorps. http://www.citizencorps.gov/

Disaster Help. https://disasterhelp.gov/portal/jhtml/index.jhtml

Former Secretary of the DHS, Tom Ridge. http://www.issues2000.org/Tom_Ridge.htm

Threat Alert System Information for Citizens. http://www.dhs.gov/dhspublic/display?theme=29

U.S. Centers for Disease Control and Prevention, Public Health Emergency Preparedness and Response. http://www.bt.cdc.gov/

U.S. Department of Education, Emergency Preparedness Plans for Schools. http://www.ed.gov/emergencyplan/

U.S. Department of Health and Human Services, Disasters and Emergencies. http://www.hhs.gov/disasters/index.shtml

U.S. Department of Homeland Security. http://www.dhs.gov/dhspublic/

U.S. Department of Justice. http://www.doj.gov/; http://www.lifeandliberty.gov/; http://www.ready.gov/

U.S. Environmental Protection Agency, Emergency Preparedness. http://www.epa.gov/ebtpages/emeremergencypreparedness.html

U.S. Federal Citizen Information Center. http://www.pueblo.gsa.gov/

U.S. Federal Emergency Management Agency. http://www.fema.gov/

U.S. Freedom Corps. http://www.usafreedomcorps.gov/

The White House. http://www.whitehouse.gov/

Nongovernmental

Byrd, Robert C. "Homeland Security Act of 2002." Congressional Record, November 14, 2002, at www.truthout.org.

CNN.com. "Labor Rights Issue Still a Stumbling Block." November 11, 2002. www.cnn.com.

Freeman, Franklin. "The Homeland Security Department and the Northern Command." http://geocities.com.

Kaus, Mickey. "The Trouble with 'Homeland.'" *Slate*, June 14, 2002. http://slate.msn.com.

King, John, Kelly Wallace, and Jeanne Meserve. "Bush Wants Broad 'Homeland Security' Overhaul." June 5, 2002. www.CNN.com.

Laurier, Joanne. "Bush Administration Moves to Suppress Documents on Vaccines." WSWS: News and Analysis, December 10, 2002. www.wsws.org.

Leahy, Patrick. "The Homeland Security Department Act." November 19, 2002. www.leahy.senate.gov.

Light, Paul. 2002. "Assessing the Department of Homeland Security." Brookings Institute, June 25. www.brook.edu.

Meruru, G. "Oppose the Department of Homeland Security." www.meruru.tripod.com.

Mullins, Brody, and April Fulton. "Controversial Provisions Could Delay Senate Homeland Vote." *Congress Daily: Daily Briefing*, November 14, 2002. www.GovExec.com.

PBS NewsHour. "Securing Our Homeland." *PBS Online News Hour*, November 20, 2002. www.pbs.org/newshour.

Progressive Management. *21st Century Complete Guide to Homeland Security: Policy, Oversight, and the New Department*. Core Federal Government Information Series. 2-CD set. ISBN 1–59248–207–4. 2003.

Saletan, William. "Ballot Box: Reorganizing Government; Does Bush's DHS Make Sense?" *Slate.* June 7, 2002. www.slate.msn.com.

Seiple, Chris. "DHS: Security in Transition." *Institute for Global Engagement,* November 2002. www.globalengagement.org.

Sirota, David, Christy Harvey, and Judd Legum. "Homeland Security: Dangerous Holes." *Center for American Progress,* March 4, 2004. www.americanprogress.org.

Index

About the Author

Howard Ball grew up in New York City, attending Taft High School and Hunter College–CUNY. He went to Rutgers University, where he received his MA and PhD degrees in political science in 1970. He has taught at Hofstra University, Mississippi State University, the University of Utah, and the University of Vermont. He was a sergeant in the U.S. Air Force, serving in Germany when the Berlin Wall went up in 1961.

Ball's areas of teaching and research competence are judicial politics, the U.S. Supreme Court, civil rights, civil liberties, international law, and war crimes and justice. Ball has authored more than three dozen articles in refereed political science, public administration, and law journals and more than two dozen books, including a biography of Thurgood Marshall (*A Defiant Life*), and biographies of Hugo Black and William O. Douglas. He has written texts for students of the U.S. Supreme Court as well as books touching upon the international criminal court. His most recent publications are *War Crimes and Justice* (ABC-CLIO, 2002); *The Supreme Court in the Intimate Lives of Americans* (NYU Press, 2d ed., 2004), and *Murder in Mississippi* (University Press of Kansas, 2004). Ball is presently at work on a book for the University of Press of Kansas, about the legal and ethical controversies surrounding America's treatment of enemy combatants at Guantanamo Bay and in America in the war on terror. He has just returned from the murder trial of Edgar Killen, the Klansman who planned the murders of three civil rights workers in Mississippi in June 1964. *Justice in Mississippi: Mississippi vs. Edgar Ray Killen* is now in process and will be published in 2006.

Ball lives in Richmond, Vermont, with his wife of forty-three years, Carol. They are surrounded by their two Chessies—Maggie and Charlie—and their three horses—Stormin' Norman, Smokey, and Dirty Harry. They have three grown daughters, Sue the actor, Melissa the teacher, and Sheryl the occupational therapist. They are blessed with three grandchildren, Lila, Nate, and Sophie. The daughters visit, two with husbands and children, occasionally.